Feb. 2018

Matt,

Thank you very much for your support. Hope you enjoy the read.

Old friends are always cherished

B. Phoenix

INADMISSIBLE

The Life and
Secret Files
of an
HR Professional

B. PHOENIX

Copyright © 2017 B. Phoenix.

All rights reserved. No part of this book may be used or reproduced by any means, graphic, electronic, or mechanical, including photocopying, recording, taping or by any information storage retrieval system without the written permission of the author except in the case of brief quotations embodied in critical articles and reviews.

This book is the work of non-fiction based on the experiences and recollections of the author over time. The recreation of events, locales and conversations are mostly from the memories of the author. The names of the people and places, and identifying features such as physical properties, occupations and places of residence, or details of events, have been changed to protect those involved.

LifeRich Publishing is a registered trademark of The Reader's Digest Association, Inc.

LifeRich Publishing books may be ordered through booksellers or by contacting:

LifeRich Publishing
1663 Liberty Drive
Bloomington, IN 47403
www.liferichpublishing.com
1 (888) 238-8637

Because of the dynamic nature of the Internet, any web addresses or links contained in this book may have changed since publication and may no longer be valid. The views expressed in this work are solely those of the author and do not necessarily reflect the views of the publisher, and the publisher hereby disclaims any responsibility for them.

Any people depicted in stock imagery provided by Thinkstock are models, and such images are being used for illustrative purposes only.
Certain stock imagery © Thinkstock.

Scriptures taken from the King James Version of the Bible.

ISBN: 978-1-4897-1401-5 (sc)
ISBN: 978-1-4897-1402-2 (hc)
ISBN: 978-1-4897-1400-8 (e)

Library of Congress Control Number: 2017914235

Print information available on the last page.

LifeRich Publishing rev. date: 9/27/2017

"Verily, verily, I say unto you, Except a corn of wheat fall into the ground and die, it abideth alone: but if it die, it bringeth forth much fruit."
John 12:24

Contents

Preface ix
Introduction xiii

PERSONAL DEVELOPMENT

Chapter 1	The Master	1
Chapter 2	A Long Ride	7
Chapter 3	Parents	17
Chapter 4	The Early Years	27
Chapter 5	To Be or Not to Be	45

PROFESSIONAL DEVELOPMENT

Chapter 6	In the Beginning	59
Chapter 7	The Lunch Thief	63
Chapter 8	Down by the Train Track	73
Chapter 9	X-Rated	81
Chapter 10	The Northwest	87
Chapter 11	Oh Fudge	93
Chapter 12	A Diamond in the Rough	97
Chapter 13	Black at Work in the Twenty-First Century	103
Chapter 14	HR Nightmare	115
Chapter 15	Finding a CEO	127
Chapter 16	Cash Cow	143
Chapter 17	The Controller	153
Chapter 18	Blackballed	165

Chapter 19	The Midyear Checkup	173
Chapter 20	Changing Tides	185
Chapter 21	Bloopers: "Go Ahead and Check"	197

Epilogue   237

Preface

While working at my first law firm, I was introduced to a well-known, extremely popular newspaper entitled *Legal Times*. This paper reported on current news events in the legal community (i.e., new regulations, job changes of high profile attorneys, lobbying activities, special legal reports, etc.). One section of the paper, which was very popular in my office, reported on issues, many of which were a shock to the legal community. Some of these reports were of well-known attorneys leaving, or joining firms, attorneys who were disbarred, and law firms taking on landmark legal cases. This section was entitled "***Inadmissible***."

> **Inadmissible**: not capable of being accepted;
> not allowable; not worthy of admission.

My *Inadmissible* gives you a glimpse of life as I've known it and shares the unbelievably wacky and wild events of my career as an HR professional for several multimillion-dollar law firms and other companies over several decades.

> Some things we should accept;
> Some things we should allow;
> Some things we should admit;
> and
> Some things should just be *inadmissible*!

B. PHOENIX

**In honor of my great-grandmother,
Cicely C. Heel**

Feeling led by God to keep me, Cicely raised me like no one else could. She taught me more than I could ever express in one book. I find myself quoting her constantly and am forever trying to stay on the path she started for me before I took my first step. Today, I realize she gave me more love than I could ever hope to have. The wisdom she imparted to me can never be taken away. As she promised, I would not realize how much she did for me until she was gone. How right was she! Not only do I realize the magnitude of what she did for me, I am fully aware of her greatness. And it is because of her greatness, her powerful teachings, and the example she set in her strong faith in God that I could deal with some of life's most challenging tests.

Thank you, God, for Cicely Heel and thank you Cicely Heel for your obedience to God!

In loving memory of my great grandmother
Gracie Beck

Although Ms. Gracie kept me close to her side, she could
see right on through them. She looked and people
quit being mean to me. She sat with me until she was satisfied
for the next task. My first memory of how she gave me more love
than I could ever hope to know. I love how hard she opened the
room up. As she prayed, I would just smile and listen. She did turn to
me and she was gone. I ran, I ran as fast as I could. I notice the rain outside
of what she felt for me. I am fully aware of the greatness, and it is because of
her presence there is such a teaching. I am so sure He is the sea. He heard my
faith in God that I count, and welcome of life, and H-ill mighty Jesus.
Thank you, God. For God is real and the place I used to see a life for, will
always be a God.

B. PHOENIX

Introduction

Two days after I celebrated my forty-seventh birthday, I decided to begin writing my story. I figured, at that point, I had so much to tell I needed to put it all down in an organized fashion. You know, gather all my notes from napkins, notepads, notebooks, journals, yellow post-its, and minicassettes, and bring them all together (for those of you who don't know what minicassettes are, Google it). I knew that with the help of God, I would have something worth printing. And although this is the work of an infant, what you won't find in its infancy is my story. It has been growing and developing before me, in me, and around me for more than one hundred years. And besides, in the words of one of my old friends, "I need a new gig." The one I had was enough to drive a person mad! So there began the writing of my story. I did my best to tell as much as I could, but in this one book, I could not tell it all!

Most of my adult life has been spent working as a human resources (HR) professional for nonprofit organizations and some of the most prestigious law firms in the nation. In the legal arena, these law firms ranked highest in many different categories (e.g., practice areas, prestige, and profitability). In terms of profitability, one of them ranked in the top one hundred law firms in the United States. This was a ranking Wilcox & Andrews boasted for many years. Although it was one of the most profitable law firms in the nation, it was not one of the largest, or one of the most well-known. And just as the firm ranked in the top one hundred law firms for profitability, in its later years, many people would have ranked it one of the top five law firms for the ridiculous. In an earlier version of this book, I said the firm would have ranked one of the top five law firms for "bull_____"; but my Pastors encouraged me to use cleaner language.

You probably think you can imagine all the ridiculous things I must have experienced as an HR professional, but you can't—trust me, you cannot. In this role, I was subjected to some of the most unbelievable stories, lies, and situations that anyone could possibly imagine. And although I worked with many brilliant, good citizens, I also worked with individuals who personified the darkest level of ambition, and I saw greed at an unprecedented level. Mind you, I did not walk a chalk line myself, but I must say, some of the things I witnessed were just beyond beyond!

My colleagues and other HR professionals had stories to tell, but not quite the stories I could tell. At one point, I started to wonder if it was me. I thought maybe I was just a magnet for foolishness. I began thinking that perhaps I just looked for problems. Then I realized I could never even fathom most of this stuff, let alone look for it. I was constantly trying to rationalize why folks came to me with such nonsense. One theory was that people found it very difficult to read me, so they would try it all. In addition to being difficult to read, it has been said that I am very unpredictable. Most people never knew what answers or responses they would get from me. Oftentimes, they thought I was snobby when I was not, angry when I was firm, hurt when I was thankful, easy when I was hard, strict when I was enforcing the rules, bad when I was good, good when I was bad, and mean when I was painfully honest. This was the case with me long before the beginning of my career.

My career began over thirty years ago. In the beginning, I was being further prepared to work in HR without even the slightest awareness of it. My early supervisors, from whom I learned so much, were all very intelligent, hardworking, highly educated individuals with a keen sense of how people fit into an organization and the importance of every role. There are also many other people I must credit with molding me and teaching me the right way. Thus, I held positions in administration and HR at every level from administrative assistant to vice president to executive director. In each of these roles, I was required to maintain confidences. From the very beginning, people confided in me, and they have always felt comfortable doing so, even when I was a young girl. As a teenager, I had adults trusting me with their confidences. And in some cases, the information these adults shared placed an extremely heavy burden on me.

Ironically, carrying heavy burdens early in life proved beneficial to me personally and in my career. Also, at the beginning of my career, I learned that you must be strong, uncompromising, and willing to be politically incorrect when doing the right thing. Another important lesson I learned was that you should get to know an individual before you can fully trust what he or she tells you. And I mean get to know who the person is, not who he or she may choose to show you. I know this sounds very pessimistic, but as I have learned, some folks are extremely skillful manipulators and can convince many people of just about anything.

Our society has bred generations of people who are not principled, but rather have been taught, in many ways, to lie, cheat, steal, manipulate, and deceive. Perhaps we are all guilty of some of this. If we want a thing and don't want to ask for it, we may drop a few hints expecting an offer. We tell people what they want to hear, even if it is not true. We tell people only what we want them to know, when they should be told more, even if it hurts. What about the price tag on the item we want that is more than we can afford, or are willing to pay, and so we switch price tags, or even destroy the tag? For some people, this behavior is very natural. However, in many cases, people are taught this behavior—reared to be liars, manipulators, and purely disingenuous.

For instance, we all know lying is not good, but we sometimes believe it is better to lie than to tell the truth. Some people are very bad at lying while others are exceptionally good at it. Manipulation, however, is a process that can be good or bad. In some cases, the skill of manipulation is used for good and is totally harmless. On the other hand, manipulation in the form of exploitation can be extremely harmful. In terms of being disingenuous, this behavior became so prevalent in the workplace some years back that one of the well-respected national television networks devoted an entire segment of one of its programs to discussing people in the workplace who are deceivers. I recall there was a woman who was being interviewed as an "expert on the subject." And although she used a different term in referring to these individuals, in this manuscript, I've chosen to use the term "disingenuous." This expert stated that the art of disingenuousness had become a job. I'm sure these positions have existed for a while; however, I was surprised to learn that someone was bold enough to make it an official role and give it a job title.

The problem I've found with people who are disingenuous in the workplace is that they can greatly interrupt the flow of productivity, and thereby the loss of time and money. And, unfortunately, disingenuous people exist at every level of many organizations. Even most recently, you can barely get through a day without hearing news reports of high level government officials who are disingenuous with the public. Sadly, these are the people who should be providing us with the naked truth. If, in fact, these people (some of whom are the most powerful in the world and leaders of the largest employer in the nation) are disingenuous, I know you must have had one or two in your workplace as well. I have experienced these types of characters on a personal and professional level and will introduce some of them to you in this book.

Also, in this book, I share a variety of information from files I maintained working in HR—many of which describe some real doozie disingenuous artists. Additionally, I share short files of even wilder behaviors I encountered in over thirty years as an HR professional. But before I tell you about the dirt, lies, and scandals I encountered in my career, I will give you the straight skinny on how I came about—and please know—there is irony in growing up around someone who was poor, uneducated, and had no real work training, but was a master disingenuous artist, and then spending most of your career around some of the richest, most highly educated, well-trained disingenuous individuals in the world.

Your past does prepare you for your future!

B. PHOENIX

The Master

HARMON'S GAMBLING CAREER was extremely profitable for many years. When he won, he won big. I mean so big that he would hand out large sums of money to his family members and would still have plenty left for himself. Harmon was on a multi-decade-long winning streak. He got up most mornings, got dressed in a suit and tie, freshly laundered and starched shirt, professionally polished shoes, and a dress hat. He was a professional and looked the part. Not only was he a professional gambler, he was a professional con man. He could convince most people of just about anything. Harmon was extremely well groomed, clean-shaven, and could have easily been mistaken for a prominent businessman back in the '60s. He was articulate and a smooth operator. He dined at the best restaurants and showcased some of the most beautiful and educated women in Washington, DC. He was well respected by many people in the DC area. In his circles, he was known as "a lucky man." However, his luck was just like every other gambling con man—sometimes you win, and sometimes you lose.

In the early '70s, Harmon suffered a major downfall—a losing streak that went on for many years and a near fatal encounter. One of his physical identifying marks was the result of him being shot by a man to whom he owed $5,000. He had conned the man for the money in a fake real estate deal. It was said that this man nearly killed Harmon with several buckshots. A buckshot is a bunch of pellets inside a shell that is used in a shotgun. When the shotgun is fired, the pellets spread out, resulting in multiple wounds from one shot. The marks from Harmon's wounds were small and round (almost perfectly round and a little larger than the size of a pea) and there were about fifteen to twenty of them all over his torso. He was hospitalized for weeks and spent many months recovering. That's enough to change one's behavior. In Harmon's case, he did change his behavior; however, the change was that he turned to other illegal activities.

Harmon, being the con man that he was, was very cagy and tricky. As I said before, he could convince most people of just about anything. He took the old expression "poker face" to a whole 'notha level. After his luck with gambling drastically changed for the worse and his near fatal encounter, he thought he could transfer his skills from gambling tables to courtrooms and insurance companies. Harmon decided to employ himself by scamming the legal system and a few insurance companies. He studied the legal system under some of the best attorneys in the DC area. He would get all dressed up, go into different courtrooms, and observe attorneys arguing cases before the court. He studied their moves, gestures, and comments as well as the judges' reactions and responses. After many courtroom observations and countless hours watching *Perry Mason* (a television show about an attorney who never lost a case, and Harmon's favorite television program), he was convinced he could do the work of an attorney and get paid for it, and he did.

For many years, Harmon counseled individuals with legal problems and, in some cases, spoke on their behalf. Most of the problems were petty issues, such as traffic violations. He convinced his "clients" that he could do what the attorneys did for a lot less money. After many of his "clients" obtained favorable court decisions, Harmon developed a reputation for being the man to call. He later expanded his services to include taking the written driver's exam for people who had difficulty passing it. The word of Harmon's ability to get a driver's license for someone who could not get one legitimately spread quickly. This news brought people seeking help with all types of legal problems. However, Harmon was unable to solve many of them. So, he, being the businessman that he was, enlisted the help of a real attorney. The attorney made a ton of money from Harmon's referrals, and Harmon was receiving very handsome referral fees from the attorney. Business was booming!

Like most people who develop an illegal scheme that "works," Harmon got greedy. He decided to offer services he could not deliver. He convinced people who lost their driver's license, due to drunk driving, that he could get it back for them. For this "service," he charged anywhere from $1,000 to $1,500. When Harmon had to face the music, and tell these people he could not get their driver's licenses, in almost every case, he convinced them that not getting the driver's license was somehow their fault. He told them things like, "I didn't know you had been charged with drunk driving in the past. If you have a previous charge, it's hard for my people to work with you." Of course, he did not obtain this information until after he paid money to "his court connection."

These people believed the entire lie. In some cases, Harmon convinced them that maybe in six months the records would be clear, and they could try again. This retry would require an additional fee, of course—so tricky. In the end, a really brave, smart judge gave him a severe warning—you stay out of my courtroom, and if you come within a five-block radius of this court without a subpoena, I will have you arrested. Harmon took heed to the warning, and that was the end of his career as an "attorney." However, he did not stop his con games; he just moved to a different arena, deciding he could scam insurance companies. So, he starts a new career.

Harmon would fake neck injuries from car accidents and would have the nerve to incite an accident so he could collect payments for "damages." I can remember overhearing some of the adults talking about an instance where Harmon was near a multicar accident that involved several pedestrians. Although he was not part of the accident, he quickly went to the area and lay in the street moaning and groaning as if he had been hit by one of the cars involved. Apparently, there was so much confusion that no one noticed Harmon's fake fall to the ground. He would go to the hospital and immediately follow up with his "doctor." You could often find Harmon in a neck brace—you know, the old whiplash problem. There was much talk about doctors who participated in Harmon's scams. He sought assistance from these characters on a regular basis. At one point, reportedly, he had these "quack doctors," as the elders in my family called them, on retainer.

In addition to the quack doctors, Harmon solicited help from a couple of his female companions to assist him with some of his scams. These scams ranged from claims of tainted food in restaurants to chipped glass in soda bottles purchased from local grocery stores. Harmon received thousands and thousands of dollars using these lies and scams. Most of the insurance companies paid him early in the investigation without ever involving the court system. However, just like every other criminal, all of Harmon's years of illegal activities were coming to an end. His final scam was with one of the nation's largest insurance companies. This company decided it was not going to roll over and pay, and met Harmon in court. The company called his bluff and caused him to shake in his boots.

Harmon, who was not known to be a religious person, suddenly was reaching out to God. He went to a nearby Catholic church every day for prayer and brought candles home, which he burned in his bedroom every night. This caused a lot of whispering in the family about how Harmon may have pulled his last scheme and how he may be going to prison for a very long time. These whispers only took place when Harmon's mother, with whom he lived, was not around. The family had always sheltered her from Harmon's illegal activities. However, one of the elders in the family decided it was time to let her know what was happening.

Many people in Harmon's family were still not sure of exactly what was going on, but they could hear little bits and pieces of conversations. What most of them were sure of was that Harmon had crossed a major line, something had gone wrong, and he was in big trouble. As it turned out, he had been charged with eighteen different counts of illegal activities, including fraudulent insurance claims, and was waiting on a decision from the court. The local newspaper wrote articles about Harmon and his female accomplice. At this point, people were making statements such as, "Harmon and his girlfriend are like a modern-day Bonnie and Clyde." Well, they made this statement as if they were referring to some type of accomplished celebrities.

When Cicely was finally told about Harmon's trouble, she asked if it was true, and her only other words about it were "everything is going to be all right." Okay, everything was going to be all right. Everyone knew what that meant. Cicely had sent an SOS up to God. She was very close to God, and God took care of her. Some of the family told the story that they imagined Cicely having a red telephone hidden in her bedroom that was a direct line to God. This phone was said to be the same color and look of the candy used on a red candy apple, and it was stored in a beautiful crystal box. Cicely didn't use this phone very often, but when she did, the story was that God **always** answered her call.

Well, the family didn't know what, but they knew something good was about to happen—and it did. It was how Cicely and God rolled, and her call was answered yet again. The court dropped all the charges against Harmon except one, and his penalty was that he had to repay $58,000 and was placed on probation for several years. After years of worrying about how his case was going to turn out, Harmon gave up the life of scams. He did, however, return to gambling, but only to realize very small winnings. Harmon was truly a master manipulator and a professional con man who, at an early age, could find no other turns to make, and when he reached the end of this road, death was there waiting for him.

CHAPTER 2

A Long Ride

CICELY C. HEEL, Harmon's mother and my maternal great-grandmother, was a woman of average height with a beautiful, light walnut brown complexion. She was born in 1906 in Red Springs, North Carolina. Red Springs is a small city located south of Raleigh, North Carolina, and northeast of Columbia, South Carolina, very close to the South Carolina border. Cicely lived in Red Springs with her parents and four siblings. Her parents were in business for themselves. They were farmers, and they owned and operated a small country general store in Red Springs. This was the place where many of the locals shopped for small miscellaneous items. As the times would have it, Cicely was pulled out of grade school to help her parents with the farm and the store. She was a very strong worker. Considering the times, Cicely and her family enjoyed a nice, comfortable life.

Cicely got married and left home at a very early age. She met an extremely handsome man who wined and dined her to the altar. Syris Heel was about twenty-three years old, and Cicely was only thirteen. Syris was originally from Richmond, Virginia. He and Cicely "courted" for several months. One hot summer afternoon, Syris showed up at Cicely's house. He told her parents he wanted to take her to Sanford, North Carolina, for lunch. Sanford was a big city to folks from Red Springs. There was a restaurant, a dress shop, and other businesses accessible to blacks. This was going to be a very special day for Cicely. When she and Syris arrived in the city of Sanford, Cicely was very happy and excited. What she did not know was that Syris had planned to ask her to marry him. He wanted to propose to her when no one else was around. That way, he could influence her answer. Syris was a very persuasive man. He wanted Cicely as his bride, but he knew she was not old enough. He knew he would need her parents' consent, but he also knew her parents would never agree to this marriage.

Cicely was very excited about her short courtship with Syris. She had found a man who was handsome, strong, and intelligent. When Syris asked her to marry him, she said yes immediately. Unlike Syris, Cicely believed her parents would give their consent and be very happy for her. She did not believe her age would be a concern. After all, in those days, lots of young girls were married at an early age. When Syris asked Cicely's parents for their permission to marry her, they made it very clear it was out of the question. Not only did they feel Cicely was too young, they needed her to help with the family business. Although Syris expected Cicely's parents to disapprove, he was still disappointed when he heard it from them. He began working feverishly to develop a plan that would get Cicely away from her family. When he did, he took her for a ride—a ride straight to hell!

Syris got one of his closest friends to go with him and Cicely to the local courthouse. There, Syris's friend swore to a judge that he had known Cicely for most of her life and that she was sixteen years of age (the legal age for marriage without parental consent). I remember that Cicely, who was a very devout Christian and one who would never hurt a fly (except the two times she tore my tail up for being disobedient), told me if she ever saw the man who lied about her age so she could get married, she would "slap his face." Well, this was wildly violent for Cicely. In the nineteen years I lived with her, I never heard her speak of doing anything that would remotely resemble violence. So, for Cicely to say she would slap someone was totally out of character for her. This was how strongly she felt about the injustice that had been done to her by Syris. I'm sorry; I must stand corrected about Cicely's appetite for violence. I almost forgot about the time my aunt (Cicely's granddaughter) was kidnapped by her much older boyfriend. This man was closer to Cicely's age, and I always thought she secretly had a crush on the old man until the kidnapping. The one thing I remember her saying about the kidnapping was, "I never tried to fight a man or woman, but this man, I would fight."

Cicely and Syris were finally married. To the dismay of Cicely's family, Syris moved her to the big city of Richmond, Virginia (which was practically on the other side of the world for Cicely and her family). Cicely and Syris lived in Richmond until the early 1920s when they moved to DC. They had two children, James G. and Warren T., before Cicely was sixteen years old. By the time she was nineteen, they had three children. Their third-born child was my grandfather, Harmon, born in DC on June 25, 1925. Cicely was never happy in her marriage. Syris was very mean to her. He was also a very heavy drinker. He would come home regularly as drunk as "Cuta Brown." He treated Cicely as if she was a live-in servant—and from the stories she told, she was not a wife, but a domestic slave.

As a domestic slave, Cicely was required to cook, clean, care for the children, have sex with Syris ad nauseam, and take care of all the other domestic chores. In addition to being physically and mentally abusive, Syris never allowed Cicely to leave the house, other than to get food from a nearby grocery store. She was not even allowed to visit her parents and siblings in Red Springs. After working as a domestic slave for over fifteen years, Cicely decided she could not take any more of Syris's abuse. With very little education and virtually no money, Cicely bravely took matters into her own hands. She decided she had to get rid of her biggest problem. One morning after Syris left for work, she packed up her few personal belongings and, with her three sons, moved on, not letting Syris know her whereabouts for many years. This great escape made her three sons furious; however, they knew Cicely's life would be much better without Syris.

THE BEGOTTEN OF SYRIS HEEL

James G., Cicely's oldest child, and my great-uncle, was over six feet tall and weighed about 250 pounds. He had the same beautiful light brown skin as Cicely and looked more like her than his brothers did, but had the character traits of Syris. His eyes were more piercing than a dagger. His body was in excellent condition, and he moved like a royal king. Uncle James faithfully served in World War II, where he received a near fatal injury that left him with a permanent head injury. People in my family were always commenting that the metal plate in Uncle James's head caused him to act mean and crazy. But I say, as Cicely used to say, "An apple doesn't fall far from a tree."

Uncle James was released from the military on 100 percent full disability.

B. PHOENIX

When he returned home from the war, he moved back into Cicely's house. He was the child that gave Cicely many fearful nights. His alcohol consumption rivaled most. Unlike his father, who drank most days, Uncle James was what Cicely called a "binge drinker." He would go months without a drop of alcohol. Then he would go months loaded with alcohol, and we would not see him until the binge was over. The person he was varied greatly when he was drinking versus when he was not.

During his drunken binges, you could have easily mistaken Uncle James for a street person who was dirty, bloody from drunken falls, smelly, and full of liquor. Cicely never knew when he was going to come home drunk at the end of one of his binges. This was nerve-wracking for her because Uncle James was the type of drunk who would shout profanities at anyone, including Cicely. In addition, he was a destructive drunk. He was never physically violent to anyone in our home, but he would not hesitate to destroy our property. One day, he came home so drunk that everyone in the house refused to acknowledge his knock at the door. After he banged and banged (shouting profanities) for about thirty minutes, Cicely decided to let him in. She did not want to continue the embarrassment he had already caused in our neighborhood. To show how destructive he was, once allowed in the house, he proceeded to take the front door off the hinges. Can you imagine? He was so crazy drunk, he thought removing the entire door was going to prevent anyone from keeping him out ever again.

To the contrary, during Uncle James's dry spells, he could have easily been mistaken for a college professor. He always walked very tall with perfect posture and spoke perfect English. He would firmly correct anyone in my family who spoke incorrect English to him, and he despised ignorance. I remember once when I was about ten years old, I asked Uncle James, "Can I have something to drink?"

His response, (with the diction of James Earl Jones) in the harshest of tones, was, "I don't know, are you capable?"—putting emphasis on each syllable of the word *capable*, while staring with laser precision directly in my eyes.

Cicely's middle child was Warren T. Uncle Warren was about five feet seven, handsome, and very intelligent. He was a real ladies man, but a man's man also—one who always surrounded himself with fine people and fine things. Like his father and older brother, he too was a heavy drinker of alcohol. He smoked very expensive cigars, yet he was a very particular eater. He always maintained an extremely healthy diet—eating lots of fish, fresh fruits, and vegetables, and he refused to eat pork and was disgusted by anyone who did.

Uncle Warren became a DC businessman in the 1940s. He owned a clothing store and a grocery store. In addition to his retail businesses, he was one of the biggest numbers men in the city. He managed and operated an illegal lottery system using the horse races. In those days, this was called the numbers game. Uncle Warren made tons of money in the DC numbers market, and he was extremely generous when it came to Cicely. He always made sure he looked out for her. The gifts he gave her (china, draperies, rugs, and clothes) were always of the finest quality, and he made sure she never had financial problems. He loved Cicely more than anything in the world. However, Cicely never knew about his illegal activities.

Uncle Warren lived a very affluent life in the black community. He owned a very large beautiful home on the gold coast—an upper Northwest section of DC. He married Lillian Johnston, a beautiful young woman who was a registered nurse at one of the best hospitals in the city. Lillian was average height with extremely light skin. She had a shapely body and a very pleasant personality. She was a perfect bride for Uncle Warren. Not only was she beautiful, she was smart, classy, and very well-groomed. She always wore the finest clothes money could buy, and their home was full of all the best furnishings and modern technology. This lifestyle was impressive to a lot of people in the 1950s because unemployment, reportedly, had reached its highest level in nearly twenty years and many people were negatively affected by this.

Uncle Warren and Lillian were totally unaffected by the woes of unemployment. They had a great life, and their friends and family thought they were the perfect couple. He was the envy of all the men in town, and she was the envy of all the women. Uncle Warren, however, had another life. He maintained an outside relationship with a beautiful young woman who was not only very attractive but very sexy with dark exotic features. She was faithful to Uncle Warren and bore him five daughters during the many years of their affair. Eventually, Lillian could not take any more of Warren's infidelity, so she left him and relocated to New York.

Harmon (the gambler and con man you met earlier) was Cicely's youngest child and my maternal grandfather. Harmon, or Daddy, as I called him, except when certain people were around, and he introduced me as his niece because he didn't want people to think he was old, was a real momma's boy. He always stayed close to home. Even when he was married and had his own home, he still spent a lot of time at Cicely's house. Harmon was a short man, about five feet four, with a dark brown complexion. He was of a small stature, but had a very large, brave heart (no short man complex for Harmon). Unlike his father and two brothers, he never touched liquor, and he despised heavy drinking. He wouldn't even drink in social settings. Harmon married a beautiful young woman, Virginia Carpenter. Ironically, Virginia loved to drink liquor, but she hid her drinking from Harmon for many years. They had two daughters, Marie and Carla (my mother). They were very beautiful girls. Marie had reddish brown hair, and her skin color was a reddish-orange tone. As a child, she was very quiet and a little shy. Carla had very dark hair, but unlike Marie was a social butterfly and very outspoken. Harmon loved Marie and Carla more than life itself.

Harmon worked very hard to support his family. His first real job was in the 1940s as a messenger for the government. He was the best messenger ever. He dressed in a suit and tie every day. Nobody made deliveries as fast as Harmon, and he was looking forward to getting his first real paycheck. On payday, he arrived to work extra early. He knew he would be dealing with the bank on that day, so he dressed extra nicely. Harmon had a legitimate job with real income, and he was looking forward to getting to the bank with his first legitimate paycheck.

As per ThePeopleHistory.com, in the 1940s, the average income was about $1,725 per year, and by 1949, the average annual income was about $2,950. You can imagine that as a messenger, Harmon's salary was much lower than the average salary. I never knew for sure, but based on these average salaries, I think it is safe to say that Harmon's annual income would probably have been no more than $800 per year. At that rate, his two-week paycheck was probably $33.00 before taxes. When Harmon opened his first paycheck, he almost passed out. He went straight to his supervisor and told him that there was a big mistake made on his paycheck. His supervisor apologized profusely and asked to see it. Breathing a big sigh of relief, his supervisor proceeded to explain that the check was correct. He thought Harmon was confused about gross pay vs. net pay. Well, Harmon wasn't confused about gross vs. net pay; his issue was the amount of money he was being paid, before and after taxes. He could not believe that people worked two full weeks for the pay he received. Again, his supervisor assured him the money was correct and apologized for any misunderstanding.

After taking a few minutes to compose himself, Harmon shook his supervisor's hand, thanked him for the opportunity, told him he would not be back, and walked out. Due to the degrading manner in which he was treated, and what he thought was unbelievably low pay, he would find some other way to care for his family. That was Harmon's first and last legitimate job. He was a gambler at heart and decided he could far better support his family by gambling rather than working as a messenger. This was the reason Harmon decided to try gambling as a full-time job. So, he used the two weeks' pay to start his new career as a full-time professional gambler.

Harmon made huge amounts of money gambling, but believe me, this career path was paved with lots of heartache and pain. On many occasions, he lost every penny he and Virginia had saved. It was a frustrating life for Virginia. Soon after their oldest daughter, Marie, started school, Virginia decided she was sick of their lifestyle. She wanted out of the marriage, but could not bring herself to leave. She was so unhappy that she started drinking more and more. Well, the stuff hit the fan the day Harmon came home, found Marie and Carla unattended, and Virginia in the bedroom passed out drunk. This was totally unacceptable to Harmon. He was a Heel, and the Heel men were strong and had everything their way, or no way. He, on that day, moved out and let Virginia keep the house. He took his daughters and went back home to Cicely. When Virginia sobered up and realized Harmon had left with her daughters, she was extremely upset and said she would do whatever she could to stop him from keeping her daughters, but there was nothing she could do. Harmon threatened to kill her if she, in any way, tried to interfere with him and/or his daughters.

Marie was five years old, and Carla was three when Harmon moved back home with Cicely. Virginia went from being a loving and devoted wife and mother to an alcoholic who smoked like a chimney. After many years, Marie and Carla were finally allowed to visit Virginia, but they were never allowed to stay long and never overnight. Years later, Virginia developed throat cancer and eventually died—not from cancer, not from sclerosis of the liver, not from a broken heart, but from indigestion. She ate a half-smoked sausage, lay down, went to sleep, and never woke up. Can you believe that? You survive losing your husband and your only two children, throat cancer, heavy doses of alcohol and nicotine, and you die in your sleep from indigestion. Unbelievable!!!

A LITTLE SISTER

In addition to Marie and Carla, Cicely became the surrogate mother to another young girl. Annette was the niece of Uncle Warren's wife, Lillian. Lillian was contacted by someone who lived in the same apartment building as her sister. This neighbor informed her that her sister's children had been left alone in the apartment for several days. Lillian's sister was a drug addict and often worked as a prostitute to support her addiction. She had two children—Joey, five years old at the time, and Annette, ten months old. Lillian had to rescue her abandoned niece and nephew, but she and Uncle Warren were very busy and did not have time for children. She asked someone in her family to raise Joey, and she asked Cicely if she would be willing to raise Annette. Cicely, who could never turn anyone away, agreed. Annette was a beautiful little baby girl. She had light brown skin with light green eyes. She became Marie and Carla's little sister. Cicely was now raising her second generation of children.

CHAPTER 3

Parents

MY MOTHER WAS a beautiful girl with very light skin and dark brown short hair. When she was thirteen years old, she had the body of a twenty-one-year-old woman. She was short with shapely legs and a full, firm body. Guys of all ages were attracted to her. She was extremely popular at school, and many of her peers (male and female) wanted to be around her all the time. She had a great personality and was the perfect social butterfly—a real party queen. As a young adult, she was known as Carla Steen the party queen.

My father was a few years older than my mother and, in many ways, the total opposite. He was tall with very dark skin, much like the skin of Nat King Cole. His body was strong and large in stature. He was the scholarly type with a very promising future—you know the type, very boring with nutty professor style eyeglasses—a real future leader and apparently an extremely gifted lover and athlete. He was a star football player in high school who could have received scholarship offers from several colleges and universities.

At my birth, I was a bundle of conflict for most people who were affected by my arrival. God, however, knew I was truly a bundle of joy—born to spread this joy to his people. Of my generation, I was the first born on my mother's side of the family and one of the last born on my father's side. Weighing in at close to ten pounds, I was extremely well nourished, had red skin with dark brown soft curly hair, was as fat as a Butter Ball turkey, and was admired by all. I was a beautiful round-faced little girl who won the hearts of all, but one, who encountered me. My father's mother refused to accept me as her son's child. She felt her son was the victim of a cunning trick. After all, she felt I had no resemblance to anyone in her family.

> Out of a secret pregnancy of a teenage girl, I was born.
> With all the odds against me, still I rise.

THE SECRET

At age fifteen, Carla could barely understand what was going on with her body. She had been "fooling around" with a boy but had no idea of the correlation. Under Cicely's strict Christian upbringing, sex was not allowed before marriage. In 1957, Christians and non-Christians alike understood that "good girls" never "fooled around" with boys before they were married. In those days, it was very much taboo to have a child out of wedlock, let alone a teen pregnancy out of wedlock. Carla knew it was going to be a complete tragedy for her family when it was revealed that she had been having sex. Therefore, being the young adolescent that she was, she decided to simply keep her condition a secret. In the summer of 1957, Carla was preparing to go to high school, but she had one problem. She could not start school with a big belly, so one of her closest girlfriends helped her solve this problem. They decided a girdle was the answer. In Carla's mind, hiding this pregnancy, at least initially, was a lifesaving exertion. She wore a girdle from the moment her stomach began to expand and maintained her regular lifestyle as a teenager. She continued to attend church, go to parties, and hang out with her family and friends.

Carla was a freshman at Ellson High School in DC. When she began school, no one suspected that there was anything wrong with her. She participated in physical activities of which most expectant mothers would be horrified—Carla was a cheerleader. Because Ellson High School had a very large athletic department, there were always athletic games with rowdy young teens around. Ellson participated in many team sports, which kept the cheerleaders very busy. Can you imagine being fifteen years old, a freshman in high school, a cheerleader, and three months pregnant? When God intends to use you, he will bring you through the worst.

This was a big secret, and only Carla and her best friend knew about it. Her sisters, who slept in the same room with her and were closer to her than anyone, did not know. They were all so young and naïve. So much so that Carla would make bets with her sisters that she could, by pressing her stomach muscles outward, make her stomach expand "five times bigger than normal." The wages were always candy and bubble gum. Obviously, Carla always won the bets. This game was usually played while Carla was in the bathtub with lots of water and bubbles. Isn't it ironic that no one, not a teacher, preacher, neighbor, or family member, discovered this huge secret? When God wants something to happen, it happens!

Suddenly, Carla felt trouble coming. She started to feel discomfort from her restricted stomach. The girdle was doing an excellent job concealing her condition. However, six months later, Carla knew she had to reveal her secret because she was literally about to pop. Around this time, one of her friends planned a huge party. Of course, Carla, being the party queen that she was, was invited. There would be less fun if Carla were not there, and if she was to attend the party, her sisters had to attend as well. Carla decided that this would be the perfect time to reveal her secret. So, before she went to the party, she left Cicely a note explaining her situation. When Cicely read Carla's note, she was terribly upset and very disappointed. "Dear Momma, I have been fooling around with a boy and I am going to have a baby." Cicely could not believe what she was reading. Carla was pregnant. How could this have happened? Little did she know, not only had it happened, it had happened about nine months before. Cicely's first great-grandchild was going to be born at any moment, but Carla's note failed to include the critical "any moment" detail. One week later, I was born.

THE YEAR 1958

I was born in DC on a beautiful Thursday morning in March 1958. There was a lot going on in 1958. Ironically, like me, many of these things were insignificant at the time. However, all of them stood the test of time and made a significant mark in our society. **Sharon Stone** was born a few days after me; **Madonna** and **Michael Jackson** were also born that year; **first class mail** increased from three cents to six cents (I'll bet that almost caused a riot); **television game shows** were being investigated (the investigation must have worked in their favor); a pack of **Life Savers** cost a whopping five cents;

B. PHOENIX

Prince Charles, son of Elizabeth II, became the prince of Wales; talking on **the telephone** was being advertised as "fun" (what a brilliant ad campaign; almost sixty years later people still find talking on the telephone fun—so much so, you can find one glued to the head of almost every adult and child; Ma Bell would be proud); the United States launched its **first satellite** (We have one on every corner now, don't we?); 1958 was also the year of the debut of **American Express** (just like me, they got stronger with time); *Wagon Train*, *The Rifleman*, and *Maverick* were all the favorite television shows (what a man's world); **the Hope Diamond** was donated to the Smithsonian Museum (wow, maybe it was a sign that there was hope for me—either that or it was a sign that I would be a real jewel lover); and General Mills created the **Trix cereal** and, like any good ad campaign, the slogan fit the times (one of General Mills's 1958 ads read, "Logic won't work but Trix will!"—how about that—fifty-nine years later many people still accept tricks over logic).

THE PRINCE OF PEACE

On several occasions, Cicely made it very clear that her girls would not be allowed to bring a baby into her home if they were not married. This was a real concern for everyone in the Heel family. They all knew Cicely always said what she meant and meant what she said. Many of the family members tried to convince Cicely to commit to accepting me when I arrived, but she would not. However, she could not resist the strength and opinion of one of her nephews (who I always called Uncle Bradford, but he was my third cousin).

Cicely loved and respected Uncle Bradford more than most other people, and he was one of my favorite people in the whole world. I remember as a child, wishing he was my father. Uncle Bradford was a giant of a man (as tall as a tree), but was the most gentle, charming, loving, and handsome man I knew. He was my knight in shining armor. He was admired by all and was the prince of peace in our family and among all his friends. Uncle Bradford would not speak to Cicely about Carla's situation until the very end. He was like a family secret weapon. However, his power was no secret.

Everyone knew Uncle Bradford had unprecedented negotiating skills. He went to Cicely to try and convince her that I needed to be brought to her home—and finally she agreed with one stipulation—that I would have to be brought in through the back door of the house. In the good old '50s, a single woman was practically executed for having a baby. Okay, they weren't executed, but they were treated as if they were lepers. So, you can imagine the type of treatment an unmarried teen mom must have received. In many cases, not only did society ostracize these girls, their own families did as well. Most of the black girls who got pregnant out of wedlock had no choice but to suffer through the horrific treatment they received from society. They were forced out of school and, in many cases, missed an entire school year. For some, the shame was so great that they never returned to school.

To the contrary, many unwed white girls who got pregnant were sent away to "boarding schools." At least, this is what people in my family often said. These girls, supposedly, were sent away to have the baby and continue their education. However, many of them, I was told, would leave the babies in the places where they had them and return home without a blemish on their reputation. Others would be taken to doctors who would perform "safe procedures" to get rid of the unborn child, while many black girls had no choice but to birth and keep their babies or go to a butcher to get rid of the baby—and you know the type of butcher, a back-alley abortionist.

About five days after my birth, Uncle Bradford went to the hospital to get Carla and me and took us home. He pulled his brand new 1958 Chevy Bel Air right up to the front of our beautiful, red brick row house on Capitol Hill, parked his car, took me in his arms while helping Carla get out of the car, and walked us straight through the front door. It was days, however, before Cicely would even look at me. Finally, the family called the secret weapon again. One afternoon, Uncle Bradford came into the house, picked me up, handed me to Cicely, and said, "This is your baby, your first great-grandchild." He told her he believed God needed her to care for His child. At that point, she took me in her arms, stared at me, and as the elder Christians used to say, "It was all over but the shoutin'." Suddenly, no one knew what to do for me or how to care for me but Cicely. One look at me, and I became her child. At this point, Carla was merely a helper—there to assist Cicely with the chores of her newborn baby. Insofar as my father was concerned, he was forbidden to visit our home. Who would ever have guessed that Cicely, after having been so adamant about not allowing me to come into her home, could love me more than life itself? Round three—Cicely was now raising a third generation.

THE CALL

Carla knew I was her child, but who was my father? I remember that when the father of a child was unclear, the elders in my family would say "momma's baby, poppa's maybe." My father and certain members of his family believed he was my father. One of his sisters and his grandmother were very happy about my birth and looked forward to being part of my life. On the other hand, his mother and other family members refused to believe I was his child. The family was in a total uproar over this illegitimate child. Supposedly, his mom stared at a photo of me and could not believe I was her son's child. She believed Carla was blaming this on her son, and she wasn't having it. After a couple of months of suffering with the fact that this disaster had occurred in her family, she decided to do something about it. She was sick and tired of hearing about this bastard child and was going to put an end to it, once and for all.

One Saturday afternoon, Cicely was in the kitchen baking one of her famous chocolate cakes when the telephone rang. In her normal clear and pleasant voice, she answered. After about thirty seconds, her face began to turn red, and her jaw dropped. At this point, everyone in the house knew this call was big trouble. One of Cicely's nieces told me that after many seconds of silence, Cicely said in a very stern and chilling voice, "Let me tell you something, lady. I never called you for help with raising this child, and I had no intention on calling you, your son, or anyone else in your family. This is our baby, and we fully intend to raise her and give her all the things she will need in life. This will not include you, your son, or anyone else in your family. Please have a wonderful day, and may God help you." Cicely hung up the telephone, reached across the table for some eggs and began adding them and other ingredients to the bowl for her cake, as if nothing had ever happened. No one asked Cicely anything about the call. They all knew who the caller was and later learned that she had called to inform Cicely that her family did not accept me and that they would have no part in raising me. This was Cicely's final conversation with my paternal grandmother.

BACK TO SCHOOL

At six months old, I was the pride of the family. It was the fall of the year, and my father visited our home to inform Cicely and Carla that he was leaving DC. He had joined the army and was heading to Fort Bragg, North Carolina. This was great news for Cicely. The thought of Carla possibly having another baby out of wedlock was completely sickening for Cicely. She did not want Carla anywhere near my father. She wanted Carla to return to school, finish her education, and hopefully find an "appropriate" suitor. Shortly after, Carla returned to Ellson High School without a blemish on her record. Her pregnancy had been hidden from most people. Her teachers thought she had been sick with pneumonia. The family doctor was a key player in this cover-up. Thus, the school was very supportive of Carla. They allowed her to do schoolwork at home.

When Carla returned to school, everyone was happy to see her. Her girlfriends were very anxious to update her on the new school happenings. One important happening was that the school had recruited several new male athletes. At that time, Ellson was ranked one of the top ten high schools in DC for its football and basketball teams. Thus, many of the top athletes in the area were being recruited there with hopes of a scholarship and a chance to get into the pro leagues. One of the new athletes, Paul Steen, had transferred to Ellson as a junior and was of interest to Carla. The first time she saw him, she had an immediate attraction. When Paul saw Carla, she was walking down a hallway near the gymnasium. At first glance, he thought, "Look at that beautiful redbone girl. I have got to have her."

Carla was a sexy redbone. Her lips were colored with a rich red lipstick. She was wearing a bright white, heavily starched blouse, as crisp as fresh lettuce, with nicely fitted black pants and red shoes. Carla was very fashionable, and Paul was mesmerized by her. He was a star basketball player with a promising future. He was being recruited by several top colleges in the country. He was bright, athletic, almost seven feet tall, and although not very handsome, he was a real ladies' man. The girls at school were wild for him, and although Carla was who he wanted to be his main girl, he was very lascivious by nature, lusting after all the pretty girls.

At the time, Carla was maintaining a long-distance relationship with my father. However, she started dating Paul, and they were soon madly in love. They dated through the end of high school. My father's closest friends began writing letters to inform him that Carla was dating Paul, but he did not believe what his friends were telling him. By the end of Paul's twelfth-grade year, he had received several scholarships offers. He and Carla, however,

B. PHOENIX

began making long-term plans for their future. At this point, Carla sent my father the infamous "Dear John" letter. He was crushed. And meanwhile, Paul informed his parents that he had taken the United States Post Office exam, scored high and was planning to take a job with them after graduation. His parents were outraged. What could possibly make Paul turn down opportunities of a lifetime for any young man, especially a young black man? His mother felt sure he would be ruining his life if he did this.

The Early Years

THE HEEL FAMILY celebrated my first birthday, and it was a big hit. There was plenty of food and refreshments. All of the family and close friends of the family were present. Cicely was in her role of forever present. Carla, of course, was there. Marie and Annette, who also played a role in caring for me, were there. Harmon, who was in love with me, was always very protective of me, and played a major financial role in raising me, was there also. However, my maternal grandmother (Harmon's wife), who I did not know at the time, was forbidden from participating in any of the Heel family events. Nor were any of my father's family included in the celebration. Nonetheless, it was a great party, and one of which the family talked about for many years.

In September 1963, I began kindergarten at Middletown Elementary School in DC. By that time, Carla and Paul were married, living in Cicely's house and had two other children. In the spring of 1964, Carla and Paul moved into his parents' home. Paul's mother was totally against them moving into her house (she always blamed Carla for ruining her son's life), but his father insisted they be allowed to move in. Carla and Paul started a new journey. However, Cicely made it very clear that it made much more sense for me to remain in her care. With no ability to win a fight with Cicely, Carla moved on with her life and left me in Cicely's care.

Elementary school was very good for me. Cicely made sure I was always well prepared for school. I showed up every day well fed, perfectly dressed, and ready to learn. My kindergarten teacher was Mrs. Farmer. Mrs. Farmer was a true educator. She was passionate about her students, and I was her favorite. She loved me, and I loved her, and we both knew it. I always did well in all my subjects and got along with my schoolmates. I was precise and tried to go by the book. I had developed a level of meticulousness that was far beyond my years. I was extremely organized. My teachers loved this about me, but it drove most of my peers and young relatives crazy.

I experienced my first crush in elementary school. It was Stevie Edson, a very thin, beautiful, brown-skinned fellow. Outside of Jermaine Jackson, of the Jackson 5, Stevie had the largest, most beautiful afro I had ever seen. He made it very clear that he liked me. I received my first billet-doux from Stevie. It read, "I love you very much. Do you love me?" I loved Stevie, but I'm not sure he ever knew how much of a crush I had on him. Girls in those days just did not let boys know how they felt. And besides, Cicely would have killed me if she found out I had expressed any type of feelings about a boy. My elementary school days were some of the best days of my life. All my teachers made learning fun. We also enjoyed school plays and great field trips. May Days were huge events in our school. They were days where lots of festivities took place over multiple days in the spring—and no school work. It was great!

Elementary school, however, is where I performed my first bad deed. I was probably about nine or ten years old. About four of us girls played together at recess every day. One of my playmates was Lisa. She was a nice person, and because she was an only child, having a small group of girlfriends was great for her. Lisa's parents were older than most of the parents and had the means to give her a very privileged lifestyle. They both worked, and Lisa was one of the first latchkey children I knew. Her house was across the street from the school, and she went home alone each day after school. One other girl in our group and I were also from nice homes and had families that cared about us as well. They raised us to be nice to other people. Unlike Lisa, the two of us always had someone at home when we got out of school.

The fourth girl in our group, however, was from a large family, and as I look back on it, I don't think she got the love and nurturing she needed to be a good citizen. She was strong and tall, and towered over most of the boys. She was a bully and quite frankly had the three of us scared to death of her. But for some reason, Lisa was the one she picked on the most. She would make Lisa carry her books, wait on her hand and foot, and bring food from her home to give us—mostly apples, oranges, and cookies. Lisa did not want to do it, but the mean girl was brutal. She would push and punch and yell at Lisa and me, and the other girl would not do anything. We were so afraid.

I remember on one occasion, Miss Meany would try to make us hit Lisa, and when we refused, she would literally grab one of our arms hard and swing it at Lisa. On many occasions, Lisa would be crying and crying. I used to feel so bad about it but could not think of anything to do that would not result in Miss Meany killing us. There was always peace among the three of us when Miss Meany was not around, but when she showed up, all hell broke loose. We would try to avoid her, and if we saw her before she saw us, we would run fast in the opposite direction. Can you imagine your child being so tormented by one person? This went on for a couple years before somehow it just stopped. I don't remember, but I think Miss Meany moved or got transferred to another school. Nonetheless, this is a deed I regret, and if I never formally apologized to Lisa—I am so very sorry for not stepping up and defending you in that madness!

When I was in elementary school, my father was released from the military. One afternoon, he showed up at my house, and Cicely, although she had no interest in seeing him, was kind enough to let him in. No one had ever mentioned my father, or who he was, and it never occurred to me to ask. After all, my last name was the same as Carla's, so I must have belonged to Paul. At least this is what most outsiders thought, but the family knew better. And although I would tell people Paul was my father, I always got a sinking feeling in my stomach when I said those words—"My father." I believe somehow, buried deep in my soul, I knew that Paul was not my father.

My father, however, was a total stranger to me, and it was obvious that this visit was putting Cicely in the awkward position of having to explain who he was. So he, to ease Cicely's apparent discomfort, told me he had known my family for a very long time and that he had been away for many years. He said he had just returned to the area and wanted to see how we all were doing. I still didn't understand why Cicely was making me sit in the living room with her and this man. I knew something was different about him because our living room was reserved for formal visits and special occasions only.

During this pretty lengthy conversation, mostly with my father asking for updates on all of the family members, Cicely told him about Carla and

B. PHOENIX

Paul having two children, Marie having been married with several children, Annette also being married, and how they all had moved out on their own. After all the updates, my father told me he would like to come around more often and wanted us to be "pals." He asked, "Will this be okay with you?" Thinking that perhaps I would be dismissed sooner if I agreed, I cheerfully said, "Okay." It worked. Cicely told me I was excused, and I rushed out and left her and my father, who I obviously did not know was my father, in the living room talking.

For many years, my father came around from time to time, like he said. In addition, one of his sisters made her way around and introduced herself to me as my aunt. However, in terms of the relations, none of it fit together in my mind. I never connected my father and my aunt. To be honest, I never attempted to put it all together, and no one else put it together for me. Besides, we had several family members that were cousins, but I called them aunt or uncle. When I first started visiting my father's sister, he would always be around. Initially, I wasn't sure if he was her friend, brother, or what. He was always very nice to me, and he and I had short but cordial conversations. He bought me expensive gifts and always signed the cards "Your Pal." I accepted my aunt as my aunt and the man who was my father as my "pal," and life moved on.

As it turned out, I spent more time with my aunt than with my father. She would get Cicely's permission to take me to her house for weekend sleepovers. This was unique because Cicely would not entrust my care to most people. My aunt lived with her mother, and although her mother refused to accept me when I was an infant, she was always cordial to me when I visited her home. Hanging out with my aunt was great! She was young, educated, and very well-groomed. She worked as a professional in the federal government. She received her bachelor's degree during the time when many blacks still could not read and write. She had an excellent position in the government and was paid very well for a black woman in the '60s. She was not married and made it her business to reserve time for me. She introduced me to many of the finer things in life. I thought she was rich because she and I would do things that cost lots of money. We would dine in very expensive restaurants and shop in high-end stores in DC and New York. Life was good. My aunt was a very special person in my life.

My childhood never lacked anything. Cicely always provided the best foods; I wore the best clothing, and there was peace in our home. I was very happy and never aware of any hardships Cicely experienced. Life for me was full of fun and joy. By the end of elementary school, Cicely decided there was no way she was going to allow me to attend junior high school in the public school system. One morning, she called me into the kitchen. She wanted to give me the "good news." She had applied for me to attend a private school on Capitol Hill, and the application was accepted. While Cicely was very excited about the news, I was very sad. I did not want to attend private school. None of my lifelong friends were going to this school, and I would not know anyone there. It made no sense in my head why Cicely would make this decision. And besides, the tuition was very expensive. This just seemed crazy to me.

I let Cicely know I did not want to go to private school. However, it didn't matter because several of my elementary school teachers had recommended this to Cicely. They told her I was one of the best-rounded students in the school, and I had the ability to master anything if I put my mind to it. They explained to her that a good private school would nurture and develop my natural abilities. Carla, however, believed that private school was a big waste of money. She informed Cicely that she would not be able to help her with the expense of private school. Cicely didn't care. She wanted nothing but the best for me, and if it meant she had to go at it alone, it was fine with her. Cicely trusted only God to provide for her and truly believed He would continue to look out for her and give her the desires of her heart.

TEENAGE YEARS

In the fall of 1970, I began the seventh grade at one of the finest private schools offered to blacks in the DC area. It was a big adjustment for me. My first days at St. Mary Comforter School were exciting. Most of the boys and girls at St. Mary Comforter seemed very happy to be living. This was different than the environment from which I had come. Some of the students from my old school seemed to have serious domestic and social issues. The students at St. Mary Comforter seemed to have no real issues. They were all neat and clean, very well-groomed, and most of them seemed very happy. Suddenly, I was in an environment where the students were, at least outwardly, the same as me, and their parents seemed to have the same mind-set as Cicely. They wanted the best for their children, and they had a strong belief in God.

The students at St. Mary Comforter were far ahead of me in their studies. This required me to work extra hard to catch up. Since Cicely had not completed elementary school, she was ill-equipped to assist me with my homework, but she always made sure that someone was around to help me and that I had every resource necessary to succeed. And before long, I pulled my grades up and became one of the top students in my class. These students, however, were also far ahead of me in the level of freedom they had, of which I was not accustomed. This freedom afforded them money to do what they saw fit—one thing was purchasing and smoking cigarettes. Well, once I got over the initial choking, I too became a real smoker. Of everything I learned in private school, smoking was the one thing Cicely never knew about. If she ever found out I was a smoker, I believe she would have killed me. And there was one occasion, in fact, when I feared for my life.

A student, one of the lower classmen, caught five of us older girls smoking in the girls' restroom. We threatened the student, telling her that she would be in deep trouble if she reported us, but she reported us anyway. And guess who was in trouble—each of us. Suddenly, one of the nuns came walking down the hallway. We knew she was coming because we could hear her loud, clunking shoes, and her pace was clearly hard and fast. Before she entered the restroom, each of us had gone into one of the stalls and stood up on the toilet seat. Well, she was smarter than that. She proceeded to open each of the stall doors—slamming them open one at a time – bam, bam, bam. We were all trembling like a leaf. We knew a severe punishment was coming, but we had no idea what type of punishment it would be.

Sister Sarai Antony marched us to our lockers and told us to get our lunch money and coats. Lunch money and coats? We had no idea what was about to happen. We followed Sister Antony down a long hallway and down the staircase that led to the front entrance of the school. She opened the front door and said, "Follow me!" We followed her to a nearby grocery store. While there, she purchased five packs of cigarettes. We went back to the school, and she made us sit in one of the classrooms. She then proceeded to forcefully open each window (at least eight to ten large windows) and told us to "light up!" Light up? We didn't know what to do, so none of us made a move. She repeated herself, but this time screaming, "Light up," as she slammed a yardstick on the desk. At that point, we were all so frightened that we nervously opened the cigarette packs and began to smoke. Near the end of smoking the first cigarette, we were all thinking, "Okay, this is fun."

Well the fun soon ended. She made us smoke the entire pack (all twenty cigarettes), one after the other. A couple of my friends were fine, but the rest of us were sick as dogs. After we finished all twenty cigarettes, she slammed her yardstick on the desk again and said, "Don't ever let me catch you smoking again. Now get out!" We all quickly scurried out of the classroom. For the rest of that day, the five of us were quiet, and most of us were sick to our stomachs, or had serious headaches. When I got home that day, Cicely took one look at me and asked, "What in the world is wrong with you?" For fear of being murdered, I lied and told her that I started feeling sick after lunch. She immediately began nursing me. I felt so bad that I went to bed early and, of course, never mentioned a word to Cicely about what happened.

Because Cicely was a very strict parent and, as I thought, overly protective, many of the delinquencies in which a lot of my friends and other young people my age were engaging, I was not. You know, things like stealing the family car, sneaking out of the house after everyone was asleep, and coming in after curfew—none of that for me. I was only allowed to play on my side of the city block, and my curfew was when the street lights came on, I had to get home quickly. I was rarely allowed in other people's homes and was only allowed to accept food from certain people. Cicely had tons of rules, all of which now I know were to protect me, but back then I thought they were the worst—like being in prison.

Another one of Cicely's many rules was that I had to attend Sunday school and regular church service every Sunday. We were members of the Church of God in Christ (COGIC). For those of you who don't know, back in the day, COGIC was a very strict Pentecostal denomination. There was very little you could do with the secular world. With Cicely, if extracurricular activities didn't happen with the school or church, normally I did not participate. Cicely kept close tabs on my whereabouts. I knew teens and even family members, many of whom were younger than me, who could go places and do things that I was never allowed to do. For instance, leaving the street on which I lived. I couldn't even go around the corner from my house without checking in with Cicely, and I only got to go if she had spoken to an adult at the place where I wanted to go, and she felt comfortable about it.

B. PHOENIX

I remember once, Cicely sent a neighbor to the Safeway, our local grocery store. The neighbor's little sister, who was a friend of mine, was going with her and asked me to go along. It was an enjoyable trip. My friend and I played all along the way. We picked out our favorite houses and cars—claiming ownership of those we liked—"that's my car," "that's my house." Once at the Safeway, the nice man in the produce section gave us so much sample fruit that our bellies were full. It was a fun trip. When we headed back home, I was so excited and couldn't wait to tell Cicely all about my adventure. As we neared my house, I could see Cicely, from a distance, standing on the corner of my street. Why on earth was she there? The closer I got to her, I realized she was waiting for us. Well, she was waiting for me—waiting to tear my tail up! Whew! I was very leery about going to the store because Cicely had not given me permission to go, but I went any way. After all, they were going for Cicely—doing her a favor—bad decision. She got me good—so good that I never went anywhere else without her permission. So even though I loved adventures, there were no more unapproved adventures for me!

I also loved to sing. When I was thirteen years old, I joined my church choir. I enjoyed singing in the choir on Sundays and looked forward to choir rehearsal every Wednesday. I grew to love church very much. The Spirit of God constantly flowed through my church. There were happy and positive people, good music, and very cute boys—especially one boy in particular—John-John—a real stereotypical preacher's kid (PK). PKs had a reputation of being wild and worldly children. John-John was by no means the exception. He was a very bad boy—the epitome of a stereotypical PK. He was also my second love. John-John was tall and handsome with rich, beautiful brown skin. He had very full lips and was interested in kissing me at every moment. He so desperately wanted to do more, but Cicely had put the fear of God in me about having sex, and John-John knew I would never go any further than hugging and kissing.

It seemed as if we would kiss and hug more than the minutes or hours we were together. We kissed and hugged everywhere—in the main sanctuary of my church (when no one was around, of course), in the kitchen of my church, in the pastor's office, in other churches, in the backseat of his dad's car, in his house, other church members' houses, in restaurants, and on buses. We always found a way to lock lips, everywhere we went. Sorry, not everywhere—the one place we never kissed was in Cicely's house. There was no way a boy would get past her eagle eyes. Cicely liked John-John and his family very much, but she would never have left us alone in her house. John-John had a great family, and we had lots of great times together!

Another family I spent a lot of time with had a daughter, Patty, who was my best friend at church. Patty and I were like soul mates. We coordinated outfits and always ensured that we were both engaging in all the same church activities. Patty's parents were much younger than Cicely and not as strict, so at Patty's house, we could listen to secular music, and during many of our regular sleepovers, we would be up into the wee hours of the morning dreaming about our future and talking a lot about boys and clothes. I was also often included in family vacations with Patty. We went many exciting places, such as Atlantic City and New York City.

After successfully completing elementary school (Catholic schools during that time did not have middle school), I moved on to St. Margaret's Academy, an all-girl Catholic high school. St. Margaret's had a great college prep program, and by the time I was in the tenth grade, I was already taking college-level courses. I enjoyed private school very much. In the end, I was pleased Cicely made sacrifices so I could receive an excellent education. She made sure my life was complete. I got most of the things I wanted and all the things I needed. This was a philosophy Cicely taught me very early. She would often say, "You should never give children everything they want, even if you can—you'll ruin them, but you must give them everything they need."

Another reason Cicely raised me with the philosophy that you "give a child all of what they need and some of what they want" was because she believed that a child that received everything he or she wanted would not be able to deal with some of life's most difficult tests, and she wanted me to be prepared. Cicely was all about preparation. She was very organized and always planned, and didn't give much attention to spontaneity. She took every task as a project and sat down and thought through every step and every requirement for completing each task. Our weekends were planned like excursions every week. At some point on Friday, Cicely and one of her nieces would sit down and make lists and strategize on how to accomplish the most out of each weekend. For those of you who know me, I guess you know that jumped all ova' me—so see, it's not my fault.

We were not rich, but I thought we were. There were friends and relatives who thought we were rich also. However, whenever I spoke of this to Cicely, she would always say, "You have more than a lot of people and live better than many, but we are not rich. We are blessed with God's favor, but always remember we are no better than anyone else." And blessed we truly were. Cicely owned a beautiful house in DC, and sent me to the finest schools around; we always had the best foods, and she dressed me in the finest clothing offered for children in those days. All of this was done with the help of family and on the salary of a domestic worker.

Cicely cleaned the Senate House Office Building at night and the apartment of a very wealthy diplomat during the day. Her salary was extremely low, but over many years and after having raised several generations, she learned how to make a little go a long way. Also, her sons, nephews, and nieces always looked out for her. Her sons bought her expensive household furnishings, all of which lasted most of my life. Her nieces and nephews raised cattle and hogs and owned huge fruit and vegetable gardens. They made sure we had fresh meat, fruit, and vegetables. Our home was the place that people could always count on having a warm bed and a great meal. Cicely never prepared meals for just us. She always prepared "just in case someone comes by and is hungry," and most of my life this happened quite often, especially on Sundays. Being the only child living in the house for many years, I loved having guests at our home. Especially since I couldn't do much outside of the house.

During my teen years, I spent a lot of time in my room reading, listening to music, organizing my closet and drawers, and cleaning my room. When I got my own private telephone line, talking on the phone took up a fair amount of my time, especially since I was not allowed to go many places unsupervised. Although Cicely tried to control the amount of time I spent on the phone, I managed to talk to my friends more often than she knew. I was a daydreamer, and my dreams were almost always about my future—the kind of house I wanted, the job I wanted, the places I would go, and, last, but certainly not least, the man I wanted. In my world, many young girls wanted a good man. However, not many of them believed in the "knight in shining armor" man. But I did. And the "knight in shining armor" man is who I wanted. I always had my antenna up to try and decipher who he could be.

In addition to dreams of my knight in shining armor, I also dreamed a lot about having a great job. I never dreamed much about college. When I was a very young child, I remember Cicely saying she wanted to live long enough to see me graduate from high school. For her, graduating from high school was a major accomplishment since she never finished grade school. Therefore, graduating high school seemed to be the bar that I needed to reach. Then, I could get a great government job and move on with my life. Well, I graduated high school and Cicely did, in fact, live long enough to see that happen.

Cicely's days left on this earth, unbeknownst to us, were few. It was very hard for me to leave St. Margaret's Academy. Out of nowhere, everything was changing. The tuition at St. Margaret's increased drastically. I was being forced to return to public school. Cicely was experiencing medical issues and was no longer able to afford private school. As you know, Carla never agreed with paying tuition and thought it was ridiculous to pay for an education when you could get one for free. After all the many discussions and arguments about sending me to public school, amazingly, just fourteen years after my mother graduated from Ellson High School, I was enrolling at Ellson. Although Cicely never said how she felt, I could see the disappointment all over her face. She trusted God for everything, but I could tell she was disappointed about this change in her plan. This is a perfect example, and more confirmation for me, of how sometimes our plan is not God's plan and His plan is *always* better, no matter how it looks in the beginning.

Ellson High School, founded in 1890, is an old, gigantic, historic school building. There were massive columns in front of the building, a huge stone circular driveway, and beautiful stone corners on all sides of the building. The building and its property covered all four sides of a full city block. The halls were longer than any school building in which I had been. There was a full football field with lots of wooden bleachers; a full-size gymnasium and multiple basketball courts, the largest cafeteria I had ever seen in my whole life, and a beautiful concert choir room with a baby grand piano and stadium type seating. The construction of this school was purely a masterpiece. And although the school had taken a beating over the years, it was still a grand sight to see.

The first week of school, one of my neighbors, Breen Tallwood, spotted me in the hallway. She rushed over to greet me and said, "I sure am happy you finally broke out of that prison you were in." We both laughed and headed to class. Suddenly, I was feeling a little better about leaving St. Margaret's. Breen was a very outspoken person and was extremely popular in school. I, on the other hand, was very shy, and being a new kid at the school, didn't know many people. I also wasn't the type to put myself out there. From a young child, I was very shy. I was friendly, but I needed to be approached first. Breen and I were like night and day in terms of our personalities. When we reached my class, she asked me when I was scheduled to take lunch. As it turned out, we both were scheduled for lunch on the same period, so we planned to meet in the cafeteria.

During lunch, Breen introduced me to at least one hundred people. It seemed to me that everyone in the entire school knew her—teachers and students. She identified many of the people she talked to as members of the school's gospel choir. She told several of them that she was going to take me to the music room after school to try out for the gospel choir. Breen never asked if I wanted to join the choir, but I had been singing in my church choir, so I had no problem with this new endeavor. However, at church, all you needed to do was have the desire to sing; you didn't have to have a real voice, and you could still be part of the choir. To be a member of the Ellson High School Gospel Choir, you had to pass a real audition. Man, was I nervous.

After school that day, Breen met me at my locker, and we headed up to the music room. I was trembling in my boots. As we walked in, I was in awe at the choir room. The music teacher, Mrs. Joan Green, was sitting at the baby grand piano, playing music like I had only heard before on television. It was simply beautiful, and I knew at that moment that this was a woman I admired and would look up to forever. Breen introduced me to Mrs. Green and told her that I wanted to try out for the gospel choir. I was petrified. I had to sing for this woman by myself and in front of several other people that were hanging out in the music room. For as painful as it was, I made it through the audition and was deemed to sing good enough to be part of the Ellson High School Gospel Choir. At this point, Ellson was beginning to feel even better to me. Mrs. Green informed me of the rules and welcomed me to the choir. I was so excited I could barely wait to get home and give Cicely the good news.

As I expected, Cicely was very excited as well. She loved God more than anybody I knew, and for me to be in a choir singing the gospel outside of church was just icing on the cake for her. My siblings, who lived with Carla, and other members of my family thought it was queer that I joined the choir. For them, this was confirmation that I was a "goody two-shoes church girl."

Most of the time, I could care less about the names they called me because I was used to hearing negative comments from them about positive things I did. When I received good grades, they teased me. When I was selected to participate in other extracurricular activities (such as ballet), they teased me. If I tried to do the right thing, this was grounds for their teasing. Merely the color of my skin was, in some of their minds, worthy of teasing. They called me "yellow girl," "white girl," and "rich girl" all the time. Although the teasing did sometimes bother me, Cicely was the only one I wanted to please, and I never let on that the teasing bothered me.

I was very excited about my first day at choir rehearsal. I thought about it all day long and couldn't wait to get there. When school let out at three that day, by 3:05, I had booted it up to the third floor and rushed into the choir room to find no one there but Mrs. Green. She greeted me with a huge smile and again welcomed me into the choir. She told me to take a seat and that the others would be along very soon. A few moments later, the herd began coming into the room. Breen was in the crowd. When she spotted me, she made her way over and sat next to me. We engaged in small talk as the others were entering the room. Breen told me about all the wonderful trips we would be taking, and she explained how we were "going to have a ball" with the choir.

Mrs. Green was one of the smartest women I knew. She was a brilliant music teacher and choir director. She was innovative, and under her direction, the concept of a high school gospel choir was taken to a new, higher, level. She was a true maestro. She taught us about all types of music, and we sang songs from all genres—classical, pop, gospel, and opera. We never knew what Mrs. Green was planning for us. She introduced us to it all. She also taught us lessons on being responsible adults—always holding us accountable for our actions. One of her infamous statements was, "No excuses." That philosophy is one by which I have tried to live my entire life. Being part of the choir was a very exciting and educationally cultured experience.

Just before Mrs. Green began class, a couple of guys walked in. One was very tall, with dark skin, and handsome. The other was tall with very light brown skin, and was the most handsome guy I had ever seen in my whole entire life. My heart skipped several beats as he made his way to the back of the room. He was neat, clean, and very well-dressed. I wanted so desperately to turn and look at him more, but I was far too afraid that he would catch me looking. I couldn't possibly let him know that I was immediately interested in knowing everything about him. In just a few seconds, this young man had made a deep imprint on my heart. Now, Ellson High School was even better than all the days before!

Every day we would go to choir rehearsal after school, and my dream man would come into the room and light up my life. It was an unbelievable attraction—something I had never felt before. Nothing like I felt with Stevie Edson in elementary school. Nothing like I felt with John-John as a young teen. Each day, I seemed to feel more and more attracted to this young man. I watched him every chance I got. He was always very nice and seemed to be a perfect gentleman. There was something different about him than all the other guys in school.

Different was something to which I was always attracted. I established a taste for things that were different as a young girl. I always looked for clothes that were fashionable but different from what everyone else wore. Every day, there were guys making passes at me and trying very boldly to get with me. I had no interest in any of them. In all honesty, I was afraid of bad boys, and getting too close to most boys made me nervous. Part of my fear was due to Cicely's forceful warning that "you better stay away from those boys. When you start fooling around with boys, trouble starts." I also feared I might miss my "knight in shining armor." Many of the boys at school were fast at putting moves on girls, but I knew my guy would not be as forward as most of the guys that approached me, and that is what I wanted.

Even as a teenager, I was very in tune to what I wanted, and very seldom did I change my mind once I decided. This guy was the one for me. He was always very polite, and although he never made a pass at me, I always felt there was a common attraction. There were lots of rumors about this one girl in the choir who everyone thought he was dating. She latched onto him every chance she got, but none of us knew if they were really an item. After about six months of watching and listening to him talk to his friends, I decided I was feeling way too strongly about him to let him get away without knowing how I felt.

One day during his lunch period, I was walking through the cafeteria and saw him sitting and eating all alone. My heart began racing about one hundred beats per minute. I decided this was my chance. The two of us would be alone, and I could tell him just how I felt. So I walked right up to him, and, in all honesty, I don't remember what happened. What I dreamed I would say was, "I love you so much. I think you're my knight in shining armor, and we should date." I don't remember what I said, but what I do remember is that everything suddenly seemed foggy. He gave me the most beautiful smile, and whatever he said, I rushed away. How could I have been so forward? Or was I? I don't know what happened that afternoon. I would never approach another guy ever again! That experience was far too painful and embarrassing. I went on with the rest of my day even though I felt humiliated and didn't even know why I felt that way. To this day, I don't know what was said, but from that day forward, he always gave me the most beautiful warm smile.

When I walked out of school that day, heading to work, there sitting parked right in front of my school was a guy who had been chasing me for years. He was there waiting for me. He was handsome, well-dressed, with a beautiful singing voice, and a real gentleman (or ladies' man, as it turned out). He attended COGIC as well and knew me and my family. Cicely, many years before I was born, had known his parents. This guy was a bit older than me and was very charming. He sensed right away that something was wrong and zoomed in to console me. I never told him why I was so sad, but the attention did me good. He drove me to work that day, and we scheduled a date.

Mr. Charming courted me hard. He convinced me that he was very much into me, and he knew I was becoming more and more attracted to the attention he was giving me. What he didn't know was that Cicely had already warned me to "stay away from that guy." She never explained why; I just thought she didn't want me to be around any guys. And although I spent a fair amount of time with this guy, I was always reluctant to get too close to him. This reluctance was mainly due to the forcefulness in Cicely's voice when she told me to "stay away from that guy." It was like a serious warning. And besides, Mr. Knight in Shining Armor was who I wanted.

I returned to school the next day, and my knight walked into the choir room as usual. This day, the other girl walked in with him with a huge smile on her face. Watching how she looked and interacted with him sickened me. They were never openly romantic but were together way too much for me. By June, my knight graduated and moved on with his life, but he never moved from my heart. I remained in the choir, which was the highlight of each of my days. I thought of him often and especially every time I entered the choir room. For many years, whenever I encountered anyone or anything associated with Ellson High School, I thought of him, but life moved on, and my last year at Ellson was a lot of fun. Because I had completed more credits than needed to graduate, in my twelfth-grade year, I went to school in the morning for a half day. In the afternoons, I worked as a clerk in the federal government for a few hours and returned to school for gospel choir rehearsal. Life was grand!

WORLDLY POSSESSIONS

Almost immediately after I graduated high school, Cicely began showing signs of serious memory loss. In late 1976, she had a stroke and was admitted into the hospital for several weeks. In the spring of 1977, Cicely died. The one person I knew, without a doubt, loved me more than life itself, had died. I had no idea what the future held for me, but I believe Cicely did. At her funeral, although I didn't know either of these things at the time, seated to my right was the man I would be married to for more than thirty years, and in my womb was my first child. In addition to wanting to see me graduate from high school, I believe Cicely also wanted me to meet a good man that would look out for me as she did. Could she have asked God for one last blessing? "God please give my great-granddaughter a man who will love and look out for her as I did"—was that one of her final prayers? Perhaps she felt praying for a good man for me would help me survive this cruel world without her.

Could Cicely have known that, although her intent was that all her worldly possessions be left for me when she died, there would be nothing for me after she was gone? I wonder. After Cicely died, I had virtually nothing material. Throughout my entire life, I heard the adults talking about Cicely leaving her many possessions to me. However, none of her worldly possessions ended up with me except for a small wooden table, one chair, and a beautiful teapot. All her other worldly possessions were taken by other family members and either lost or destroyed. Precious items such as expensive crystal and china were taken and used for everyday meals; beautiful, expensive drapery destroyed; antique furniture abused, scratched, and then eventually trashed; and the grand finale was a million-dollar piece of prime real estate on Capitol Hill lost in a card game. Although I didn't inherit any of those things, I received the best inheritance of all—a strong belief in God and the understanding of His largesse on me.

CHAPTER 5

To Be or Not to Be

IN JANUARY 1977, my closest friend invited me to a party hosted by one of her friends. It was a party that had become a big annual event. Several of my friends had been attending this party for years. They came back every year with stories about all the fun they had and the cute guys that were there. For years, I was never allowed to go to this party. You know Cicely. She was not about to give me permission to go to a party where there were boys and drinking, oh no! Finally, I could make the decision to go. I was very excited to be going to this party, and my friend and I began preparing, days in advance. We made sure our outfits, shoes, and hair were just right. I didn't wear much makeup, but I always loved wearing beautiful lipstick. So, needless to say, that was right too.

We left Capitol Hill in my friend's brand new apple green, two-door Camaro with pure white interior and headed to the other side of town. After days of preparation and much excitement and adrenalin, the trip to this party was a disaster. We got very lost and were riding around for hours trying to find this party. We could not find a phone booth anywhere. Yes, I said phone booth, and if you don't know what that looks like, ask anyone over forty years old. This was pre-cell-phone days. To make matters worse, believe it or not, we ran out of gas. At this point, I was thinking I had been waiting at least three years to attend this party, and it was starting to feel as if I was going to miss another one. My friend and I were so upset! After sitting in the car for about thirty minutes trying to figure out what to do, we saw some people come out of a nearby house and asked them if we could use their telephone. My friend called this guy she was casually dating, and he came to bring us gas and escorted us to where we were going.

By the time we arrived at the party, it was almost over but still in full swing. There were plenty of men at this party. I mean full-grown men. I was just eighteen years old, and most of the people at this party were in their twenties and thirties. However, it wasn't uncomfortable for me because I had been used to being the youngest in most of my circles. My friend was twenty-three years old, and she introduced me to her world. And most of the people in her world were young professionals—all of whom were much older than me and all of them employed by the federal government.

As I made my way around the room, I had been asked to dance by several guys, most of whom were tall and sweaty. This grossed me out so badly. It was superhot in this place! After walking around trying to keep a low profile, I began to feel a need to sit down. I looked across the room, and there was an empty chair in the kitchen next to a window. As I approached the chair, a young man was approaching it at the same time. He graciously offered the seat to me, but I declined and began to walk away. This guy followed me and asked me to dance, and I agreed. He was an excellent, smooth dancer. He wasn't all sweaty like many of the other guys, and he remained a gentleman the entire time. We spent the rest of my time at the party together. We talked and danced and talked and talked.

His name was Lewis, and he seemed to be a pretty nice guy. He was handsome and very well groomed. He was very unassuming and seemed to be a bit less confident than the other guys at the party. Lewis asked for my telephone number, and I gave it to him. Shortly after, my friend came to me and said she was ready to go. It was music to my ears because, although we arrived late, I had been ready to go soon after we got there. We left and went to a pancake house to get a bite to eat. We talked about every aspect of the party including Lewis. After about two hours, we left and went home.

Lewis began calling me on a regular basis, and we started spending time together. It was easy to spend time with him. Unlike most other guys I met, he did not put a lot of pressure on me to have sex. It never came up until three months later. It was early April and Lewis's birthday. At the time, he was renting a very quaint apartment space from a young couple who were friends of his. Lewis's living space was very neat and clean and quite lovely. I was very impressed at how well he kept it. Lewis worked for a subcontractor under an electric company. He told me he was an electrician, which I later learned was a lie. He was a laborer on a construction site and was laid off not long after we started dating. He had apparently worked in the electrical field in the past, but was laid off from that company as well. I encouraged him to take some electrical classes, and he did. Before too long, Lewis was offered a position as an electrical helper and began a very strong career as an electrician.

Lewis was born in a small beach town in Virginia. He is the second and only living child of his parents. His parents' firstborn child died as a baby. Lewis's father, supposedly, came from a very-well-off family and was an only child who had all the pleasures he wanted in life. His mother was raised by adopted parents who basically used her and her brother to labor on their farm. Lewis's father's parents never felt his mother was good enough for their son and had nothing to do with her after Lewis's father's early unexpected death. A horrible car accident took his life when Lewis was just a toddler. After his father's death, his mother was left with a very handsome amount of money. However, as the story goes, that money was used up prematurely, and there was nothing for Lewis when he became of age.

When Lewis was about seven or eight years old, his mother and her new husband packed up and moved him and their other children to DC. Lewis's stepfather was not in the home a lot because of his military duties. His mom always worked at least two jobs, and for many years, she depended on Lewis to care for his younger siblings. Per Lewis, he had a very challenging childhood. He said that he rarely received the things he needed and that by the time he was fifteen, he dropped out of school so he could work to earn money for necessities (e.g., toiletries, shoes, and clothes). By the time I met Lewis, he was already a strong survivor.

After dating Lewis for a short amount of time, I became pregnant. Although shocked, I was not upset about becoming pregnant. Lewis and I had a seemingly strong relationship and spent most of our time together. We spent so much time together that my friends began to resent me not spending time with them. I will never forget the day I announced to Lewis that I was pregnant. His response, which shocked me more than the fact that I was pregnant, was, "What are you going to do about it?" What are you going to do about it? What kind of question was that? Did he mean what I thought he meant? Yes, he did. He wanted to know if I was going to have the baby or have an abortion. This question made me furious. After I went off on him, he quickly changed his tune, and we moved forward without ever having discussed that again.

In December 1977, my first child was born. Kendal was a beautiful baby girl. Everyone marveled over her. I remember Lewis's grandmother commenting on how beautiful she was and how she reminded her of Lewis's mom's firstborn child. Grandmamma used to say that her mother said, referring to this child, that "this child is too pretty to live." That made me wild when she said that, and she said it on more than one occasion. I could not understand why she would make such a statement in relation to my child. It was very bizarre for me, but I ignored it and moved on. My child was healthy and strong and a joy to be around. Lewis was the perfect father. He and I made sure to take care of all her needs before doing anything else. Lewis didn't make much money, but we did well with what he and I made together. We moved into the house on Capitol Hill where I grew up. My Uncle James and my grandfather, Harmon, were both still living in this house. Life was going very well for us; well, with a few exceptions.

One night, I was awakened by the voice of a woman screaming, "help me; please help me; somebody please help me!" I sat straight up in the bed and began rubbing my eyes to be sure I was not dreaming. As I looked around the room, everything seemed in place. Lewis, at this point, sat up in the bed as well. We conferred with each other that the sound seemed to be coming from the back of the house. Then suddenly, we both agreed that the sound was coming from the alley behind the house. This woman's voice was so piercing with fear that I just knew she had been dragged into the alley and was maybe being raped. We both jumped up to go look out one of the back windows, but Lewis insisted that I stay in the room and let him check first.

As he slowly opened the bedroom door, the voice seemed louder and much closer. It seemed as if the sound was coming from the bathroom that was at the back of the house. Perhaps someone left the bathroom window opened. Lewis insisted that I close our bedroom door behind him, and he went to the bathroom to check. After about two minutes, I could hear Lewis pleading with Uncle James, saying, "James, let him go." That's right—let "him" go. Uncle James in his drunkenness had picked up a man in drag thinking it was a woman. Well, he became sober very quickly and chased the guy up two levels in the house and had cornered him in the bathroom.

After hearing Lewis's pleas, repeatedly, I went into the bathroom and could not believe my ears or eyes.

Uncle James was holding this guy up off the floor in a corner of the bathroom with his left hand around the guy's neck and with his right fist was beating him in the face unmercifully. The guy was butt naked, and his legs were literally dangling (along with other body parts). His face had already started to swell, and blood was gushing out like a baby experiencing projectile vomiting. I know it sounds gross, but it was gross! As I approached the bathroom, I could hear the guy screaming, "Please let me go; I'm sorry I'm not a woman; I'm sorry I'm not a woman." I, too, began pleading with Uncle James to let the guy go, but he would not. He was so enraged; he was not beating the guy's face with a constant punch. He would punch him extremely hard (Uncle James was a very strong man) and then pause with his piercing laser-like eyes staring at the guy for at least thirty seconds, and then hit him again. This was repeated many times.

Not knowing whether to call the police or what, I finally decided to call Mrs. Elise Broady, who was a long-time neighbor and close family friend. Although in the wee hours of the morning, Ms. Elise, as we called her, picked up the telephone quickly. In an extremely exacerbated voice, I said, "Ms. Elise, Uncle James has a man in the bathroom, and he is beating him to death, and I don't know what to do." She said, "Hold on; I'll be right over." She rushed over in her bathrobe and silk cap on her head and went upstairs to the bathroom. Well, she couldn't believe her eyes and ears either, but she remained calm and began talking to Uncle James in an extremely commanding voice. Ms. Elise coached Uncle James for about five minutes, then he let the guy go, and the guy went running down the steps and out the front door, butt naked, never to be seen again. Just another one of Uncle James's continued drunken, crazy antics.

The electrical field was very profitable, but it was made up mostly of white guys. This was a huge disadvantage for Lewis. It was almost like a fraternity, and black guys were not welcome to join. However, as God would have it, the administrator of the law firm where I worked was dating a guy who was the owner of a very profitable private electrical service company. This company serviced most of the office buildings on a prestigious corridor of Connecticut Avenue in DC. My office administrator spoke to her friend, and he met with Lewis and offered him a position as an electrician helper.

B. PHOENIX

Lewis, of course, accepted the position, worked very hard, and life continued going well for us.

It was very odd, but the subject of marriage never came up with Lewis and me. We were, for all intents and purposes, living as a married couple, but not legally married. And although Lewis and I never discussed marriage, my neighbor, Ms. Elise, discussed it every time she saw Lewis. She was a retired nurse and was one of Cicely's biggest fans. If she saw Lewis leaving for work, or returning from work, or just in her presence for any reason, she would ask him, "When are you going to marry that girl?" Her tone was always very serious, and she was relentless about it. She told him on many occasions, "I know Mrs. Heel is turning over in her grave. You are over there living with that girl and getting her pregnant and not marrying her." This relentless pressure went on for about two years. Ms. Elise loved me as if I was her own child, but for some reason she never uttered a word to me about Lewis and me living together. She never pressured me. The pressure was always put on Lewis and always when I was not around.

In December 1978, we celebrated Kendal's first birthday. Our families and close friends joined in the celebration. It was a great party with lots of fond memories. One day in early January 1979, Kendal appeared to be having pain in her left arm. We took her to her doctor, but he could not find anything wrong. He asked us to take Kendal to the hospital to get an x-ray of her arm. We left the doctor's office and went directly to the hospital. They took her in for the x-ray and told us that she had fluid in her left arm and that they needed to run further tests to see if this fluid was anywhere else in her body. After the first test results, they decided to put her on antibiotics and were going to admit her until the other test results were complete. I immediately felt pain and did not understand what could be going on when my child was perfectly normal the day before. Also, she was always very healthy and got clean bills of health from her pediatrician.

As we started the admission process, my heart began racing at an extremely high rate. We got Kendal settled into her room, and I stayed overnight with her. On Sunday, her doctor came into her room to inform us that they were not sure how long she would be there and that we should go home and get some rest. He said Kendal would be fine and that they would call if they needed us. So, after Kendal fell asleep for the night, Lewis and I went home to shower and change clothes. I called the hospital several times

INADMISSIBLE

to check on her, and the nurses informed me that she was fine and still sleeping. Shortly after, not even an hour later and right before we were ready to return to the hospital, my telephone rang. It was the hospital calling to say that Kendal had awakened, was not doing well, and that we should get to the hospital immediately.

We rushed to the hospital, which took about fifteen minutes. As we reached the floor where she was, the nurse was waiting for us and said they had moved Kendal to the intensive care unit. How could this be possible? She was outwardly perfectly fine when she went to sleep. There my one-year-old only child lay, with no movement in her body and hooked up to all types of machines and equipment. Suddenly, alarms began going off on the equipment, and they rushed us out of her room. At this point, I lost it. I began crying uncontrollably. I remember hearing her doctor being paged to "ICU stat!" I thought I was going to lose my mind. I just knew my child was dying, and I could do nothing about it. Nor did I know why. Finally, a family friend who was a doctor on staff at the hospital was being paged to ICU. This was bad. I knew he would be the one bringing the bad news to us, and he did. Kendal had died, and no one knew why. The hospital requested that we allow an autopsy and we did. The next day, we returned to the hospital to retrieve her personal belongings. Everyone at the hospital was very sad about Kendal's death, and they all were very sympathetic to us.

As we were leaving the hospital, a very tall, very heavyset white man in a white doctor's coat with a pure white beard came running after us. He was yelling, "Mr. and Mrs. Phoenix, Mr. and Mrs. Phoenix." We turned and saw that he was desperately after us. We were on the escalators going down, and when we reached the bottom, we waited for him. He came up to us and said that he was considered a great physician by his peers. He said the hospital had called him in to give an analysis of the autopsy. He also stated, "I am great at what I do, but I want you to know that there is someone greater than me, and He wanted this child."

The doctor informed us that Kendal had died from an exorbitant amount of fluid around her heart. He explained that the heart has a sack around it and that typically when people have "fluid around the heart," the fluid is around the sack. However, in Kendal's case, the fluid was inside the sack. He also told us that it was miraculous that she lived the entire one year of her little life without symptoms or pain. He then offered his condolences. We thanked him and walked away. By the time I reached the car, I could not believe that although I was still very sad, I suddenly felt a sense of calm. In my mind, I immediately started recalling what the doctor said and something that had happened several weeks before Kendal died.

One night, Kendal and I were home alone. I remember she would not go to sleep this night. She was not fussy at all, but just would not go to sleep. She lay in her bed, and I remember hearing her say, "Look, look." Finally, I went in and got her and sat with her on my lap at the foot of my bed. She had the most beautiful smile on her face, and she continued saying, "Look, look." Suddenly, not knowing why, I broke down in tears and could only think to myself, *I wish my grandmother (Cicely) could have seen you.* I cried for, I know, an hour, and the entire time Kendal sat on my lap, lay her little head on my chest, and occasionally looked up at me with that beautiful smile, saying "Look, look." After the doctor's statement and my recollection of that night with Kendal, it all started to come together. I knew then that God wanted her and that I had no right to be angry about it or question God's decision. From that point on, I was strong.

Kendal's funeral was very, very sad. Hundreds of people came to express their sympathy. Most of them had never known a child so young to die. It was my first as well. The pain was something I had never experienced—not even when Cicely died. And although the pain I felt was great, I could remain calm. I remember my family and friends wondered whether I had been given drugs to keep me so calm through such a horrible experience. It was not drugs, but like always, it was God's hand on me that gave, and continues to give, me unexplainable strength even in severe pain.

To describe the pain, this is what I remember: it felt like I had a big hole in my heart, and air was constantly blowing back and forth through it. That is how it felt, and I walked around with that feeling for months. Then, there were moments when I would just break down into tears. Even at this writing, I can barely see the words I'm typing because of the tears. This, next to Cicely's death, was the most pain I had ever felt, but, thank God, I recovered. Also, I will always remember what the physician said the day after Kendal died—he was a great surgeon and well respected by his colleagues, but there was someone greater than him who wanted this child.

A couple years after Kendal's death, I was at work as busy as I could be and my phone rang. It was Lewis. He asked me, "Do you know what we would have to do to get married on Wednesday?" I was shocked, but for some reason the question struck me as a research request. I was in work mode, and I never skipped a beat. I said, "I don't know, Lewis." He then asked, "Would you find out and call me back?" I said yes, hung up the telephone, and proceeded to research the matter. I learned that you, in DC, needed a blood test and paperwork, which would not allow the marriage to occur that same week. In Maryland, however, you only needed a birth certificate and a completed application, and you could be married two days after submitting your application. So we were married in Maryland.

Unbeknownst to me, Lewis was under pressure and needed this to happen that week. After I called him with the information, he asked, "Can we go tomorrow (which would have been Tuesday) and complete the application, and get married on Thursday?" I answered in a very matter of fact manner and said, "Yeah, I guess we could do that. We would have to go into work late tomorrow and probably put in for the whole day on Thursday." Can you imagine how crazy this conversation must have sounded? Lewis said, "Okay. I'll see you later." We hung up the phone and this guy (one of my coworkers) who was near me and overheard my conversation, came over to my desk. I looked up at him and said, "I think Lewis just proposed to me." He was ecstatic and wanted to hear everything that was said. I told him the whole story, and he thought it was so romantic. Romantic was not at all what I was thinking. I was, at that point, very confused.

When I got off work that evening, I asked Lewis what in the world made him call me with that on that day. He, in a very exhausted fashion, said, "Ms. Elise was about to drive me crazy! For the last time, she said, 'Lewis, when are you going to marry that girl?' When she asked me that today, I yelled back and said, Wednesday!" On Tuesday, we applied for the marriage license, and on that Thursday, we got married. My family and a friend of my family, as well as a couple of Lewis's sisters, all piled into a very small room, and Lewis and I were married. That Friday, we left for Diamond Beach, Virginia. Our honeymoon was spent that weekend with Lewis's aunt and uncle, whom we adored, and with whom we spent many vacations afterward. On Monday, we returned to work and life as we knew it, and moved forward as if nothing had happened.

By the end of that next year, Harmon had passed, and I was delivering my second child. Harmon died from colon cancer. It was very sad, and I remember the night before he died, Lewis and I were at the hospital visiting with him. He was scheduled to have surgery the next day, and because he was always concerned about good grooming, he asked Lewis if he would shave him. As Lewis was shaving him (using a straight razor as Harmon always had), Harmon declared, "I must be getting ready to die if I'm allowing this nigger to shave me." As most of you know, the word *nigger* has had its own career, and as spelled out in Randall Kennedy's *Nigger, the Strange Career of a Troublesome Word*, this was a time when the word's career was on the downswing but not ended. After making this comment, Harmon and Lewis shared the biggest laugh. I then said, "Don't say that, Daddy." All I could think about was his statement about dying. Well, Lewis completed a very nice shave, and Harmon looked in the mirror with a big smile (pleased with the shave Lewis gave him) and thanked him. Lewis and I went home late that night, and the next morning during surgery, Harmon died.

Shortly after Harmon's death, my second child was born. She was a beautiful baby. She apparently was born with a heart murmur, but believe it or not, I knew that she would be okay. I truly believed that God would not subject me to losing another child. He also gifted me with a beautiful baby boy. He was born two years after my daughter, and not only was he handsome; as it turned out, he was extremely bright. These two children brought a lot of joy to my life, and I thoroughly enjoyed raising them. Lewis and I worked very hard to provide our children with the best life we could. Hard work was something we both learned very early. We got along very well and had a great marriage. Many people we knew thought we had a perfect marriage. And obviously, it was not perfect, but I can truly say that we enjoyed a wonderful life together. Life was going very well for us, and in terms of my career, I was a long way from the beginning.

"Thou shalt not muzzle the ox when he treadeth out the corn."
Deuteronomy 25:4

PROFESSIONAL DEVELOPMENT

THE FOLLOWING SECRET files are all based on real events over many years and from many different workplaces. They are written to share what often goes on behind the closed doors of an HR Department. In all instances, names were changed so as not to reveal the true characters. In some instances, workplaces were combined, the nature of businesses changed, and these files are not necessarily in any specific order. They were purposely changed or reordered to avoid the precise timeline.

B. PHOENIX

CHAPTER 6

In the Beginning

I BEGAN MY career working full time in the federal government and worked as a civil servant for about three years. One of my assignments was to assist a young attorney. Berlin Shor was Jewish, handsome, and extremely smart with a very promising career in the legal community. I was assigned to be his secretary. Berlin worked very hard and was a perfectionist. He had extremely high standards for work product and expected—no, demanded—the same from those who worked with him. He was a short man but very confident, and although just about five feet four, he had the confidence of a giant—no short man complex for Berlin. I witnessed him stand with and against some powerful giants, and he was always right at home and very comfortable. I used to tell folks I didn't believe Berlin knew he was short.

Berlin exuded confidence, and although very nice most of the time, he could unleash his fury on demand. However, he was always very nice to me and extremely generous. He never let a holiday or special occasion go by that he did not give me a thoughtful generous gift. He and his wife would always remember me when they vacationed. No matter where they went in the world, they would always purchase a beautiful gift for me. Berlin and I had an excellent relationship, and when he received an offer from one of the area law firms, he asked me to go with him, and I accepted.

Hobart & Johns, PC (H&J) employed about 150 people. It had beautiful office space in downtown DC. There were upscale establishments of all types—fine leather shops, spas, boutiques, and other specialty shops, with a very famous hotel just a stone's throw away. It was truly a posh section of town. At H&J, each attorney had an exquisitely decorated private office. It was like nothing I had ever seen in the workplace or on television. I had only worked in the federal government and at a small local college in DC, and, trust me, they had none of the frills that were provided by this law firm. There were free soft drinks (any kind or flavor you wanted, soda, juice, coffee, tea, milk, and very expensive bottled water). They served delicious food at most of the office meetings, which was provided by some of the finest caterers in the country. There were unbelievable parties. Everything was top of the line, and every affair was fit for a king. I thought I had died and gone to work heaven.

I will never forget the day I walked into Giovanna Gustina's office for my interview. Giovanna was the office administrator. She was responsible for all aspects of the firm's administration and human resources, including hiring and firing. She was tall, dark, and very handsome with an extremely cavernous voice. I use this description for her, not because she was masculine in any way, but because she was the first white woman I had ever met who could hold her own in a man's world. This woman had balls of steel, and they were larger than most of the men's in the office, all of whom were white except two. Giovanna was a beautiful Italian woman who was always extremely well-dressed, had the most beautiful hair, and was a looker in the highest sense of the word. As folks in my family would say, "She was as sharp as a tack, from head to toe." Both men and women either loved her or hated her. She was one of the first women I had ever met who was what I call an "IW"—international woman—one to whom men of all races were openly attracted. Giovanna knew she had this quality, and she made it work in her favor.

My interview with Giovanna was very lengthy. We talked and laughed and puffed away at least six cigarettes each. At the end of the interview, Giovanna told me she would be very pleased to have me join the firm as a legal secretary for Berlin Shor. They hired Berlin as an associate attorney in one of the firm's largest practice groups. When Giovanna informed me of what the compensation package would be, I thought I had misunderstood what she was saying. I thought my insides were going to explode. I began praying silently, "Oh God, please help me keep my cool." Cicely taught me to remain calm and cool when a white person was giving me something. She said, "If you show a white person too much excitement over something they give you, the next time they were able to give you something, it would be less, or not much more than what they gave you the first time." So needless to say, I remained calm.

The salary offer was $16K per year. This was more than double what I was earning in the federal government, and it would be the same as a legal secretary today earning $150K per year. I was so excited, and there was one thing I knew for certain; I, unlike Harmon, would not be quitting after my first paycheck. In addition to the great salary, the firm was going to pay 100 percent of all benefits for my family and me, give me a holiday bonus that ranged from $1 to $5K, and the potential to earn merit bonuses as well. The pressure of following Cicely's instructions and my extreme jubilation were clashing. I thought I was going to pass out right in Giovanna's office. I started praying again—"Oh God, please help me get through this calmly," and I did. This was it. Yippee, my ship had come in. Life was grand! I found a pot of gold, and I could not wait to get home to tell my family.

My start at H&J was great. I learned so many new things about work life and life in general. Being surrounded by extremely bright, hardworking people afforded me an educational experience that would prove to be extremely beneficial later in my career. Well, the honeymoon lasted a little over a year. After I was assigned to assist one of the hiring attorneys with the firm's recruiting efforts and other administrative duties, I began to see another side of the firm and the people—the real human resources—and they were real and human. There were all sorts of human relations issues that came up in the office, which I found shocking. I expected more from these wealthy, highly educated individuals.

However, what I learned was that, in fact, they were just human. The education and the money disguised some of their defects, but in the flow of a Dr. Seuss book, some were nice, and some were naughty; some were sweet, and some were bitter; some were honest, and some were not; some were good, and some were very bad. Although these are all human characteristics, the fact that this crop of people exhibited some of this behavior in the workplace was, again, shocking to me. So here began my observation of human behavior in the workplace, and some of its triggers.

B. PHOENIX

CHAPTER 7

The Lunch Thief

ONE BEHAVIORAL PROBLEM was the stealing of employee lunches. We sent out notice after notice to all staff. We posted notes in the employee lounges and made all sorts of threats of what would happen to the thief if he or she was caught. Nothing my supervisor did seemed to phase this thief. Well, while I can't say who, someone decided to take matters into their own hands with regard to this naughty human behavior. A couple of weeks after a very strong notice went out to all employees, homemade fudge brownies were brought into the office in a small brown bag. There was a note on the bag (written in large bold letters, "DO NOT TOUCH") and it was placed in the refrigerator in the main employee lounge. Later in the day, the owner of the brownies discovered that several of them were missing, and reports were being made that certain people in the office were behaving strangely—walking around the office laughing uncontrollably. Everyone was perplexed at what could have happened to these individuals when, finally, the culprit let a few people in on what had been done—they had made and brought in "magic brownies." These brownies were made with marijuana as one of the main ingredients. *Yes!* The people who ate these brownies were as high as a kite. And not only were they high, they had now been revealed as the office food thieves, even though none of them ever admitted to eating the brownies. However, the truth slowly leaked around the office, and I do believe a lesson was learned, because we had no more problems with employee lunches being stolen.

B. PHOENIX

IVY LEAGUE BRAWLERS

One night while viewing the nightly news, I saw two of the partners from my office being interviewed. The reporter was questioning people about tickets that were being scalped at one of the popular venues in DC. There was a telecast of a heavyweight championship boxing match. It was one of the biggest prize fights ever. Everyone wanted to witness this competition. In the interview, the partners were telling the news reporter that they had paid $1K each for the tickets. They reported purchasing the tickets from someone outside the venue—suggesting it to be a scalper. When the reporter asked the two partners if they would give their names, they agreed. However, they gave the names of two of the firm's most prominent senior partners. I could not believe what I was seeing, or hearing. When I went into the office the next morning, I asked my supervisor if he had seen the news report. He said he had not and insisted that I report what I had seen to one of the senior partners. I was so nervous and afraid to go to this man's office and was shaking like a leaf. Although I didn't want to report this information, being pressured by my supervisor, regrettably I did. After I went to the partner with my report, all hell broke loose, and it led to a major street brawl. Adult men rolling around on the floor fighting. One punch after another, some landing, some not, but all shocking to me, and I recalled a story the elders told many times about a dispute between Harmon and one of his card players.

Although Harmon was small, he was a fiery man, and you could not chump him, ever! He would always stand his ground. As the story was told, after claims of cheating in a card game, Harmon got into a heated argument with a much larger man. The man made reference to his small size, and Harmon said, "You know what people say; the bigger they are, the harder they fall." Well, this guy wasn't backing down either, and he said, "Yeah, but the smaller they are, the farther they fly." Unlike the guys in the office, Harmon and his opponent passed words only. They dropped the matter and walked away, which I think was a smart move. So, watching these Ivy League guys rolling around in the floor made me realize that education doesn't necessarily make you smart.

WORK INTIMACY

I had never been in an intimate social setting with a large group of coworkers until I attended my first corporate office party. As it turned out, this party was very educational. It seemed to bring out the worst in many of my coworkers. I had attended big parties hosted by family and close family friends, but this was unlike those parties. At the parties I attended, people came in fine clothing, enjoyed delicious food and drinks, and had a wonderful time, rarely with any trouble—just fun for all. To the contrary, at the office parties, many of my colleagues would tipple, and in their idiocy, were simply "off the chain." There were couples who practically had sex on the dance floor, not to be mistaken for those who had sex in the restrooms, closets, and even in back hallways of the facility while the party was in full swing. As the liquor consumption continued to increase, there was dirty dancing and spouse swapping right in the middle of the dance floor. Even though the term "sexual harassment" had yet to be born in the workplace, a party such as this was full of sexual harassment and would be an HR nightmare today!

The place was pregnant with what today is called a "hostile work environment." The things that were common in the workplace then (disparate treatment, racial and sexual discrimination, harassment, sexual harassment) would be an employment attorney's dream in today's workplace, or perhaps nightmare depending on which side they represented. This behavior was from young attorneys, old attorneys, staff, and spouses. It was during this time that I realized one of the sayings of the elders in my family was so true: "You can't buy, teach, or give class." Another thing folks in my family used to say is, "You can take the person out of the ghetto, but you can't take the ghetto out of the person." We know this is not true in all cases, but we do know it is true in many cases.

THE BREAK UP

After working at the firm for several years, Berlin Shor was very well respected by most of the senior attorneys. They often referred to him as a "hot shot" and a "whiz kid," and a hot shot he was. Berlin was a perfectionist. His aim for perfection in his work product was unparalleled, and he accepted nothing less from me. He was also totally devoted to providing his clients with the best service. Therefore, Berlin gets most of the credit for my foundation of a strong desire for perfection in my work product and my loyalty to clients and supervisors. He was one of the best young attorneys in the DC area. He and I enjoyed a very pleasant, close working relationship. We also shared many personal moments.

Berlin and I both lost our first child. His was miscarried, and mine, as you know, died very unexpectedly at age one. We were there for each other through both these tragedies. Several years passed, and Berlin was finally up for partnership (owner of a piece of the pie—a huge pie, I might add). Back in the day, if you were an attorney in a private law firm, being a partner was the ultimate career move. However, it was a move primarily made by white men. There were very few female or minority partners in any DC law firms. For that matter, there were very few females or minorities at any attorney level in private law firms. In all honesty, females in law firms during that time were typically in secretarial positions, and the majority of them were white.

When an attorney was in his fifth to seventh year of practicing law, he was eligible to become a partner. This required a majority vote into the partnership by those who had already reached this pinnacle. The partners would get together one evening or weekend and vote on which of the associate attorneys should be made partner, or not. This decision was based on who had demonstrated the ability to bring in substantial business (a "rainmaker") and/or who had reached a high level of expertise in an area of practice (a subject matter expert).

In law firms, this period of eligibility was a critical time for most young attorneys. It was the time when they were labeled successful or not, and could mean the difference between owning a BMW and owning a BMW and a yacht. Berlin wanted to become a partner and was very nervous and anxious about the big palaver that was going to be held where a decision would be made about his future. As time drew closer to the big day, he was more and more edgy and almost impossible to satisfy. Many of the secretaries would tell me, "I don't know how you put up with him." Sometimes I didn't know either, but I respected Berlin and didn't take any of his bad behavior personally. However, everything changes.

One very cold wintry morning at about 8:15 a.m., I was in the restroom fixing my lipstick and checking my hair before beginning the workday. One of the other secretaries in the firm came rushing into the restroom and in an almost breathless voice said, "The receptionist is looking for you. She said it is urgent that she speak to you, now." Assuming something was wrong with my family, I rushed out to the reception area to find the receptionist anxiously awaiting my appearance. She said in a very nervous and frightened voice, "Berlin has been calling repeatedly looking for you. I have him on the line now." As she transferred Berlin's call back to my desk, I rushed to take it. I knew there must have been something horribly wrong.

When I picked up the telephone, Berlin began speaking to me in an extremely loud, angry voice. I was so taken aback by his behavior that I allowed him to rant and rave for several minutes. The only thing I remember him saying was that he was expecting a very important telephone call, and he needed me to stay at my desk. Mind you, at this point, he was yelling at me, and his words began ringing in my head repeatedly. Finally, I yelled back at him. The fact that this conversation was taking place a half hour before I was due to begin work was infuriating me. In a very strong voice, I said, "This call can't be that important to you, or you would be here to receive it yourself." I then hung up the telephone. I slammed it down. I was angry at Berlin for treating me this way. So I sat at my desk for at least ten to fifteen minutes stewing in what had just happened. Then I started wondering what the result of my insubordination would be.

Shortly after, Berlin arrived in the office. I was at my desk still fuming over what had happened. He said "Good morning," and I said, "Good morning," and he went into his office as if nothing had happened. For the rest of that day, I could hear his voice ringing in my head repeatedly: "I am expecting a very important telephone call, and I need you to stay at your desk." This statement seemed to haunt me all day. By the end of the day, I decided I could no longer work for Berlin. His behavior was unacceptable, and I could not risk him feeling free to treat me that way again—especially after I had been so loyal to him over many years. I went to Giovanna and told her what happened and asked for an assignment change.

Giovanna tried to talk me out of leaving Berlin, but I needed to move on. As Cicely used to say, "Fool me once, shame on you; fool me twice, shame on me." I gave Berlin my all and was more loyal to him than I had been to any other supervisor. Routinely, I protected and covered for him when he was out of the office goofing around instead of working. He was one of the biggest

B. PHOENIX

procrastinators I had ever met. Berlin would procrastinate all day (from gossiping with the other attorneys and staff to midafternoon racquetball). Then he would often keep me working until 7:00 p.m. when I was scheduled to end work at five thirty each day. On many nights, while I was working like a madwoman to get his last-minute filings completed, my husband sat in our car on Connecticut Avenue for nearly two hours waiting for me. Berlin never gave me fair notice about working overtime, but I never complained. I just suffered through intense arguments between my husband and me. After Berlin's latest behavior, it was time for me to move on.

Giovanna told me she would find another place in the firm for me. She said she would move me before the beginning of the next week. I had mixed emotions about moving to a new assignment. Berlin and I had worked together for so many years that I grew to love him and his family. He had been very good to me, but for some reason, I could not shake his yelling at me that morning. And as it turned out, the very important telephone call was from one of the top corporations in the country. Berlin had been in negotiations with them about retaining the firm to handle a large case, and he was expecting the call that day. Although I understood his nervousness—landing that client would surely seal his partnership—I was still very hurt at how he treated me. Thus, our relationship ended.

Berlin got the big client, and the firm made him a partner. He was assigned a new secretary, but as it turned out, I was Berlin's first secretary, and the last one to stay with him for the time I did. I must admit that moving to a new position was a little scary, because at that point in my life, I did not like change. However, I understood the inevitability of change and was ready to make the move. When Giovanna informed me that my new role would be assisting one of the senior attorneys who practiced litigation and assisting her with administrative tasks, I was very excited. I did not want to seek employment elsewhere, so being given another position in the firm was a win-win situation. And although I felt strongly that Berlin spoke inappropriately to me, I still loved him and am forever grateful for the training I received under his leadership.

SEX, MONEY, AND POWER

I had no idea this new position would bring so many challenges and life lessons. My new assignment was working for another bright young attorney. She was, as it turned out, madly in love with her married supervisor, a senior partner in charge of the practice group. The young attorney had been sharing her feelings about her supervisor with me. What she did not know was that the partner was "hot and bothered" by another. He had been chasing someone else in the firm for years, and they had just recently become sex partners. Both these women were confiding in me. I could not believe what was happening. The partner was married with several children. He was having sex with one coworker while encouraging a relationship with another coworker. The young attorney was pouring her heart out to me about her feelings for the partner and had no idea the man of her dreams was having sex with another. This other woman, although she admired this man, was not in love with him. She was in love with his power and money. This love triangle went on for many years and taught me much about life and love.

This position was providing me with an education no school on the planet could provide. I found everything about law firm administrative work interesting, intriguing and at the same time unbelievable. This was the place I learned the truth about people, and where I developed an entirely new vocabulary. Working in law firm administration brought a whole new meaning to words such as "brown-noser," "kiss-up," and "suck-up." I had heard some of these terms before and knew of individuals who were described this way. However, I reached a whole new level of exposure and understanding, gaining firsthand experience with these types of people. I also learned the danger of power as well as the difference in accepting the power that comes along with a position and seeking a position purely because of the power it holds. Either can be extremely dangerous or extremely positive. However, I didn't realize how dangerous workplace power could be until later in my career.

As the top administrative person at the firm, Giovanna used her power very creatively. One afternoon, things in the office, seemingly, were running very smoothly. Suddenly, you could smell Giovanna in the air. She wore a very expensive perfume that would lightly enter your space well before you saw her. We used to joke in the office about how we could always "smell her coming"—no pun intended. As she breezed by my desk, she said, "Unplug your typewriter; the people are here to take it" (yes, typewriter—no computers during this time). I had no idea what was going on, but there was a gentleman running behind her, begging her to stop and listen to him. I mean this guy was literally running to keep up. Giovanna was a very fast walker and a fast talker. The man was telling her how sorry he was for the way he spoke to her. He was timidly saying, "I'm sure we can work something out."

As it turned out, the firm was behind in its payments for the rental of the typewriters and "Mr. Typewriter Man" thought he was going to threaten Giovanna into giving him the payment. He had, in a very erratic manner, threatened to take the typewriters back if the bill wasn't paid that day. Instead of paying the bill, Giovanna told him to come get the typewriters. He did not believe she would give them to him. After all, she needed to run a law firm. Once he arrived at our office, he realized this was not a bluff. This guy was so nervous and panicked about possibly losing a pretty decent account that he begged Giovanna for forgiveness. To his chagrin, he was reduced to a begging fool. Finally, she agreed to "work with him." Can you believe it? Giovanna was a brave heart. This is the kind of power she rendered over most people. We owed this guy, but by the time she finished with him, he was acting as if he owed us. In the end, they "worked something out," which did not include paying him on that day. He thanked Giovanna, and she sent him on his merry way.

On another occasion, one of the vendors called Giovanna making threats over a very small amount of money the vendor was owed. After a pretty short but exhausting fight over the telephone, Giovanna told the vendor to send someone to our office, and she would have the payment in full. When the vendor rep arrived, he was stunned. I was pretty stunned myself but very amused. Giovanna had one of our messengers go to the bank to pick up a package for her. She was very good friends with the bank president and got him to agree to her request. When she escorted the vendor into her office to receive the payment, there were two very large wicker baskets full of change. That's correct, nickels, dimes, quarters and pennies—the vendor's payment in full. This poor man was so shocked he didn't know what to do. He begged Giovanna to "keep the change," and he would wait for the payment. She agreed.

Effectively keeping a firm running from an administrative perspective is one thing, but the owners must work together and do their part as well. H&J, after many years of success and wealth, experienced some infighting among the partners. I don't mean just the kind that happens around boardroom tables, I mean real fights—very loud arguments in the hallways that would turn into street brawls with fists flying, profanity being yelled out, and bodies rolling around on the floor. And everyone thought southeast DC was the place for street brawls. These brawls eventually led to the destruction of the firm, and, in the end, the attorneys all moved on to other firms, and most of the nonlegal staff found good positions. However, Giovanna was left without a new position, and she never again returned to law firm administration.

Many years after H&J ceased to exist, I went to one of the area's premier employment agencies seeking a new position. While the recruiter was reviewing my resume, she asked who I had worked for at H&J. Before I could get his full name off my lips, she yelled out of her office, "Kathy, get in here. I have Berlin Shor's former secretary in my office!" This woman flew into the office where I was and began bowing down to me. She told me Berlin's firm was one of their clients. She said they had been dying to meet this "goddess." You can imagine the shock that came over me, and it felt uncomfortable. They told me that they had placed fifteen different secretaries in one year to support Berlin and that none of them lasted more than a few months. They said he was constantly comparing secretaries to me, and, in his mind, none of these people could measure up. I had no idea this was going on and found it hard to believe. Apparently they could see disbelief in my face because they pulled out a file that had documentation of all the candidates they had placed with Berlin. The file was huge, and they called it the "Shor File."

B. PHOENIX

CHAPTER 8

Down by the Train Track

WHEN I WALKED into the offices of Wilcox & Andrews (W&A), I could not believe my eyes. This place was so beautiful—so much so that being at work was a real pleasure. There was amazing artwork, much of which had been done by local DC artists. The collection included oils on canvas, watercolors, etchings, and photographs, as well as sculptures. W&A was a colorful place. I especially loved the quaint private terrace overlooking the city. The terrace sat above one of DC's most popular restaurants. You could see hotels, bridges, and beautiful parks, as well as landmark buildings, and it was walking distance to the train station. At that time, W&A was the only law firm in town with office space that included restaurants, shopping, salons, and other specialty shops.

In addition to beautiful office space, the people at W&A seemed very nice. They welcomed me with open arms. The firm was young and very progressive. It was founded by seven local attorneys. These attorneys were true "partners." Many people in the DC legal community thought these attorneys would never make it as a law firm. They, themselves, weren't sure how well they would do either, but they were bound and determined to give it their all. They worked tirelessly to build an extremely profitable business from nothing, and they did; and then came some spiders and sat down beside her and scared poor W&A away.

In the beginning, the partners at W&A were extremely selective about who they allowed to join the firm. They recruited only the best and the brightest. They pulled powerhouses from government and the private sector.

B. PHOENIX

They attracted young law students from the finest law schools in the world. Insofar as support staff, individuals were reaching out to the firm on a regular basis seeking employment. In its heyday, the firm received hundreds of resumes each week, and it became more and more sought-after each year. At its peak, the partners were earning so much money, not only could they not believe it, some of them claimed to be embarrassed about the amount of money they were earning. One of the partners told me how shocked he was when he received his first partnership draw (paycheck). He said the amount was so great that the numbers on his check had to be printed on two lines. I remember thinking, *if you were that embarrassed, you should have given some of that money away*. Another thought entered my head, and I told him, "If you still feel that way, I will be more than happy to have some of the numbers moved from your paycheck to mine." We both laughed.

Many years later, W&A published, in a popular legal magazine, the average partner's salary. I will never forget how the staff and younger attorneys went crazy. The article reported that the average partner earned an average annual salary of $500,000. Why would you unnecessarily publish this type of information if it was not required? Are you bragging? Is it advertisement? If advertisement, for what? There was a time when law firm partners did not make their salaries public information. The law firm partnership was an exclusive private club and private was their business. I personally don't understand why owners' salaries would be published. I guess law firms decided to join the athletic industry and some others in corporate America by publicizing their annual salaries. I'm sure law firms would be able to survive without this public display of personal income. Besides, it drives the nonpartners *wild*!

I believe it does a firm a disservice to publicize the partners' compensation, and I found this to be especially true when partners earn far more than the average partner in other similar law firms. When this is the case, the staff considers it a good reason for them to earn salaries far above their market value as well. Can you imagine the problems a business would encounter from employees who felt they were somehow not getting their piece of the pie? I lived through many of the problems. Some employees will get it one way or the other. Some will steal it, some cheat to get it, some lie to get it, some sell their souls, some their bodies, but either way you slice it, some of these folks feel entitled, and, in many cases, it is only because they have information that is none of their business. In my management training days, I was taught that all information in or about the law firm, its clients, or its employees should be provided on a very strict "need-to-know basis" only. One of my former supervisors taught me this valuable rule, and he is the person I credit with building a solid structure on the foundation that Berlin Shor and Giovanna Gustina built years before.

The owners at W&A were young, smart, and very rich. The firm was growing like weeds. At one point, we were conducting new hire orientation every Monday. The employees and owners of the firm were all very happy to be working there. During my early years at W&A, I enjoyed the tremendous amount of cohesiveness of the partners. The environment was fun and stress-free. The office administrator had been with the firm for many years but had not fully grown with the position. Although she hired her son to manage the firm's money, hired her very good friend to inventory and sell the firm all its office supplies, and used firm money to purchase a full wardrobe of maternity clothes for one of her direct reports, many of the partners trusted her to manage the firm's business and employees.

W&A employed many young nonattorney professionals, most of whom were white and were recent college graduates. There was lots of fun going on always. However, it was the type of fun you typically experience on a college campus. Nameplates were being switched from door to door (once someone switched the nameplate of the chairman of the board with one of the young interns); telephone headsets were being glued to the bases of the telephones; employees' offices were totally rearranged in their absence; belly dancers were being ordered to surprise young attorneys; and prank telephone calls were being made all the time.

One of the funniest prank calls happened to a young paralegal. The managing partner was asked to speak to the paralegal and give him a horrible assignment. The paralegal was told that the managing partner wanted to speak to him on the telephone, but he felt there was no way the managing partner would waste his time on the telephone with him. Nevertheless, he got on the telephone and immediately proceeded to say things such as, "What do you want, you big fat pig?" and, "You need to go on a diet and stop playing games with people. You look like a big tub of lard." The managing partner was a very tall, very heavyset man. The paralegal hung up the telephone and laughed hysterically at us. Well, the laugh was on him because, as you know, it was the managing partner on the telephone. After we convinced the young paralegal of the truth, he spent the rest of his tenure with the firm hiding from that managing partner.

I also worked closely with the event manager. We planned lots of events for the firm, and I met so many wonderful people through our efforts. Namely, there were unbelievable events planned for the summer legal interns. These events included expensive parties—many of which were held at different attorneys' homes. The attorneys hosted the parties, and the firm paid the bill. The total cost of these events ranged anywhere from $2,000 to $15,000 each. The entire program ran about three months and cost the firm close to $100,000 in event expenses. Believe it or not, some of these expenses covered things such as pottery classes and bowling and were justified with statements such as, "We need to do team-building activities," "We need to get to know these law students on a personal level," and the award-winning, "All the other firms are doing these types of extracurricular activities, so we have to do the same to be competitive." It was all a bunch of nonsense, if you ask me. All of this "playtime" was far from what I had been accustomed. The reality is that you can learn a great deal about a person just working closely with him or her for three months. Many people can fake it for a few weeks, but for most people, it's hard to fake it for several months.

The programs at W&A were totally opposite from other programs with which I had worked. The summer programs I previously worked with were more like training grounds—much like boot camp for attorneys. One of my old supervisors once said, "It is not fair to the young law students, or the firm, for them to be recruited into an environment that is nothing like the real world." He believed the firm should work these young people to the max and teach them as much as possible, and the social aspects of the program should be minimal. After having worked closely with both types of programs, I totally agree with this concept. My supervisor once stated jokingly that he believed, "The young law students should be worked so hard that their tongues would be hanging out of their mouths when they left the office." Although none of the young attorneys left the office with their tongues hanging out, they did work very hard, and we never had a problem with top-level recruits accepting our offers of employment. I believe this concept, if it hasn't been already, should be revisited.

W&A's summer program was more of a country club environment

that got out of control. My theory about how law firms allowed the whole attorney recruiting process to get out of control has very little to do with the attorneys, but more to do with the individuals who needed to justify a position for themselves. The law students at W&A were wined and dined at every moment. I used to wonder how those young aspirants would handle the reality of working as a regular full-time attorney. How were they going to deal with paying for their own lunch every day, working late-night hours, the pressure of meeting a twenty-two hundred billable hours requirement each year, people who practically kissed their rear ends for three months and suddenly having those same people not even willing to say hello to them, producing new work with very little guidance, and living with the reality that many of their superiors really do not think they are "all that" even if all of their lives everyone else told them they were. How does one deal with this?

Most of these young attorneys were slapped down before they could even attempt to climb the ladder. The process of climbing the ladder could be so brutal. These young attorneys were lured in with all that is shiny and sweet and then thrown into deep water having to sink or swim. Many of them were given little support, and they had to complete extremely complex assignments the best way they could. The minority attorneys were in a worse situation because many of them were basically given no support. Most of them never even got an opportunity to get into deep water. And if you did not attend one of the Ivy League law schools, you could forget about getting into one of the top-law firms in the country, no matter your race.

I felt so sorry for the law students from non-Ivy League schools who would call to find out how they could get an interview. Unfortunately, the answer was always that they could not. Most of the top law firms followed the same recruiting practices. We received thousands of resumes from attorneys and law students each year. The only keepers were those who had attended or were attending one of the Ivy League law schools. And even then, the only people who were brought in for interviews were those who were in the top 5 to 10 percent of their class. All the others were rejected—all of them. No exceptions.

I remember young law students calling and breaking into tears—none of the top firms would interview them because of the law school they attended. Please remember that some of these schools were excellent law schools, but because they were not considered one of the top law schools, most of

B. PHOENIX

the big firms would not interview their students. Sadly, most of the big law firms were all after the same group of people. As far as I was concerned, too much emphasis was placed on the school attended, and not enough on wisdom, intelligence, and strength—the qualities I found in each of the truly successful attorneys I encountered over many years, some from Ivy League schools and some not.

CHAPTER 9

X-Rated

WHEN ONE FIRM closed, most of the white secretaries moved on with the attorneys they supported. Of the four black secretaries, only one was asked to move on to the next firm with her attorney. The rest of us struggled to find jobs that would pay us what we had been earning. To make matters worse, we learned from some of the white secretaries that not only had they interviewed at some of the same law firms, but they were receiving offers of greater salaries than the black secretaries with equal experience. It may have been a little more palatable if the white secretaries were already earning larger salaries than the black secretaries, but many of them were not. Each of us black secretaries were earning more money than the white secretaries who were sharing the information with us. You can imagine how much of a low blow this must have been. We all passed the tests, we all came from the same firm with as much or more legal experience, and we all were as professional, if not more so, than the white secretaries, yet we were not receiving the same types of offers.

After exhausting searches, each of us black secretaries finally found employment. And we did receive salary offers that were more in line with what we had been earning. My salary offer was a little less; the other three black women received a little more, but guess what? Three of us were hired to work for undesirables—attorneys for whom no one else would work. Normally, these types of legal secretarial positions came with "combat pay." Perhaps these law firms thought giving us a little more, or a little less than our previous earnings, for "us" was combat pay. It is so sad that in these days racism was still very much alive and well. These were all hard pills to swallow, and the low blows did hurt, but the Fabulous 4 were all strong black women who refused to let ignorance hold us back. Being the youngest of the group, I paid close attention to their every move. These women were intelligent and not shy at all about putting me in my place and letting me know in no uncertain terms when I was approaching a dumb move. I have tons of stories and life lessons I learned from these women, and it is to them that I credit my sense of who I am as a professional and my understanding of the plight of black folks, particularly black women, in the workplace. I love these women deeply and am forever grateful to them for the nurturing they gave me.

I moved on to a small law firm that was founded by a famous attorney who was also a politician. This firm was small but extremely wealthy. I was assigned to assist one senior partner, who was a writer approaching the deadline to finish a new book on legal ethics. This was a great job and an opportunity for me to perform at a higher level. At that time, working for a partner, especially a senior partner, in a DC law firm was very glamorous and extremely prestigious for a legal secretary. After all, legal secretaries who supported one partner in a law firm were at the executive level. This position was a real bonus because in those days, black secretaries were rarely given positions working with one attorney, let alone one partner. Most black secretaries worked for associate-level attorneys, and two or more of them.

Penn Folger was a medium height, medium build Italian who was very bald in the top of his head. His hair was very dark and straight, and he proudly wore the infamous "whip-over." He wore a suit and necktie every day. However, his clothes were always scruffy. His shirts were a little dingy and never crisply starched. Penn was a workaholic. I arrived at the office each morning by 8:00 a.m., and he was always there already. He never stopped working for lunch. In fact, the entire time I worked for Penn, he never took a lunch break. He was a coffee fanatic! He drank at least ten to fifteen cups of coffee in eight hours. When I left the office, normally at 5:00 p.m. each day, he was still at his desk working and drinking coffee. He truly was a workaholic and rarely socialized with anyone in the office.

I will never forget my first day at the firm. Penn greeted me with a big smile and was careful to introduce me to all his colleagues. After my formal introduction to everyone, he took me into his office to lay down the ground rules. He made it crystal clear that I answered to him and him alone. He informed me of the importance of keeping up with him on his book because he was working under a strict deadline. Penn told me his former secretary had not given any notice when she left the firm, and it had put him in a real bind. He said he felt very lucky to have found me and was extremely confident that my skills were just what he needed. He informed me that if I stayed with him through the end of the book project, he would give me a $20K bonus. Well, at that time, bonuses were given to legal secretaries all the time, but rarely as substantial as this, especially not for black secretaries.

After my first week on the job, Penn was very impressed with how well I could keep up with him. As expected, I could type much faster than he could write. However, as a fast, sharp typist, I could crank out chapters at a rate that was far ahead of his writing pages. Although Penn was impressed with the speed at which I worked, this was a much slower pace for me. I had come from an environment where I had to keep up with many people all at once. Whenever Penn was a couple of hours behind me on his writing, he would tell me to go out and take a break. He would say, "Go for a walk, or do some shopping." On many occasions, this would happen at ten in the morning or midafternoon. Being a person who loved to shop, this was great for me because I was often in the stores when most people were at work. I loved every moment of it. I could not believe I had landed such a wonderful position.

A couple of weeks later, Penn began to act strange. One morning before lunch, out of the clear blue, he called me into his office. He gave me some cash and sent me to an office supply store to buy these special ink pens. Although this happened on several occasions, I never knew why these pens were so special. On one occasion, when I returned with the special ink pens, Penn informed me that he was planning to travel to North Carolina. He gave me explicit instructions that I was not to give his North Carolina contact information to anyone. He said he would inform everyone that if they needed to reach him, they should contact me. He reiterated these instructions and added, "including my wife." I was to call him, and he would return the call of whoever was looking for him, including his wife. Obviously, this was odd, but I had experienced much stranger things.

Before Penn left for North Carolina, he asked me to organize the files in his office while he was away. So, one quiet afternoon, I decided to get the filing project under way. I went into Penn's office and began looking for the files to see what shape they were in and how much work I had cut out for me. While going through his file drawers, I discovered something shocking. I rushed out of the office frantically looking for someone I could trust to treat this information as confidential. I immediately thought of one of the attorneys, Micah Comings, who had been very nice to me. Micah gave me the first warning about Penn. Quite honestly, it wasn't a warning; he flat-out told me that Penn was an "asshole," and he could not stand him. For some reason, Micah and I bonded right away and became office buddies. I wasn't sure if Micah was my guardian angel or if he had the hots for me. We shared laughter, cups of coffee, and lunch on many occasions. I never told him this, and I don't think I gave him any signals, but my heart did a double flutter whenever he was around. Micah was a fine white boy and someone I could have dated. He was from Annapolis, Maryland, and he, like me, loved the water, boating, and other outdoor activities. He was tall with very dark hair, and his skin seemed to be tanned most of the time. He had a very nice body and a walk that exuded confidence. If I wasn't married at the time, we could have been an item.

Well, I was so shaken by what I had found in Penn's office that I immediately ran to Micah and told him about it. He could see the shock on my face and told me, in a firm and angry voice, that he wanted to see for himself what I had found. After making him swear to keep it a secret, Micah and I went to Penn's office. I pointed to the large, deep file drawer where I had made this discovery. Micah could not believe what he was seeing. He was outraged and began calling Penn all kinds of bad names. In this drawer, there were boxes of edible underwear, X-rated videos and magazines, a variety of sex toys, condoms of all kinds, and X-rated magazines, one of which was entitled something like *Black Meat*, or *Sweet Black Meat*. I can't remember the title; however, it was an X-rated magazine that featured all black women.

Call me crazy or delirious, but when I looked down at that magazine, it was opened to a page where the woman, at least in my frantic and freaked-out mind, looked just like me. Micah was furious. He wanted to slam this guy up against a wall, but, again, I made him swear not to say anything about this to anyone. At this point, I decided to get out of that firm as quickly as possible. One week later, Penn returned from his travel, and I submitted my resignation. He tried to convince me to stay, but I had to go. This was a scary experience for me.

Well, God was there for me once again. I called one of the young female attorneys that I trusted, with whom I had worked in the past. When I told her the story about Penn, she could not believe it and told me her firm was looking for a secretary for the head of one of their practice groups. She gave me the HR manager's contact information and told me to call her right away. I did make the call, and within a few days, I was given an offer, which I accepted. To try and keep me, Penn upped the ante to a $25K bonus and got approval to raise my salary by $10K. As tempting as it was, I could not accept it. It went against every fiber in my body. I declined the offer and left after having worked on this job less than six months.

B. PHOENIX

CHAPTER 10

The Northwest

BERNSTEIN, EPPS & COY, PC (BE&C) was a rich law firm in many ways. The firm had its own office building in DC. It was a beautiful modern building full of glass and chrome. There were life-size paintings of stairwells, doorways, and windows, all of which gave the illusion of being real. The office space was extremely neat and clean, and exquisitely decorated. Everything was organized and in its place. The employees dressed very professionally, and the work environment was palatable to the eye with very low stress.

I was hired as an administrative assistant for David Toona, a partner in charge of one of the firm's largest practice groups. David had only been with the firm about six months. He had previously worked for the federal government. He was a short, petite white man with dark black hair. He had a full head of hair, and every strand was always in place. During the interview, Peggy Windpost, the HR manager, told me David was a nice person. She said he was a great guy to work for, and it was an excellent opportunity for me. The pay was great, and I agreed that it was an excellent opportunity.

After my first week at BE&C, I learned that David was a tyrant—Peggy lied to me. I started getting reports from attorneys and staff that David treated his prior assistant so badly that she was in tears just about every day. I also learned that every administrative assistant in the firm had refused to work for David. Here I was again, assigned to someone that no one else wanted. More and more stories started coming at me about how poorly David treated his former assistant. Although, I had not experienced any of the things that were being told to me, so many people felt compelled to share stories that I knew there had to be some truth in what people were saying. The stories ranged from David yelling and screaming at his former assistant, calling her degrading names and blaming her for anything that went wrong, to lying on her in her presence. After the first couple of weeks, I could see that David was intense and could lose his cool very easily, but for some reason he controlled himself with me. He would yell and scream at other people but not at me.

One afternoon while sitting in his office, David was so angry at one of the younger attorneys that he took a letter opener and began digging into his desk with it. This was not just any desk. It was a beautiful, expensive, hand-carved, oversized oak wood desk. The damage was so extensive that the firm had to call in a mill worker to make the repairs. David was a time bomb waiting to explode. He was also extremely regimented. Every couple of weeks, he would give me cash to keep locked in my desk drawer. My instructions for this cash were that each day he was in the office, I was to go out and buy his lunch—a tuna fish sandwich on rye bread with lettuce, tomatoes, and mayonnaise; a piece of fresh fruit (my choice); and a small carton of milk. He ate this every day that he was in the office. If he came into the office five days in a row, he would eat the tuna fish sandwich five days in a row. The only variety in his lunch was the fresh fruit that I got to pick for him. I worked for David about ten months, and this was the routine the entire time.

SOMEBODY'S WATCHING YOU

One Friday morning, the office administrator, Carl Fairvet, came up to my desk and asked, "Would you meet me in my office in thirty minutes?" This was a very strange request because I had never had one conversation with this man. Carl was well-respected in the firm. He was a wise man and much older than most of the people there. In his early seventies, he was very handsome and well groomed, with a full head of beautiful hair. The owners all trusted his opinion, and his experience was impeccable. Carl had retired from the military as a colonel, retired from the federal government as a civilian, and was nearing retirement from the law firm. In the later years, I used to tease Carl about becoming a triple dipper.

Well, I could not imagine what Carl wanted with me. I smiled and said, "Yes, I'll be there." When I arrived at his office, he invited me in and asked me to have a seat. As I sat down, he got up and closed the door. I thought, *Oh God, what is this about?* Carl proceeded to explain that David had not lived up to the firm's expectation. He was not the expert they expected him to be. And thus, he was asked to leave the firm by the first of the year (about sixty days later). Carl also informed me that he was looking for a new assistant. He said he had polled several of the senior-level employees (administrative staff and attorneys) in the firm and asked them who they would recommend, from the current staff, to be his assistant. He told them he needed someone who could be groomed for a higher-level administrative role.

At this point, I'm wondering why on earth this man is telling me all this. I wanted him to get to the point. The only thing my brain seemed to retain was the fact that David was being asked to leave. Was Carl going to inform me that I would have to leave as well? I had no idea where he was heading with this conversation. Finally, he got to the point. Per Carl, in his poll, my name came up several times, and he was interested in considering me for his administrative assistant position. He explained the job duties and asked if I would be interested. I was shocked, but flattered. You never know when people are watching you. I told Carl I was very interested in the position. A couple of days later, he officially made me the offer. I accepted and was moved to the administrative office suite about one week later.

FIRST EVIL ENCOUNTER

At the beginning of the new year, David returned to the government. For me, life was good. I worked as Carl's administrative assistant for about six months and was given a promotion to administer the firm's benefit programs. I had no prior knowledge of benefit plans and was concerned about being able to do a good job. When I went to Carl to express my concern, he told me that I should not worry and that he had every confidence in me. He felt very strongly that I could handle the job. So, I took on this new challenge as I had with every other—with nervous jitters but confident I would do my very best, and I did. Within the first year, everyone in the office had become confident in my knowledge and abilities in administration and as the benefit specialist. Not only were they confident in my administrative skills; they began to confide in me on other matters—mostly matters that should have been taken to the HR Department.

B. PHOENIX

Many of the employees were uncomfortable with Peggy, the HR manager, and most of them, support staff and attorneys alike, were either afraid of her or simply did not like her. Peggy was the first person I had ever met whose behavior was exactly what one would expect it to be if she were possessed by demons. Even though I had been exposed to a lot of crafty and tricky characteristics in the workplace, those of a revolting nature were not something with which I was familiar. Peggy was constantly behaving in a disgusting manner. However, whatever possessed her during these times, she was very careful not to reveal it to the wrong people. Her wrath was generally suffered by the support staff and attorneys she perceived as unimportant. With these individuals, she was out of control. To the contrary, with those people Peggy considered important, she was very warm and in control.

Watching Peggy's odious behavior gave me a very strange and creepy feeling. And as obvious as her bad behavior was to me, some people could not see that side of her. The ability to see in Peggy what many people could not was often very awkward for me. The book of Hosea in the Bible says that those who are wise will realize things and those who are discerning will understand them. Wisdom was something God blessed me with through Cicely, and people were always pointing that out to me. Discernment, however, is a gift I did not realize early on that I had, and on many occasions, I stated that I hated when I got things that others did not get. However, after one of my dear colleagues pointed out to me that it was a gift from God, I never said those words again, and this gift has proven to be extremely beneficial to me in my life.

Although hundreds of people suffered the wrath of Peggy, I personally had never experienced it. Then the day came, and I got my turn. One of the secretaries told me Peggy was enraged because she had been a little late for work. She said Peggy got in her face—so close that their noses almost touched. She said Peggy screamed, "You need to call me if you are going to be late, Missy!" The secretary said Peggy was literally spitting in her face and pointing her finger angrily at her. She assured me that if Peggy behaved in that same manner again, she would "punch her in her face." I knew Carl needed to know about this, so I reluctantly told him. He asked me if it was okay for him to speak to Peggy and let her know he got the information from me. I agreed. Another lesson Cicely taught me was that if I say something to someone (anyone), I should "be prepared to repeat it."

A few days later, Peggy stormed into my office. With her finger pointing in my face, she told me she was not going to tolerate me going to Carl about her. She said if I heard anything about her, I was to bring it directly to her. While screaming this at me, her face began to turn beet red. This redness, as she got madder, began to move down her neck and then her arms to the tips of her fingers. I began praying, silently asking God to "please get this ugly spirit away from me." Suddenly, she began gritting her teeth and making a monstrous sound, opened my door, and fled from my office while slamming the door behind her. Silly me (or maybe not), I got up and followed her down the hall to Carl's office.

Peggy slammed Carl's door behind her attempting to keep me out. I opened the door, walked in, and sat down in the guest chair beside her. She jumped up and left Carl's office, slamming the door again. There was a lot of door slamming that day. Carl asked me what was going on. I told him Peggy was very pretentious; she pretended to be a pure angel in his presence and the presence of those she considered powerful and/or important, but that she treated most everyone else horribly. I told him Peggy felt she could boss me around, and I was not putting up with it. In addition to other things, Carl said, "You don't have to put up with it." I thanked him and went back to my office. Although Carl's response was appreciated, I was a little surprised because most people in the firm, including me, believed Peggy had Carl snowed, and he had no idea how bad she was as an HR manager.

For a time after my encounter with Peggy, she was calm and dealt with most people in a very passive-aggressive manner. I figured Carl had put her in her place. However, about three months later, Peggy came out of her place again and began flipping off on folks—same old story. She reduced people to tears many times after their encounter with her. Some of the employees resigned and moved on because of their bad encounters with Peggy. Some of them reported these encounters to me, and I would always encourage them to report the inappropriate behavior directly to Carl. Not only did folks begin reporting Peggy's behavior to Carl, some of them took their complaints to the chairman of the firm. And finally, Peggy began to feel pressure to permanently correct her behavior. In an effort, I believe, to test her position in the firm, she went to Carl and told him she was considering pursuing another career. I knew this was nothing but a bluff. Why would she leave? She had a great position, earning lots of money, a beautiful office, and her own assistant, who handled most of the day-to-day work.

B. PHOENIX

Surprisingly, Carl told her he thought it would be a good idea for her to pursue other career options. He also asked her to let him know when she would be leaving. Peggy was shocked and crushed! I think she was expecting Carl to ask her to remain with the firm. She left Carl's office, stormed into her office, locked the door, and began wailing like a baby. Peggy went into Carl's office selling wolf tickets, but that day, he was not buying. About six months later, Peggy left the firm, and there were many celebrations. The biggest celebration was held over the telephone when I called a friend who had been the victim of Peggy's wrath for many years to inform her that this dog had had its day.

CHAPTER 11

Oh Fudge

ANOTHER INTERESTING CHARACTER I encountered during my career was a legal secretary who worked for one of the firm's most profitable partners. The accounting department supervisor notified the administrator that they thought this secretary was fudging her overtime (charging the firm for time she did not work). The accounting department pulled all her overtime records for a six-month period. I was assigned to do the audit. What I found was that for the six-month period, the secretary had reported more than $15K in overtime. When we took the records to the partner for whom she worked, he could not believe it. He told us he had no knowledge of her working *any* overtime. We showed him the overtime sheets, and his face turned blue. He had not authorized any of the overtime the secretary reported. As it turned out, the secretary had forged his signature on all the overtime sheets.

At this point, the decision was made that I should audit the secretary's overtime for a two-year period. This audit revealed that the secretary had been paid over $100K in unauthorized overtime. The administrator decided that he and I would speak to her about it. After we approached her, she began crying uncontrollably. She was lost for words, and at one point just stared at us. Then, after realizing she was on her way out, she told us she had a drug problem. Yeah, right! We looked at her like we both were thinking, *you have got to be kidding me*. She was one of the most well-dressed, more able to maintain perfect attendance with children in private school, high-dollar-car-driving druggies we had ever seen. The administrator and I both believed she was simply living far beyond her means and decided to steal money to support her lifestyle, not a drug habit.

Most people in the office thought this woman was a model employee. But for me, it was something in her eyes. I cannot describe it, but I knew there was more to her than everyone else could see. She always seemed to avoid me. Perhaps she knew I could see more than others. I saw behavior in her much like what I had seen in Harmon—always pretending to be something he was not. This made me recall something Harmon involved me in when I was a young girl.

One day, Harmon called me into the foyer of our house to brief me on an assignment he had for me. I must have been no more than thirteen or fourteen years old. His directions were to go into the living room, with a camera he handed me, and take a picture of this man that was in there. Although I did not have a clue of what Harmon was doing, I still did not want this assignment and knew it was something fishy. Something about it just didn't feel right to me. When I attempted to reject Harmon's request, he, in his normal fast-talking manner, told me I was acting silly and said "Girl, you better get in there and take that man's picture." His final directive was, "And don't say a word; just take the picture, give me the camera, and leave." I still remember the guy's face. He looked like a very weak, vulnerable person who truly believed he was being helped.

As I looked through the camera to snap the picture, I realized there was no film in it. I remember being sickened by the entire situation. Just as I snapped the camera, the flash went off, which made me feel even sicker. As I reached over to give the camera back to Harmon, he said "Oh, sweetheart, take one more shot just so that I am sure to have a good picture." I gave him a dirty look, snapped the camera for a second "photo," handed it back to him, and rushed out of the house. As I was leaving, Harmon yelled out in an extremely sweet and pleasant voice, "Thank you, sweetheart." I was disgusted! A few minutes later, he and the man came out of the house, both laughing and talking like old chums.

This guy was sure he had found someone who could help him with his problem. I wanted so badly to say, "You dummy. You have just been tricked, bamboozled, and made a fool. There wasn't even any film in that camera"; but, of course, I didn't say a word, and the man went on his merry way. As I later learned, this was part of Harmon's driver's license scam—where people paid him money to help them get their driver's license back when it had been revoked. The image of this one guy is still fresh in my head. That poor man sat there, posing with a straight face; you know the typical driver's license photo position—head up, shoulders back, and a straight face. Like this secretary, Harmon was, again, pretending to be something he was not.

After the administrator shared all our findings with the secretary about the overtime charges, she agreed to resign and pay the firm the money she owed it. Where do you think she got over $100K? Well, the firm decided to make her an offer she could not refuse. The offer was that one of the attorneys would meet her at the firm's bank. He would bring a check made payable to her in the amount of $110K, and she would sign it over to the firm. Write her a check? It was her retirement money—all of it. All $110K signed over to the firm. I'm sure choosing this over jail was easy. But just think, it took many years to accumulate this money and in one day, it was all gone. I guess it wasn't enough to be a $50K secretary during a time when the average secretary earned a little more than half of her salary. For some folks, it is never enough.

FIRM CHARGEABLE

During my career, I learned that not only does the "little man" steal, but the "big boys" steal too. One of the senior partners in the firm, who probably earned about $300K per year, was caught with his hand in the cookie jar. The fact that he was stealing is not the kicker, but the boldness of how he was stealing is unbelievable. As you may know, attorneys track their time and expenses and charge their clients based on time and expense records. The charges that cannot be billed to a client are billed back to the firm. Many years ago, it was very easy for partners to code items "firm chargeable." Unlike client charges, firm charges were not scrutinized. No one questioned a partner's firm chargeable time and/or expenses. After all, they were "partners." This partner, however, decided the "firm chargeable" account was for his own personal use. Someone from the accounting department brought to our attention an item the partner charged to the firm that was clearly personal. He had charged $250 to the firm for the services of a clown. Yes, a colorful, face-painted, red-nosed clown.

The chief financial officer and I were tasked with doing an audit on the partner's accounts. The audit went on for months and months. We found items that had been purchased and charged to the firm from leather shops, baby shops, drugstores, caterers, upscale department stores, airlines, limousine services, grocery stores, flower shops, hotels, and maid services. The grand finale was a reception expense that totaled close to $100,000. It was his wedding reception. Can you believe it? This guy charged all the expenses for his wedding reception to the firm. And when we were done, he had a whopping $350K personal tab. How stupidly greedy is someone like this? Everything taken from the "firm chargeable" account basically is being taken from each partner. This is so ridiculous; he stole from his partners, himself, and his firm. He was voted out of the firm, and was made to pay back every penny.

A Diamond in the Rough

JEB DIAMOND WAS a genius businessman. He was tall, dark, and handsome. Jeb was so cool that a gentle breeze followed him everywhere he went. Everyone respected him, and no one, I mean no one, in the firm would mess with him. He was quiet and moved softly throughout the office—a very quiet spirit, but a fiery presence. His area of expertise was corporate litigation. And he became a master litigator. He had become the king of the courtroom. Any company going into litigation wanted Jeb on its side. He was simply brilliant. He was very powerful but humble. I always admired him. He reached a level of self-actualization like I had never seen.

I will never forget the day Jeb walked into the office with a brochure of his new boat. Well, it wasn't a boat. He had just made the purchase somewhere over in Europe, and this vessel was so big, it had to be classified as a ship to bring it into the United States. It was loaded with everything you could possibly want in a home. Yes, a home. It was a floating mansion. This "boat" was one of the most beautiful things I had ever seen. It had very soft, plush leather furniture in one of the lounging areas. Yes, I said, one of the lounging areas. I believe there were four lounges in all. There were eight bedrooms, and this thing slept twenty people easily. This boat was one of the toys Jeb purchased, which was indicative of his wealth. He was at the top of his game and very few attorneys in DC, or anywhere else, for that matter, were up there with him.

The real story about Jeb is not how rich he was, nor how brilliant of an attorney he was, but about his amazing entrance and exit into and out of the

B. PHOENIX

legal field. As the story was told to me, the very young Jeb Diamond first approached the firm about an associate position. He went through a battery of interviews, but the firm would not hire him. Even though Jeb graduated from a well-known law school, the partners at the firm felt he was not the caliber attorney they wanted working for them. Thus, Jeb decided to go at it on his own. His business had begun to grow very quickly, but he needed better office space to impress his clients. After a few months passed, Jeb approached the firm again. At this point, he offered to work for pay only from what he billed his clients. Again, he was told no. The firm did, however, agree to sublease an office to him. He accepted the offer and immediately began working in the office. Jeb was placed in the worst space you could imagine. They had legal assistants in better office space than what they gave him. Jeb never said a word about the inappropriateness of his office. He just began working and worked tirelessly to further develop his practice.

After about six months, Jeb had two large clients keeping him afloat, but he needed more resources. So, he went back to the firm and asked if they would reconsider taking him on, but, again, they said no. After about eighteen months, Jeb had a very impressive client base and requested additional office space. He had so much work; he had to hire a couple of young attorneys to work with him. When the firm understood the amount of business he built in such a short time, they finally propositioned him to join the firm. Jeb accepted the proposal, and all was well. His client base began to grow even more rapidly, and the firm was very pleased with the decision to hire him. Jeb was also happy to be a part of the firm.

As the years passed, he was made a partner and became a major rainmaker. He brought in more business than all the other partners. The firm had to hire fifty additional attorneys to support Jeb's practice. He had the largest practice group in the firm and had become the highest-paid attorney there. The billings generated from his group brought in tens of millions of dollars each month. His base earnings were more than $750K per year when most of the other partners were earning approximately $200,000 to $300,000 per year. He was the man. Jeb Diamond had proven to be far more precious than gold.

However, as the old saying goes, "all good things must come to an end." The dynasty Jeb built was no exception, but he was smart enough to know when to get out. Several years after I started working at the firm,

Jeb announced he was leaving. The news of his departure sent shock waves throughout the office. Everyone was running around trying to figure out what was going to happen next. After all, Jeb's practice was what had been carrying the firm for many years, and everyone knew it. To where was he going? Were Jeb's clients going with him, or were they going to stay with the firm? Who would inherit this huge treasure chest if his clients did, in fact, remain with the firm? Two weeks passed, and everyone, I mean everyone—from the top to the bottom—was worried about the state of the firm. Finally, we received the next big announcement.

Jeb was leaving the law practice altogether. He was going to start his own investment business in upstate New York. He also announced that all his clients would remain with the firm. This brought a huge calm over the office. Almost everyone was breathing a sigh of relief. I and a few others, however, were not so relieved. The question now in some of our minds was who could possibly fill Jeb's shoes. We didn't know anyone at the firm with the same or similar business savvy as Jeb. It would take a very special person to maintain such an impressive and enormous book of business. I kept hoping that perhaps there was someone Jeb had been privately grooming to take his place. Rumors began circulating throughout the office that Jeb would leave his clients to the partner who was the most likely choice. It wasn't a choice I felt was good, but it probably was the best choice in the firm.

I will never forget the day Jeb made his final announcement. Everyone was desperate to know who would be the beneficiary of such wealth. Handing over a client base such as Jeb's was the equivalent of someone being given all the tools they needed to gain the wealth that Ms. Winfrey has today. Jeb had decided to leave his multimillion-dollar client base and one hundred attorney practice group in the hands of Lee Falls. Well, let me tell you, the shock waves from this announcement were greater than when Jeb announced he was leaving the firm. The partner everyone thought was going to receive this huge inheritance was probably more shocked than anyone else. He had walked around the office for days with his chest out so far, his chin was behind it. You can imagine the chagrin he felt when the announcement was made. This was a big surprise to many people. People in the office and outside the office could not believe Jeb's decision.

Lee was a young partner, very popular in the office, and a very nice person. He was an artist and aspired to one day become a great well-known

B. PHOENIX

artist. Many people in the office were very impressed with Lee's artwork, and some of the attorneys purchased his artwork for their homes. To the contrary, there were few people in the office who were impressed with Lee as an attorney, and believed there was no way he could fill Jeb Diamond's shoes. For months, people discussed what could possibly have been Jeb's rationale behind this decision, but no one could figure it out. Nevertheless, most people got over the shock of it all and accepted the fact that Lee was going to be running the practice group. As time passed, Jeb left the firm, and we all moved on.

A few months into this new role, Lee began to get overly confident and started flexing his muscles. After all, every other practice group in the firm paled next to the group that he had inherited. He oversaw a client base that was generating millions of dollars each month, and he wanted to be recognized for this. Lee soon began making demands. At first, requesting a larger office; they gave it to him. He wanted a secretary all to himself; they gave it to him. He wanted to be a member of the board of directors, and he got that too. The firm gave Lee everything he wanted. Well, almost everything he wanted. One morning after a board meeting, my supervisor came into my office to discuss how grueling the meeting had been for everyone. He said Lee, who had been earning about $250K a year, requested that the board increase his salary to $750K. He told me the board members went crazy, and after an extremely long and intense discussion, they flat out rejected Lee's request.

A few months later, another big announcement was made. Lee was leaving the firm and taking "his" clients and entire practice group to another law firm. This news had a "ding, ding, ding" effect on me. Suddenly, out of nowhere and like a ton of bricks, it hit me—could this whole thing have been planned? I began thinking about my grandfather, Harmon, who often developed plans (or schemes, in his case) that spanned many years. I could see it as clearly as I could see the fingers on my hands. Jeb was not only a genius of a businessman, but could he have believed in poetic justice? Did Jeb plan this whole thing? Did he never forgive the firm for how it treated him when he was a young attorney? Did he want revenge? Was revenge something he always wanted? Was he not revengeful, but purposely let the chips fall wherever they fell? Jeb had more things and money than he would ever need. He had reached the peak of his legal career and decided to give it all up.

Jeb was a millionaire many times over. He was going out on top. Did he purposely leave his business to Lee? Did he know Lee would get greedy and ask for a $750,000 salary? Did he also know that the partners would never give Lee the salary he wanted, and he would leave the firm? With Lee's inheritance, any firm would be willing to take him. Did Jeb know what this defection would do to the firm? You know the old saying, "The same people you meet going up, are the same people you meet coming down." The partners had treated Jeb poorly in the beginning, but in the end, he was the one who came out on top. I don't want to believe this was a plan, but the way it all played out just doesn't make sense. I'm not saying Jeb spent years planning a payback coup against the firm, but it is very possible that since the opportunity knocked, Jeb opened the door and let it in.

Lee received an offer from one of the most prestigious law firms in DC. They gave him just what he wanted. The chairman of my firm was crushed when Lee announced his departure. The board made a counter offer, but Lee would not take it. The chairman contacted the clients that were going with Lee to let them know this departure would hurt the firm and many of its employees. Basically, he was a day late and a dollar short. Lee's clients didn't even know who our chairman was and had never spoken to him prior to this. This is a big mistake for managing partners and chairmen of law firms, or any business leader, for that matter. You must know and respect the hand that feeds you. Cicely taught me that very early in life. The chairman had never made a telephone call, or offered to break bread with any of Jeb's clients. Therefore, none of them felt any obligation to the firm. That train had left the station, and nothing could stop it.

Lee moved on to the new firm but only lasted there a little more than one year. He was just not strong enough to manage and maintain a client base of that magnitude. His clients became very displeased with him and began moving their business to other law firms. My firm carried on with the business it had left. However, things were very different. Costs were being drastically cut. Partners were suddenly being questioned about every penny spent. We were all seeing, for the first time in the firm's history, hard times. People were irritable most of the time, and you would often hear folks lashing out at each other. The firm was falling, and everyone knew it. However, it was unclear as to whether we would hit rock bottom or survive the storm.

One afternoon when returning to work from lunch, I ran into a partner from a previous law firm where I worked. Ron Bonsai had taken the lead on closing out that firm, so seeing him at my current office was a very bad sign. I knew something was terribly wrong. When speaking to Ron, he tried to assure me everything was going to be okay. However, my gut was telling me something different. After running into John in my office a second time, I went to my supervisor and asked what was going on, and he confided in me. He told me the firm was going to dissolve and that there was going to be a generous package offered to me if I agreed to stay and assist with the dissolution.

This was a very sad time in my career. The firm immediately started laying off employees. People were being asked to leave on a weekly basis. There were so many different emotions felt by the employees. Some people were overwhelmed with sadness; some were downright mad, and, believe it or not, some were glad—seeing the severance package as a bonus. The firm, having been one of the most productive in the area, was becoming a ghost town. No more hustle and bustle; no copy machines running, almost nonstop; no idle chatting at the water coolers; no one requesting rush messenger service; no telephones ringing nonstop; and no more excitement in the air. It was very difficult being in that type of environment, but as promised, my supervisor was correct. The firm made me a very generous offer.

I was paid four times what I had been making and worked fewer hours each day. I also received huge bonuses every six months. The CFO and I were an integral part of administering the firm's dissolution. The CFO, with a strong banking background, was simply brilliant. There was no one in town as sharp as she. She was a strong financial adviser for the firm. The arrangement we had with the firm lasted two years. I arrived to work at 10:00 a.m. and left at 2:00 p.m. each day. Life was sweet. I could spend more time with my young children, who were both in school. To top off the deal, Ron, the attorney handling the firm's dissolution, promised he would assist me in securing a position once I had completed my services with the firm. I thanked him but didn't expect him to get me a job. But, thank God! Just as he promised, one month before the completion of the firm's dissolution, my telephone rang. It was Ron's secretary. She was calling to tell me that Ron wanted me to come over and interview with a young woman in their HR department. I interviewed, received a job offer, and started working at the next law firm.

Black at Work in the Twenty-First Century

ALTHOUGH MOST OF my days in the workplace were very good, there were some days I thought I had stepped into the twilight zone. An example of this is a time I was sitting in one of the partners' offices when the partner's spouse called. The call was answered on speakerphone. They were expecting their first baby and proceeded to talk about baby names. The spouse was at home reading one of those name books and began calling out to us what they thought were "very strange names." Next, the spouse proceeds to call out names they felt were really nice names. After calling out about four different "nice" names, each one followed by a term of endearment, the spouse says, "Velveeta. They list this as a name. Can you just see some black woman naming her child Velveeta?"

I could not believe what I was hearing. The partner immediately picked up the telephone and said, "Honey, B is in my office." At that point, I thought, *Wow, B is in my office? What does that mean?* What happened to, B, I am very sorry. Or, honey, that is not nice to say. This was uncomfortable for everyone in the room. In my need to strike back, I said, "Listen, don't worry about it; maybe your baby will be born looking just like me." I got up and left the partner's office. Believe it or not, that child was born with a wide face and very, very curly hair. When I was a baby, you can figure out the rest. How could the spouse of someone who was an owner of an internationally recognized law firm be so wry? I thought the "Velveeta" comment was totally twisted.

Another morning, I was sitting in a colleague's office when one of the other administrators walked up to the office door. She was with her four-year-old son. This little boy saw my colleague from the hallway and began yelling with great excitement in his little voice, "Marcy, Marcy." He was obviously very happy to see Marcy. He proceeded to run very fast toward her. This cutie-pie turned and looked back at me sitting there smiling at his little face, and made an instant U-turn and hightailed it back to his mother, who was still standing at the threshold of the door. This baby was suddenly very frightened. As he started screaming, his little body began to tremble. He was crying, grasping his mother's leg, wildly jumping from one foot to the other. I remember thinking, *Oh God, what happened? What on earth is wrong with this sweet little baby?*

Then, after Marcy, in an extremely concerned voice, asked, "What's wrong? What's wrong?" This little child screamed, "Mommy, Mommy, it's a black person! It's a black person!" I was shocked. I thought, *Oh my God, please don't let this be a little imp. I may have to forget his age.* In all seriousness, every fiber in my body knew this was not an imp, but purely a misguided child. It was, however, very hard to believe that children so young were still being taught to hate. Marcy sat at her desk with her mouth wide open, and the other administrator (the mother of the child) said nothing. She stood in the doorway massaging her son's back but never said a word. This was one of the sadder moments I experienced at work. This child, who wasn't even old enough to attend school, obviously had been taught to fear black people. He was so frightened of black people that seeing me literally caused him to flip out.

Another senior-level administrative person in my office proved that he was on the wrong side of racism as well. He came into my office one morning to say hello. As he sat in one of my guest chairs, he began talking about his frustration with not being able to properly tie his necktie. He went on to explain how he always had trouble tying his tie just right. I told him that my husband sometimes had the same problem. Without skipping a beat or without hesitation, he looked up at me and said, "But I wear a tie every day." When I asked him why he assumed my husband did not wear a tie every day (and he had to assume, because he knew nothing about my husband or what garments he wore daily), he simply replied, "Well, I just assumed." I let it go and decided that he was somehow brainwashed just like the little boy who was afraid of me. And I was left to believe that his assumption was based on one fact—I was black.

One summer, I was at an affair, and the discussion came up about a new television program called *Socially Offensive Behavior* (*SOB*) hosted by the comedian and actor D. L. Hughley. This program addressed all types of inappropriate behavior, some of which was racially motivated. There were many people in this discussion who could not believe that most of the people on the show did not react, as expected, to such blatant racist behavior. At one point, I began to tell the necktie story and how racially motivated the guy's comments were, and a young black man (about thirty-five years old and a professional businessman) who was listening stated that he did not think the necktie comment was racist. It was amazing to me that some black folks still did not recognize racist statements even in, what seems to many, the most blatant forms.

Law firms had their share of prejudices, and even though some of the top owners knew nothing of this type of behavior, some were active participants. Much of the prejudices in some of these firms were against the young black attorneys, all of whom had been some of the brightest law students in the country. However, these attorneys were, in many cases, left to fend for themselves, while their white counterparts always seemed to get the attention and assistance they needed. The black attorneys were often ignored and not given the same work assignments, or the same nurturing as their white counterparts. They were, in many cases, isolated from the rest of the firm—in some cases they were even placed in offices far from the mainstream of the firm. They were assigned mentors, but some of the mentors were often unavailable to assist them, or just would not, or could not, provide the proper guidance. As you can imagine, these young people would never speak out. Who wants to commit professional suicide so early in his or her career? They were afraid to rock the boat. They had to be politically correct. The sad part of all this is that some of the partners wanted to know the truth, but never knew.

Speaking of knowing the truth, I was in my dentist's office one morning waiting for the dental hygienist to come in and clean my teeth. When she came in, we began talking about President Obama and what his struggle must have been like as a black president. She told me that one of her other patients was a high-level government official who told her that the top employees in her agency were all told that they were to reject anything that came from President Obama. I thought, *Anything?* Was President Obama so bad that every request should have been denied, or was his blackness the problem? It saddens me to think that racism runs deep and high.

KEY PROMOTION

I was promoted to head the HR department of a very prestigious firm in DC and was the first African American to hold a senior level administrative position in the twenty-year history of the firm. This is when the real fun began. The firm was growing in leaps and bounds, and the then managing partner felt that my predecessor was not doing a good job. She was responsible for HR, records, and the general services of the office. Right before I was promoted, she was drowning. Many of the attorneys were displeased with her performance. In all fairness to her, I felt the position should have been split in prior years. When I took over the HR function, I immediately began recruiting the best and the brightest staff possible. My goal was to maximize the use of the staff that was already there and recruit experienced individuals to strengthen the department even more.

Things were moving along very nicely. I received approval to hire an assistant, which I shared with the person in charge of finance. We hired a former colleague of mine who was an excellent assistant. She could keep all the day-to-day administrative and clerical tasks on point while most of my time was spent developing and implementing much-needed stronger, more effective policies and procedures. I, as well as the other top administrative personnel, reported directly to the managing partner. We had an excellent rapport with him, and he gave us the autonomy needed to manage the direction of our departments with very little interference.

Aside from a few minor glitches, the firm was running smoothly. Then, out of nowhere, the partners began bringing in folks who normally would never have been hired. The firm always prided itself on hiring the best of the best. Attorneys were required to be academically at the top of their game, and those who were brought in as partners were required to prove the ability to bring in a certain book of business. Almost immediately after the firm hired a young partner from a law firm in Baltimore, it began having serious problems. This is when I believe the firm's demise began. The entire culture of the firm started changing. The new guy was a real deceiver. His reputation preceded him. When the word spread throughout the city that this guy was joining my firm, I received several telephone calls from persons outside of the firm telling me that this guy was "a real loser."

One person said, "I have two things to say about this man: he cannot keep a wife, and he cannot keep a job." It befuddled me how I could obtain due diligence such as this, but the powers that be never heard this stuff, or heard it and just didn't care. The firm seemed to believe this guy was a high-level, high-class rainmaker. However, I learned early that he was a scam. There were too many things he did in my presence that gave him away. One was the fact that he was overly impressed with a hotel room he stayed in that had french doors leading out to a balcony—not only was I shocked that this was so impressive to him, the way he described the doors was "two doors that you pushed outward onto a balcony." While he was saying this, he also was demonstrating to me how to push the doors open.

Another clue was the way he behaved about a sport jacket he had delivered to the office, which he asked me to receive in his absence. When he came to my office to retrieve his package, he asked if I looked at the jacket. I told him I had, and he proceeded to brag about it being cashmere. Well, it was a very nice cashmere sport coat, but, at that time, my husband owned a full-length coat made of some of the finest cashmere around. This guy was a fake, and I knew it. I had my grandfather, Harmon, to thank for this early detection. He used to say, "You can tell a nigger who never had anything because they're always bragging about every little thing they get." I apologize for the use of the word *nigger* again; however, that is the word Harmon used, which makes me recall a statement one of my aunts made. After using the word *nigger* in a conversation with me about her disgust of certain people in the area where she lived, I told her that she should not call people that name because the NAACP buried that word. Her response to me, in a very matter of fact manner, was, "Well, they should have buried the niggers with it."

EAT WHAT YOU KILL

The new partner was trouble from the word *go*. He came into the firm making all sorts of crazy demands. He wanted special treatment for members of his staff, warranted or not. He wanted huge amounts of money for himself and thought he should be one of the highest-paid attorneys in the firm. He was a newcomer with a large, very large, promise of a huge payday for the firm. The firm rolled the dice on this guy and came up with snake eyes. He, with the assistance of all those who were willing to kiss his butt, attorneys and staff alike, turned the firm upside down. There was more infighting during his tenure than ever in the history of the firm.

You might ask why one of the most profitable firms in the country would allow some little whippersnapper to have so much control—I was told his old firm would not allow it, and that is why he left. It was all for the love of money. These guys made stupid money without the little whippersnapper. I guess it wasn't enough. He was bringing a large book of business, and the firm wanted it. What it didn't know was what came along with this large book of business. Not too long after he joined the firm, people at every level began to see that this deal was starting to look a little more unattractive each day.

The board of directors' meetings became bloodbaths, primarily because of this guy. The office environment quickly changed from a true partnership, where the wealth was shared, and everyone ate at the same table, to one in which the mentality was "eat what you kill." In this environment, if you didn't generate business, you were given very little of the profits. It would be as if you sat at a table where you are one of forty-five hungry people. There is enough food on the table to feed 245, but only ten of you may eat! The ten who are eating aren't completely heartless; they will share their crumbs (and I mean crumbs) with the other thirty-five. I'm sure you can imagine the turmoil this must have caused—the same would be true in most any environment. People go crazy when they are hungry, especially when they are constantly around tons of food, but are only allowed to have crumbs. I know women whose husbands go nuts if they don't get breakfast on time.

These partners went nuts also. Not only did the partners go nuts; some of the top administrative staff went nuts as well. They began feeling insecure. This insecurity was born from the belief that the firm's turmoil situation was going to become fatal, and just when you figured things could not get worse, they did. Some of the administrative team members became obsessed with playing the political game of disingenuousness and kissing up. This caused me to become more and more isolated from the group. These political administrators' interests were all about what they could get—just like some of the partners. During all this confusion, many of the employees were being treated unfairly, at a minimum—some were downright being abused. On many occasions, I felt like I was between a rock and a hard place. I hung in there as long as I could, then, all of a sudden, the bell rang, and I stepped into the middle of the ring. My supervisor and some of the other staff looked at me as if they couldn't understand why I had come to fight. When I reached the boiling point, and I was literally at the boiling point, I knew I had to leave—and I did.

PRIZE PEERS

My supervisor, Clarice Archie, had previously worked for one of the big corporations in DC. She had never worked in a law firm and was very political. She started sucking up to the partners early in her tenure. The day I met her, I knew working with her was going to be a bad ride. She came into the firm extremely impressed by the whole scene. I will never forget the day she came into the office to meet her new staff. Each of the senior administrative staff members were scheduled to meet with her individually in one of the conference rooms. Mistakenly (or not), the room that was chosen had a full glass wall that separated it from the hallway. When I walked in, Clarice was in a seat facing the hallway. I remember very clearly how she carefully checked out each person as he or she walked past the room. The thing that turned me off the most was the fact that she became totally distracted when one of the partners walked by. This happened, off and on, the entire half hour I was with her. For as rude as I thought this was, at least I walked away knowing a lot more about my new supervisor than she would have verbalized openly to me. And as I knew, this was the beginning of a bad ride.

Thay Hellner was the firm's chief technology officer (CTO). She came to the firm from another very well-established law firm. She was highly recommended by Clarice. People in the office thought Thay was one of the evilest persons they had ever met. Ironically, at certain times, she could be as sweet as pie. She had a department of about fifteen employees, each of whom seemed extremely fearful of her. Do you remember Peggy Windpost, the HR manager whose neck would turn red when she was angry? When Thay got angry (and this happened very often), her eyes would change colors. Once, she was so angry that I thought her head was going to spin. She would yell, scream, call her employees names, bang her fists on her desk, throw things, and slam doors for no good reason. Thay's employees would tell me about different instances where she was just downright unlawful in her conduct. These individuals were so afraid of her they would never consider formally reporting her bad behavior.

Aside from Thay's usual mean deeds, there was one act that sent me off the deep end. The technology department had just been relocated to a new suite of offices. Mary, the service manager, was supposed to have keys made for certain offices. One of the IT employees who needed to get something from his office for Thay could not get into his office with the key he had been given. When he told Thay that he would be delayed in assisting her because he could not get into his new office, she snapped. Thay, in all her fury, went searching for Mary. Well, guess where she found her? Mary was in my office. When Thay stormed into my office, I knew it was not going to be good. She began questioning why the keys were not working for her staff's new offices. I could tell she was trying to contain herself, but was failing quickly. Mary had no idea why there was a problem with the keys and could not articulate what happened.

Finally, in a choking motion, Thay put her hands around the area of Mary's neck and proceeded to scream "Should I choke you now? Should I choke you now? Should I choke you now?" She got louder each time she screamed at Mary. Well, I thought poor Mary was going to wet her pants. Her face was completely florid. She sat as still as a statue. The only visible movement was her eyes. They were moving at a very fast pace looking at me and then in Thay's direction. She looked as if she was afraid to move even the slightest bit, for fear that Thay would choke her. I jumped up and said in a very loud, strong voice, "Stop it. Move your hands away from her now! What is wrong with you?" As Thay removed her hands from Mary's neck area, she turned and looked at me with fire in her eyes. I told her she needed to leave my office immediately.

After Thay stormed out of my office, Mary sat there for a while trying to compose herself. Her body was trembling, and she was visibly upset. I did what I could to try and calm her, and after about ten minutes, she could leave my office. I immediately reported this to Clarice, but it fell on deaf ears. Most people thought Clarice was blindly fond of Thay. I wasn't sure if she was blindly fond of her or afraid of her. I could never understand how Clarice put up with Thay's inappropriate, unpredictable, snappy behavior. She behaved horribly! In the fall of that year, the firm came to its senses and insisted that Clarice fire Thay. All of her mean deeds at that firm had finally come to an end.

Another character with whom I worked was Jodi Prettener. Jodi was hired as the firm's controller. She too came from a top law firm. I was very happy about having Jodi join our administrative team. I went out of my way to welcome her and to make her feel at home. Our relationship began growing fast. We would lunch together every day and share personal stories about our families. Then suddenly, Jodi began to show signs that she was the type of person who was only interested in the people she deemed "important." She was very selfish and wanted all the attention of these "important people." To give you an example, she and I were out at a meeting one afternoon, and we saw Sharon Pratt-Dixon, a pretty well-known attorney and former mayor of DC. Jodi knew Ms. Pratt-Dixon and stopped to speak to her. They held a five-minute conversation, and Jodi never introduced us. Ms. Pratt-Dixon and I exchanged a pleasant smile and without speaking a word, seemingly communicated the same message to each other: Why is this crazy woman being so rude? I knew at that moment not only was Jodi pretentious, she had very insipid manners.

The short-term relationship I had with Jodi was finally over the day our administrator called me into her office to discuss my performance review and bonus. I was telling her that I did not feel the amount of my salary increase was fair. I reminded her of how I worked long hours and accomplished more in a few months than many of my peers had accomplished all year. Clarice, in a very snippy tone of voice said, "It is my job to look out for everyone on the staff, and everyone believes they do more than anyone else."

I said, "What we think is not as important as what you think. It is your job to decide what raise and bonus each of us should receive."

She began to get irritated and told me she was doing the best she could. She said, "It is already very difficult for me to make salary and bonus decisions, but when people discuss their salary and bonuses with others, that makes it more difficult." I had no idea to what she was referring. She then said, "I have people coming into my office telling me other employees have asked them the amount of their bonus." At this point, I immediately knew what she was talking about and could not believe what I was hearing.

Clarice was referring to a conversation Jodi and I had a few days earlier. I was walking past Jodi's office, and she called me in. She began making small talk, and it all led to her saying, at least five to six times, no exaggeration, in a very short period, "I cannot believe the bonus I got."

She repeated this so many times that it was clear she wanted me to ask her about it. So, finally, I said, "Well, what was it?" I knew I would get the information eventually and because she was constantly making comments about her disbelief in the bonus amount, I asked. I knew she wanted me to ask, and, because of my position, I felt justified in asking. When she told me the amount, I thought it was good considering she had only been at the firm for a few months. I was happy for her, but when Clarice told me how Jodi misrepresented the way in which I asked about her bonus, I felt betrayed. Again, I couldn't believe what I was hearing.

The rest of that day and night, I agonized over whether I should say something to Jodi about her comment. By the next day, I had decided if the opportunity presented itself, I would say something to her. Well, guess who was standing in the parking garage when I went down to get my car that night? Yes, Jodi. She was just standing there, and when she saw me, she had this strange look on her face. It was as if she didn't know what to do. I just jumped right in and asked, "Jodi, why did you tell Clarice I asked about your bonus?"

She said, "I didn't want her to think I was going around telling people about my bonus." So, I asked why Clarice would think she would tell people about her bonus. She said, "I don't know. I am new to the firm, and I wasn't sure who I could trust and who I couldn't."

I then said, "That is total nonsense and you know it. If you felt that way, you would have kept your mouth shut. Instead, you set me up to ask about your bonus, and after you opened your mouth, you went to Clarice with your lie."

At this point, and in an angry tone of voice, I said, "You took my question out of context. You absolutely wanted me to know what your bonus was, and you know the only reason I asked was because you wanted me to ask. I thought you and I had a lot in common, and we could become very good friends, but with this act, you have proven to me that we are nothing alike and we could never be friends." She looked very shocked to hear what I was saying, but said nothing in response. Finally, in a very calm manner, I looked her square in the eyes and said, "I actually appreciate you exposing your true colors to me." This is when I walked away and never trusted her again.

About six months later, Jodi encountered someone at the firm who too was hip to her game, and he let her know it. Unlike me, this person was an owner—a very powerful partner in the firm. Jodi claimed this partner made some inappropriate racial comments to her. The partner claimed he absolutely did not. He said that he simply refused to suck up to her as many of the other partners had done, and he let her know her place. Shortly after, Jodi left the firm to go work for a retail business and was promised a windfall. I was happy she left. She had exerted a lot of energy being disingenuous, and all she wanted was to be accepted by and to keep up with the rich and the famous.

CHAPTER 14

HR Nightmare

CHAUVIN HANSON WAS the CFO of a large nonprofit organization in the heart of DC. He went to that company after working a short time on the West Coast. He was tall with light brown hair and was very handsome. Per senior staff members from Chauvin's former firm, he displayed an unbelievable amount of rage on many occasions while working with them. Chauvin originally moved to the East Coast because of his wife. She was from California and Chauvin was from South Carolina and had pulled himself up from the "wrong side of the tracks." He was one of five children. His mother was, for the most part, a single parent and did her best to raise her five children. I'm not sure what role, if any, his father played in his life. He never mentioned his father, but he clearly had issues with his mother. If you were very close to Chauvin, you knew his mother was all kinds of bad names by which he referred to her and to his grandmother on several occasions. He referred to many women as bad names, but those women who pissed him off were called very bad names.

Chauvin was brilliant with numbers. He was granted a full scholarship to one of the top Ivy League universities in the country. College was very easy for him, and when he graduated, he went on a mission. As a child, he was one of the "have-nots," and as an adult he was going to stop at nothing to become one of the "haves." Chauvin seemed to possess a strong bitterness toward people who had wealth and power. He allowed this bitterness to eat at him. Right out of college, he landed a position as an accountant at one of the nation's largest food corporations. He moved up the corporate ladder

B. PHOENIX

very quickly. After leaving the corporation, he became the chief financial officer for a nonprofit organization on the West Coast.

Chauvin was normally very likable; however, he had an unusually short temper. The first display of his fury at this company was cast down on a group of accountants in a staff meeting shortly after his arrival. I received horrible reports from folks who were there to witness this fury. I was told Chauvin came into the meeting with fire in his eyes. Apparently, the accountants were extremely frustrated with all the problems they had experienced with Chauvin's predecessor, who was reportedly not very bright and was unresponsive to their needs. Out of frustration and aggravation, the accountants unloaded on Chauvin. They were hitting him with all kinds of questions that he was too new to answer. I believe he understood their frustration, but because he was not tolerant of this type of behavior, he lost it. He started yelling and screaming and telling them that they were free to leave the company if they were unhappy and that he could replace all of them quickly after they were gone. Then he told them he would never waste his time in another staff meeting, and he walked out. Although I was not there, I was told it was as if hell opened its gates. In the words of one of the attendees, he "ripped us a new one."

After my arrival to this company, there were reports made by several young women in the office who claimed horrific experiences with Chauvin. Each of the complaints was sexist in nature, or some other inappropriate behavior. The claims included Chauvin's inability to control his temper, his comfort in referring to women as all kinds of bad names, and how he would display fits of anger on a regular basis. These women were not willing to file a formal complaint, but wanted counsel on how they should deal with this behavior. Many employees' first reaction to inappropriate treatment is that they want to protect their livelihood—their paychecks. And these individuals were afraid to go up against Chauvin.

I will never forget my first time meeting Chauvin's wife. She told me Chauvin was "an HR nightmare." I thought *"Great, just what I need, another Peggy Windpost."* I did counsel the women, but I also went to my supervisor, and without telling him who the women were, conveyed to him what I had been told about Chauvin. My supervisor's response was as asinine as responses could get. He said, "I'm sure he meant no harm." Basically, he was afraid of Chauvin and had a problem dealing with complicated employee relations issues. This was particularly true if he felt his actions might cause some negative political ramifications. As a result, he allowed this behavior to go on, until finally Chauvin left the company to take a position at a wealthy for-profit organization.

INDEPENDENCE DAY

After working at one company for more than a decade, I went to my supervisor, Maggie Remartnoe, and told her I was leaving the company in two weeks. At first, she did not believe me and said in a very firm voice, "I don't have time for games." When I convinced her I was leaving, I explained exactly why. I told her about all the injustices I felt had been done to me as well as many of the other employees. Maggie acted surprised and asked if I would be willing to share with her what I was calling injustices. I told her: (1) many of the employees were being mistreated by their supervisors; (2) when complaints were made to her, they seemed to fall on deaf ears; (3) senior staff members were being encouraged to fight among themselves; and (4) there was a clique within the senior staff group that everyone knew about but only discussed privately.

When I put her name at the top of the list of causes of injustices, Maggie turned pasty white. I told her all the reasons I was leaving the company. The laundry list was very long and a few of my peers were on it. I told her the stress of all the wrong that was being done was more than I was willing to handle. She sat at her desk in shock. I don't think she had ever experienced anything like this. An employee was looking her square in the eyes and telling her many of the problems that existed in the company were her fault, not so much because of what she personally did, but because of what she did not do. I was walking out on a dream position—one of the highest paying positions in the company with a very large benefits package. Nevertheless, I had to go.

When people spoke to Maggie about why I was leaving, she told them it was for health reasons. Can you believe it? I guess she knew I wouldn't make waves. Either that or she was a major gambler. I considered telling everyone the truth about why I was leaving, but decided it was not worth it. However, in addition to Maggie, I shared my feelings with the president of the company and a few select people in whom I could confide. I was finally leaving the company! A big party was planned for me, and most of the employees attended. In addition to the party, I received many wonderful gifts. The abundance of lunch and dinner engagements was overwhelming. They continued even after I left. It was very sad because so many people were sorry to see me leave. However, a few people were very happy to see me go, and I was one of the happy ones. That year, it was a wonderful feeling celebrating the Fourth of July. It was an Independence Day like I had never experienced.

BACKLASH

Anna Preye was the new chief human resources officer (CHRO). She had previously worked at one of the retail fashion companies in New York. The CHRO position was a promotion for Anna. She was about four feet tall with very long, straight, light brown hair. She was born and raised in Switzerland and had only been in the United States for about five years. Anna was the daughter of a wealthy corporate executive who traveled all over the world. She owned racehorses and frequently vacationed in Europe for the Swiss National Day. Many of the employees believed Anna was in over her head, and they often talked about how she rarely interacted with them. They weren't sure if she was afraid to interact with them or if she felt she was above interacting with them. Several months into her tenure, she was met with one of the worst challenges that an HR professional could face.

Reportedly, two of the female employees from the Conference Department had begun to show signs of deterioration. Their attendance was becoming shoddier each week, and their personal appearance had clearly changed for the worse. Many of the employees described these individuals' behavior as "strange." After many weeks of this strange behavior, Anna made a circuitous attempt to get the two employees to correct their attendance, but they did not. This was all an enigma for Anna. The problem was far bigger than she could handle. Finally, the decision was made that she needed to fire the two employees. I was told Anna conducted these terminations over the telephone and arranged to have letters confirming the terminations hand-delivered to the employees' homes that same day.

Per certain staff, Anna reported to work the next morning bright and early, seemingly relieved that there was no backlash from the terminations she made the morning before. Everything was quiet on the home front, and everyone was busy about their business. Anna had successfully fired two employees, her first at that company, and she was happy it was all over and done. This problem had absorbed much of her time, and she found it difficult to concentrate on any of her other work. Thus, when this problem ended, she was happy to begin catching up on issues that had fallen behind.

Two days later, staffers were busy working to prepare for a huge conference in Chicago. Then, suddenly, all hell broke loose. The two employees Anna fired showed up at the office looking for their paychecks. Reportedly, they walked right in past the security guards and used their security keys to access the office. Several employees who saw them described their appearance as disheveled, with uncombed hair and very wild eyes. They walked through the entire administrative suite looking for someone to give them their paychecks. They went to the payroll office and were told they needed to see the CFO. They went to the CFO's office, but he was not there to help them.

Finally, they found their way to Anna's office. This is where the twigs snapped, and all hell broke loose. I was told the two employees began yelling at Anna, demanding that she give them their paychecks. Anna informed them that she did not have their paychecks and that they would have to wait for the CFO. This was the wrong answer. At that point, reportedly and sadly, one of the former employees proceeded to beat Anna with her fists as if she was beating a punching bag while training for a world championship fight. It was further reported that the other former employee, in a very cacophonous voice, chanted repeatedly, "Kill, kill, kill." Per witnesses, Anna curled up in a fetal position on the floor of her office and never tried to defend herself.

When the police arrived, the one former employee was still continuously beating Anna. Several witnesses said it took three men to pull the one employee off Anna. She was taken to the hospital by ambulance, released the same day, but never returned to the company. A couple of months later, one of the senior staff claimed that Anna and her husband made a wild attempt to get the company to pay them something like $500,000 for pain and suffering. The company thought the request was ludicrous, and in the end, gave them nothing. Anna's husband was said to be so rude and obnoxious that the company decided it would not deal with them at all and informed Anna that she needed to contact its workers' compensation insurance company. The president of the company was well prepared to pay Anna up to two years' salary, which he felt was fair, but nothing like $500,000. I never knew what happened to Anna in the end, but I pray she recovered from this horrific event.

I know people say, and I do as well, that you never know what you will do in a situation until you're in it. However, I must tell you, if it had been me in that office, the end of this story would have been written totally differently. I have never been a fighter and was afraid to fight as a child. I can't even remember ever getting into a real physical fight. I have always been a peacekeeper by nature, but let me tell you, on that day, I would have turned into a street-brawling, head-banging ghetto momma—exorcism performing wild thang! I would not have been able to help myself. And let me also tell you, if I had to be carried out by ambulance, at least one other person would have been carried out by ambulance as well.

Again, I've never been a fighter, but I grew up under that old black family rule—you never strike anyone first, but if someone strikes you, you'd better strike back—and strike back hard. It might sound crazy, but we were told if we came home crying because somebody had beaten our butts, and we did not try to defend ourselves, we were going to get beat again. I know all of you psychologists are cringing, but that is what I was taught. And you know the old saying "Train up a child in the way he should go, and when he is old he will not depart from it." So, the bottom line is that I am not a fighter, but I would have whupped some butt that day! Again, I would not have been able to help myself. And don't blame me; blame it on my upbringing!

RESTAFFING

After hearing the tragic news of one of my favorite partners and his wife being killed in a car accident, I was, as you can imagine, extremely saddened. A tractor-trailer hit a guardrail in an extremely busy intersection of Interstate 95, which contains many on and off ramps and HOV lanes—a tragic intersection that has cost many people their lives. The tractor-trailer hydroplaned many feet into the air and, unfortunately, came down on top of the partner's convertible car. This was a tragedy for the entire firm. I returned to the firm, for the first time since I left, to attend the funeral services along with most of the employees. After the funeral, one of the founders of the firm asked me if I wanted to ride with him and his wife to the cemetery. I did. He asked me a lot of questions about what I was doing and whether I enjoyed what I was doing. I answered all his questions and told him I did, in fact, enjoy what I was doing.

When we returned to the office, I spent several hours there talking to the employees. Finally, I left and headed down to the garage to get my car. When I reached the elevator lobby, two of the firm's partners were there talking. They both embraced me and asked what I was doing and whether I was enjoying it. At this point, I thought someone was playing a broken record. This was the third time in one day I had been asked the same two questions by three different partners of the firm. I gave them the same answer I had given the partner earlier that day. One of them then asked, "Do you think we would be able to convince you to return to the firm?"

I smiled and said, "I don't know, but you are certainly welcome to try."

They both smiled, and one of them said, "We will be in touch with you soon." We chatted a little longer, and I left.

A few days later, one of the attorneys in the office where I was working at the time told me he was at a party and somehow my name came up. He said another attorney who was attending the party mentioned that he had been looking for me regarding a sexual harassment case. The attorney from my office got the other attorney's name and telephone number and brought it in to the office for me. I called the executive director of the firm to find out if he knew, specifically, why this attorney was looking for me. He was not in his office, so I left him a voice-mail message. He returned my call right away. Before I could tell him the reason for my call, he asked, "Are you calling because you are ready to come back?"

I said, "No. I'm calling because I learned that an attorney has been looking for me regarding a sexual harassment case involving the firm, and I wanted to know what you knew about it."

The executive director, in a very disappointed voice, told me who to contact regarding the matter. He explained that one of the female attorneys was suing the firm for an act of sexual harassment she claimed was committed by one of the male partners. As it turned out, I was not employed by the firm at the time of the alleged harassment. A few days after I spoke to the executive director, he called me back and asked me to consider returning to the firm in my old job and made me a very generous six-figure salary offer.

B. PHOENIX

I accepted the offer because it came at a perfect time. My family was just entering some serious financial challenges. In addition, the firm had become a much better place to work. Also, a few of the partners told me the firm had hired a strong chief operating officer (COO), who would lead the firm.

When I returned to the firm, a huge mess was waiting for me. The HR Department was in a pitiable state with no one in it but administrative staff. Employees were basically doing whatever they wanted to do. The firm's rules were on paper only. Folks were out of control. Firm business accounts were being used for personal matters. Caterers were being used for personal parties, but charged to the firm. Misuse of power was prevalent throughout the firm. The firm did not have the appropriate supervision for the number of employees there. For example, there were over 120 (one of the largest demographics in the firm) secretaries, and no one was directly supervising them. This was one of the first things I fixed.

I posted a secretarial supervisor position on the firm's web page, hoping someone from within the firm would want to move to the HR Department. I felt having someone who at least knew all the players would be a huge plus. Surprisingly, many folks wanted to be considered for the position. Responses began coming in the same day the posting hit the firm's web page. Most of the applicants had no supervisory experience; however, I carefully considered each applicant. Some of the applicants were ruled out immediately because they were not in good standing with the firm. Others were ruled out because they had only been with the firm a very short time, and their performance was average at best. Once those individuals were ruled out, we were left with three candidates.

One candidate was an excellent secretary that had a great personality and very strong evaluations from her attorneys. She was my favorite, but of the three candidates, she had been with the firm the least amount of time. Another candidate was a good secretary, but she had a poor attendance record. The final candidate was a strong secretary, had excellent evaluations from her attorneys, and had been with the firm for many years. Sounds like the latter was the one, right? Right. She was the best candidate for the position. However, she was someone who was rumored to be the ring leader of a group of secretaries that were reported as, secretly and in a very circuitous manner, making attempts to have me removed from the firm. Although I knew about all the rumors, I decided I would not allow this to prejudice my decision. I had the authority to choose whomever I wanted, but I felt strongly that I had to select the most qualified person. I had personally experienced a couple of problematic issues with this woman, but I confronted her about them and put it behind me. So, I made her the offer.

I will never forget the day I called her into my office to give her the good news. I told her several people in the office had applied for the position, but after careful consideration, I had decided to offer the position to her. With a very blank look on her face, she said, "I'm shocked I got the offer."

I told her, "I really want someone from within the firm, and you truly are the best in-house candidate for the job. It is only fair that you be given the opportunity." I also told her that although I remembered the problems I had with her in the past, I had long put it behind me. At this point, she looked frightened. I then said, "If you decide to accept the position, I will give you as much guidance and direction as I can." She left my office with most of the blood drained from her face. The next day, she came to my office and accepted the offer.

A few months after the secretary was promoted, I learned why she was so shocked and why the blood drained from her face when I informed her she had been selected for the position. She and her friends were expecting me to hold a grudge against her because of her past behavior. In addition, I was told by a very reliable source that when the secretary learned the firm had asked me to return to my old position, she went around the office with a petition asking the staff to sign it stating they did not want the firm to bring me back. I never told her I knew about the petition. What was crazy to me was why anyone would want to work with a person if he or she thought so badly of that person.

Later, I was told that this secretary applied for the job as a test. She and her friends knew she was a strong candidate. They also knew that based on the other employees in the firm, this secretary should be at or near the top of the list for the position. However, they did not think, in a million years, I would offer the position to her. I was told they just wanted to be able to say, "See, she is not a fair person." Several people in the office knew how this secretary and her friends felt about me. Some of them flat out told me they would never have given her the job. Others were concerned that I would never be able to trust her. Well, as far as I was concerned, there were very few people at the firm that I felt I could trust anyway. So, I was never concerned about trusting her.

B. PHOENIX

Cicely always told me, "It is better the devil you know, than the devil you don't know," and, "You should keep your friends close and your enemies closer," and although this wasn't my purpose for hiring her, the memory of Cicely's statements brought me comfort in my decision. I wasn't sure how this woman was going to handle working directly under me. Nonetheless, I gave her the position because she was the most qualified candidate, and I never feared what she might be able to do to me. And besides, it was poetic justice to have her sit on my side of the fence. Finally, she and her little buddies would see that the view was very different from my side. This person worked under me for six years, and before long, she was running to me reporting what I felt were minor infractions by her supposedly close friends. The entire time she worked for me, she was waiting for me to drop a bomb on her, and it never happened.

Finding a CEO

MANNY MAKADE WAS the chief executive officer of one firm. He and his wife, Ellen, relocated to the DC area from Miami, Florida, where they maintained a very comfortable life with their family. They lived in a beautiful home for over thirty years. Manny and Ellen raised all their children in this house and expected their grandchildren to spend many days there as well. They were like family with all their neighbors. Before coming to DC, Manny worked in a law firm in Miami that merged with another law firm. The merged firm did not have a place for Manny, so he decided to accept the position offered by our firm. It was a very hard decision for him and Ellen, but other than the beautiful sunshine, there was no reason for them to stay in Florida. Their children were all adults, and the firm made Manny an extremely generous offer, so he decided to move.

Manny and Ellen found "the perfect house." It was in a great community in DC with a private swimming pool and lots of important people living there. Although these homes were large, they were smaller than what Manny and Ellen had been accustomed. So, they decided to sell most of their personal belongings, and they purchased all new furnishings for their DC home. Other than their clothing, they had only a few small items they could say they owned more than six months. Ellen was very sad to leave their closest friends and the place they had called home for over thirty years. Manny, on the other hand, saw this as a great opportunity to be in the mix of all the hubbub of DC. This was a new beginning for Manny and Ellen in more ways than one. Manny was perfectly fine with this new life.

He was ecstatic about his new position, the firm's office space, and location. The fact that he lived in the same community as a well-known US senator was very impressive to Manny. He found the entire DC scene exciting and very interesting. Professionally, he was flying high. He inherited a really strong team of administrators—most of whom were highly skilled and cooperative, which made his transition into the firm very smooth. There was one exception, however. His biggest problem was Whitt Kingly.

Whitt was a young, very intelligent facilities administrator that had previously been the office administrator of a small law firm in New York. He was a native New Yorker and had a very strong personality. At one of my first regularly scheduled early morning staff meetings, Whitt became very insolent toward Manny. At every meeting, he would yell and scream at Manny for some reason, any reason, or no reason at all. In some cases, he was flat out insubordinate. Manny would appropriately inform Whitt that he was crossing the line and that he needed to calm down.

This day, Whitt was in an explosive mood. His voice roared like a lion being thrown into the belly of a volcano. It was scary for most of the people in the room, but I was not afraid. I had been confronted with this type of fury before. I recognized it and refused to allow it to frighten me. Almost everyone else, however, became outwardly jittery and nervous. Manny was correct in his attempts to temper Whitt's behavior, but there was just no controlling him. If Whitt wanted to have his way, it was extremely difficult to manage him. Finally, Manny gave Whitt the option of controlling his temper or leaving." Whitt chose the latter and rushed out of the conference room.

About two weeks later, I received a call from the chairman asking me to come to his office. Whitt had already informed all the administrators that we may be receiving a call from the chairman. He told us he had informed the chairman that Manny was impossible to deal with, and he did not have a clue about what he was doing. Whitt also told the chairman he could not work with Manny any longer. I'm sure there were other things said, because we had already heard Whitt's comments about Manny on many occasions. He hated Manny. Why? I don't know, but he felt Manny was a horrible manager and knew nothing about running a law firm such as ours. I always believed Whitt's biggest problem with Manny was that he felt he could do a better job.

Walking to the elevator and riding up to the chairman's office was a long commute. I had very mixed emotions about Manny. He was a decent, fair manager who, I believed, could have handled the position with no problem if he did not have to deal with constant resistance. Manny was never one to allow the politics of the office to interfere with his decision-making process. He also seemed to do the right thing, no matter who liked it or who didn't. Manny did, however, have a few real problems. There were occasions when he would fall asleep in meetings, and on other occasions, he was just totally distracted. I often thought Manny's problems were attributable to the stress of the position; as well as the stress of dealing with Whitt each day.

I saw Whitt shortly before the chairman called me, and he had the most gratified, vindicated look on his face I had ever seen. At this point, I believed Manny's days were numbered. As I approached the chairman's office, I knew it was not going to be a good meeting. I walked in, and he said he wanted to talk to me about Manny. I sat down next to him, and he said, "I have already spoken to three other administrators, and, quite honestly, I am well prepared to ask Manny to leave the firm. I just wanted to hear what you had to say." The first thing I thought was, *Why is he calling me in if he has already made his decision?* He went on to say, "I know I can trust your opinion."

I told him, "I like Manny very much. He is a good guy, and he has always been fair in all of my dealings with him."

The chairman asked specifically about Manny falling asleep in meetings, his relationship with Whitt, and his relationship with his secretary. I told him I had, in fact, witnessed Manny falling asleep in meetings. This statement brought an incident back to my mind—it was one afternoon when the chief technology officer (CTO) and I were in Manny's office discussing a critical technology issue for the firm. Out of nowhere, Manny began to nod—I mean nodding out. The CTO and I looked at each other in disbelief. Manny would recover from a hard nod and attempt to get back in the conversation. After about twenty minutes of this, Manny moved from nodding to a full-out nap. It was unbelievable!

I continued by telling the chairman that Whitt and Manny did not get along at all. Insofar as Manny's relationship with his secretary, I told him that there had been rumors floating around the office that Manny was having an affair with his secretary but that I didn't believe the rumors. At this point, the chairman, in a very firm voice, said, "Whitt has proven himself to the firm, and the owners are very pleased with what he is doing, and I cannot afford to lose him, but I can lose Manny with no problem." He stated he felt the firm had acquired a very strong administrative team, and he was confident that the team could stand alone until a replacement for Manny was found. He expressed his exhaustion with the entire process of finding the right CEO, thanked me for my honesty, and sent me on my way.

I left the chairman's office knowing Manny's days were even fewer than I had thought. Well, a couple months later, the chairman did, in fact, ask Manny to leave, and he moved on. He landed a decent position at another law firm in DC. The position was somewhat of a demotion but nonetheless a very respectable position. I'm sure Manny knew Whitt was the cause of him being asked to leave. However, I don't believe Manny ever approached Whitt, or anyone else, about the reason for his departure. He left the firm like a true gentleman. Whitt was overjoyed, and we all moved on.

THE MISSION

After Manny's departure, everyone's adrenalin was starting to flow rapidly. *Wow* was the feeling of most people who knew why Manny was leaving the firm. Whitt was responsible for the termination of a very high-level employee, and he made sure everyone knew it. Not only did this feat boost Whitt's ego, it sent a message loud and clear that Whitt's position in the firm was secure above most. So, you know what that meant; all the administrators were subject to be let go on Whitt's whim. This hit his peers extremely hard. Suddenly, their reality was that they could not cross Whitt ever again.

Whitt was playing it very cool. He was as sweet as pie to everyone (maybe not as sweet as pie, but he was suddenly easy to get along with). He began gaining the confidence of the other administrators, and things were going smoothly. Several weeks passed, and then the chairman put Whitt in charge of recruiting a new CEO. *Wow!* Let the person that convinced you to fire his supervisor oversee recruiting his new supervisor. Whitt contacted his favorite headhunters and immediately began the search for a new CEO. He was responsible for reviewing resumes and conducting the initial screening interviews.

In the meantime, I thought of someone I knew who would be perfect for the job. I don't mean perfect, I mean *perrrrfect!* Deja Bloom had worked in very high-level financial positions for more than twenty-five years. She served as the controller/CFO of several law firms and was, at that time, the

CEO of a large law firm in New York. Before I contacted Deja, I went to Whitt to find out if he had any interest in the position. He told me that he was not at all interested and that he did not want the position. I told him about Deja and how she would be perfect for our firm. I told him I was thinking about recommending her but did not want to contact her if he was at all interested in the position. Again, he assured me he was not and encouraged me to call Deja. I later called her, and she was interested. She explained that she and her husband had wanted to move to the DC area, and she was interested in speaking to the chairman.

I contacted the chairman and first asked him if the firm was considering Whitt for the new CEO role. He told me they were not. He said he wanted Whitt just where he was, over facilities. I told him I knew someone who would be a great fit for the firm. After telling him a little about Deja's background, he agreed to schedule a time to meet with her. The meeting was scheduled, and the chairman met Deja on one of his visits to New York. When he returned to DC, he informed me that he was very impressed with Deja, as I knew he would be. After his meeting, he arranged for Whitt to go to New York to meet her. A few days after Whitt returned, the chairman called me to say he was going to make Deja an offer and was hopeful she would accept.

After taking a couple of days to think about the offer, Deja called me to say she would love to work for the firm, but because Whitt wanted the job, she felt there would always be a struggle with him. I told her I had come right out and asked Whitt if he wanted the job, and he told me he did not. She said, "He lied to you. He definitely wants that job, and he came right out and told me he wants it." Deja said she was convinced, after talking to Whitt, that he would make it extremely difficult for her, or anyone in the CEO position, to supervise him.

When I called the chairman to discuss Deja's declination of the position, he informed me that he had no interest in someone who would be competing with Whitt. *What? Wow!* I don't know what Whitt told the chairman; however, whatever it was caused him to believe Deja would be competing with Whitt. *Wrong!* Why would Deja compete with Whitt? She would not. Whitt wanted the job but knew the firm was not ready to give it to him, so he scared off a perfect candidate. This is what happens when owners and senior level management rely on information from the wrong people, especially people whose interests lie more in their own personal agenda.

B. PHOENIX

Whitt continued the recruiting process. After several weeks of "grueling interviews", he recommended a candidate for the position. He told me the guy was a wonderful fit for the firm, and he scheduled an interview for the chairman and one of the other board members to meet this gentleman. The other board member put this guy through the wringer. He asked a string of very hard questions. One of which was, "How do you expect to manage our administrative team, all of whom are much more experienced than you in law firm administration?" I clearly remember this board member saying, very early in the process, that this person was not right for the job. However, he did not press the issue. Why would he? After all, Whitt had made the recommendation, and the chairman was behind him 100 percent. By gaining the trust of the chairman, Whitt had carved a secure place in the firm for himself. Thus, some of the partners feared Whitt. However, one fearless partner referred to him as a "wild pit bull" that the chairman allowed to roam freely. Many of the partners witnessed this "wild pit bull" in action and wanted no part of it.

MR. CEO—THE FACILITATOR

Finally, a new CEO was hired—the fourth in a few years. Whitt brought this gentleman's resume into one of our weekly administrative meetings and gave each of us a copy for review. A document production and facilities background was all that was on the resume. Also, the person had never held a position at any of our levels, let alone higher. After reviewing Mr. CEO's resume, the administrators immediately started questioning how this person could possibly have been chosen to be our CEO. They were all becoming very irritated. As I looked at this guy's resume and listened to my colleagues' outrage, a thought came in my head. I suddenly felt that maybe I knew why this guy had been chosen, but I was unsure, so I remained quiet. The more my peers talked about this person's resume, the more frustrated they became with this decision.

One person blurted out, "This guy is more suited for my position. He's being hired to replace me!" Others exclaimed in total disgust, "Who are these companies he's worked for?"; "Where are his business degrees?"; "I've been expecting someone with an MBA from one of the top universities"; and "This is crazy! Who picked this guy?" The meeting fell apart at this point. Whitt answered questions very cautiously and never talked about why this guy was selected. I started to wonder all sorts of things, namely the possibility that the firm was going under and could not recruit a strong candidate. To calm the group, Whitt spoke up with this lame statement: "The firm made this decision, and we are all expected to work with this person." He, for some reason, also felt it necessary to remind the group that this guy was going to be his supervisor as well.

Well, the day came for me to meet my new supervisor. Whitt scheduled a lunch meeting with Mr. CEO, himself, and me. We walked down to a very upscale contemporary restaurant at an area marina. This is when all the fun began. As we were walking to lunch, Mr. CEO spotted the person who was assigned to be his new secretary walking near the docks. He looked at Whitt and me and said, "Every time I see her, I want to call her Connie Chung." This woman was Asian, but mind you, she looked nothing like Connie Chung, the journalist. Mr. CEO's statement hit me like a ton of bricks. I started thinking that perhaps I did get hit by a ton of bricks and that I heard that crazy statement while I was unconscious. When I regained consciousness, I thought maybe he was just nervous and made this horrible statement without any bad intentions. Still, I could not get his comment out of my head.

During lunch, Mr. CEO spent a lot of time talking about the board member he felt was downright rude to him during the interview process. Well, I understood his problem. He was a fraud, and the board member, I'm sure, called him out on it. Whitt, however, told him that the board member was an "arrogant prick" and that he should not worry about him because most people in the firm hated him. I thought I was in the twilight zone. I could not believe what I was hearing. Whitt was covering for this guy on day one. Did he already know this guy? Was this guy a relative, and Whitt was trying to hide it? It was all so confusing. A little over an hour later, we finished lunch and returned to the office.

Mr. CEO was scheduled to meet with the other administrators after lunch. They all had been waiting for days to meet this guy. After meeting him, most of them rushed into my office to express their utter disgust with the firm for hiring him. They could not find one thing this guy was bringing to the table that was useful. He told each of the administrators the same exact thing. He said he was a team player, and he would jump right in and help any of them that needed his assistance. The only team player example he could muster up was that he was "not above making photocopies." The CEO? That was a sign right there. We didn't need him making photocopies. What we needed was a high-level executive, a strong decision-maker, and a true business leader, yet Mr. CEO could only give us the expectation of his ability to make photocopies.

From the first day this guy walked into the office, his behavior confirmed he was unqualified. After a couple of weeks on the job, he came into my office to tell me he felt very confident in my opinion about the firm and the people in it. He asked if it would be all right for him to run things by me from time to time. He explained how he had relied very heavily on past HR professionals with whom he worked and would like to establish the same relationship with me. Absent the comment he made about Connie Chung, he seemed to be a nice person, but still unqualified for the position. He also seemed concerned about being fair to everyone. I had begun to think that maybe I and the other administrators were too hard on him. Perhaps he needed to be given a chance. Even if he had no qualifications for the job, he had already been hired as our new supervisor, and we needed to support him.

Our weekly administrators' meetings were moving along nicely. Mr. CEO never contributed much to the meetings and chose his comments very carefully. For all intents and purposes, the administrators ran the meetings. Publicly, Whitt kept a very low profile when it came to anything relating to Mr. CEO. He did not want our peers to know that he had, in fact, recommended this guy, which continued to be a mystery to me. Three months in the position, and Mr. CEO began to get cocky. He had a great job with a huge compensation package, a beautiful office in a luxury office complex, and an extremely experienced staff of nine. At this point, he was feeling so confident in his new role that he began to do crazy stuff. I mean crazy stuff!

One of the first crazy antics of Mr. CEO was how he started making up excuses as to why he had to leave the office early—every Friday. Before his early departures, he would always come to me as if he was seeking my approval. Many of the administrators believed he was leaving early to get started on his weekend tipple. I don't know whether this was true or not. However, whatever the reason, it must have been important to him. You could see the desperation in his eyes when the clock struck 2:00 p.m. on

Fridays. He had to come up with an explanation for leaving early, and after using all the believable excuses (e.g., doctor appointments for him and his wife, picking up family members from the airport, dog to the vet, etc.), Mr. CEO resorted to excuses that were simply sad.

I will never forget my favorite two o'clock Friday afternoon excuse. Mr. CEO came rushing into my office to tell me he had to take his wife to the airport. She was scheduled for a 4:00 p.m. flight out of Reagan National. She was going to the beach for a week. Ordinarily, this would not have seemed strange, but when I innocently asked, not realizing it was 2:00 p.m. on a Friday, "Oh, where is she going?" Not able to look me in the face, he stumbled around to find an answer. Finally, he said, "She's going to Ocean City." I thought, *you have got to be kidding me. She is taking a plane from Reagan National airport to Ocean City, Maryland?*

Ocean City is a beach resort area on the Eastern Shore of Maryland. From anywhere in the DC metropolitan area, you could drive to Ocean City in a few hours. I have known hundreds, if not thousands, of people who went to Ocean City from the DC area, but I had never heard of any one of them flying on a commercial plane from DC. Do you know what you would have to do to fly to Ocean City from the DC area? You would have to fly to Philadelphia or Boston or somewhere far and fly back. This guy was horrible at being disingenuous. He was so desperate that he just let anything fly out of his mouth. I decided it was either desperation or he thought I was, in the words of one of my old colleagues, "Susie Sausagehead." So, you know what I said? "Oooh, that's nice."

Mr. CEO rushed out of my office so fast that I imagined he probably got out in the hallway and thought, *Whew, she bought it.* In my world, I would have told him, in Donald Trump fashion, "You're fired for telling such a stupid lie; now get out of my office." His behavior became so desperate he would sneak out early (not telling anyone he had left) leaving his office lights on, door opened, and a suit coat on the back of his chair. But, hey, Whitt checked this guy out, screened his background and recommended him, as the top pick, over many other candidates.

Well, top pick or not, Mr. CEO was making a spectacle of himself daily. He referred to people from the Middle East as "tissue heads." Yeah, "tissue heads." Can you believe it? He couldn't even get a racial slur right. His lies and behavior were more and more ludicrous each day. As many of the other staff started to openly question his lame excuses and his ability to do the job, he began to show signs of uneasiness. I believe this called for something drastic—you know, someone he could trust to watch his back. Someone who would be loyal to him first. Who better to do this than a former subordinate? Mr. CEO knew the perfect person for the job. Out of the clear blue, he came into our staff meeting and announced that he had hired a young man as his new "executive assistant." There was no real need for someone in this capacity, but he felt he could make the hire. Mind you, Mr. CEO had an administrative assistant. What were both these people going to be doing? I believe Mr. CEO was so desperate that he felt he needed a really trusted cover man.

After the meeting, I went to Mr. CEO to inform him that he had no authority to hire this person before having him meet with HR. He apologized and immediately scheduled the guy to come in and meet with me. When the guy came in, I learned that Mr. CEO had made him lots of promises he could not keep. He promised free parking, a huge office, and a bonus amount for which the guy would not be eligible—all of which had to be rescinded. Nonetheless, this guy came in and immediately began his cover-up. On the days Mr. CEO would sneak out early, his "cover man" would turn off the lights and lock his office door between 5:30 and 6:00 p.m. They were a perfect pair. And to show his gratitude, Mr. CEO would take the new cover man out of the office for afternoon golf. This was causing Whitt to feel extremely uncomfortable about his recommendation, and the other administrators were completely discouraged by the situation. Not only was Mr. CEO deficient with respect to knowing how to run a law firm; he had no understanding of what was appropriate or inappropriate office behavior. He frequently made racist and sexist comments.

One afternoon, I was sitting with the office manager, and Mr. CEO walked in. He wanted to inform her that he had received approval to give the manager of client services (who was at a lower level than the office manager) a larger office. The office manager spoke up and said, "I would like to have a larger office also."

Mr. CEO looked her square in her eyes and said, "You cannot have a larger office." When she questioned why she could not have a larger office, he again looked her square in the eyes and without cracking a smile, or batting an eye, asked, "Do you really want to know why you can't have a larger office?"

She said, in a very firm and frustrated manner, "Yes!"

Then, Mr. CEO, looking at her squarely again, asked, "Have you looked between your legs lately?"

I thought I was gonna pass out! I thought, *does this guy realize what he's saying?*

The office manager said in a very angry voice, "You can't say that to me."

Mr. CEO turned to me and said, "You didn't hear that." The office manager's face turned beet red.

I spoke up and said in a very strong voice, "Are you kidding me? I absolutely heard that, and I better not hear it again. I know you're aware that those comments are inappropriate because you looked at me and said, 'You didn't hear that.'"

Then he very nervously said, "I was only kidding around."

I informed him that I had better not hear anything like that again—kidding or not—or I would report him to the chairman.

Well, the saga with this guy continued. One morning I arrived to work at about 9:30 a.m. I unlocked my office door, and as I pushed the door open, I realized there was something in the way of the door. I pushed harder, and the door opened. There was a large, thick, brown sealed envelope on my floor. My name was handwritten on the outside of it. This was not unusual because folks slid packages, letters, notes, etc., under my door all the time. I picked up the package and tossed it into the in-box on my desk. I put my tote bag and purse away and went to the kitchen to get water. When I returned to my office and began going through the items in my in-box, the package that was left under my door was the first item I opened.

As I opened the envelope, I realized it was a copy of the *Legal Times*. I unfolded the newspaper, and there was a note on a piece of yellow post-it paper. The note had been placed on one of the inner pages and folded over the front of the newspaper. I flipped the note back, and it read, "Is this where you shop?" The note was signed by Mr. CEO. An arrow was drawn to the inside of the newspaper. I opened it and followed the arrow, which led to an ad for a very seductive, X-rated clothing store in DC. The caption of the ad was, "Nothing you need, everything you want! Leather • Latex • Lingerie • Couture Toys • Corsets • Club Wear • Men's • XS—XXXL." The ad had a picture of a woman wearing a very sexy black leather outfit exposing most of her breasts and a large, black, wide-brim hat.

B. PHOENIX

As you can imagine, I was in total shock, and all I could think was, in the words of my baby sister, "What the what?" I could not believe anyone would have the nerve to send me, the director of HR, something so clearly inappropriate. It wasn't that the picture itself offended me; my problem with the package was that it was indicative of Mr. CEO's lack of respect for me, my position, and the firm. With all the press and education on harassment and sexual harassment in the workplace, I just could not believe he, or anyone else in this part of the twenty-first century, could be so stupid. I finally reached my limit with this guy. I had to escalate these problems. If Mr. CEO had the audacity to do this to me, who knows what he might have done, or said, to some of the other employees.

I went straight to the chairman and explained all that had been going on with Mr. CEO and told him about all his inappropriate comments and behavior. The chairman said he could not believe this guy was so stupid. He told me Whitt had expressed some concerns about Mr. CEO, but he had no idea the problems were so severe, and he assured me that he would deal with this problem. A couple of weeks later, the chairman informed Mr. CEO that his relationship with the firm was not working out, and gave him three months to find another job. To show how ridiculous it was to hire him in the first place, after being told things were not working out, Mr. CEO came to my office and told the office manager and me, in a very cheerful voice, "I just got fired, but I'm not surprised. I knew I was not qualified for this job. I submitted my application as a joke. I couldn't believe I got an interview. When Whitt called me and informed me that I had been selected for the position, my wife and I were in total shock."

The office manager and I could not believe what we were hearing, and for several minutes we just stared at each other. The fact that this guy was telling us this story was unbelievable. Not only did he tell us the story, he told it with no remorse whatsoever. He had put the firm at risk on many occasions, but this was of no consequence to him. Finally, he said, "My wife and I agreed that because the offer was so much money, I would accept it and ride that train for as long as possible. Honestly, I didn't think I would last as long as I did." Then he walked out of my office just as cheerful as he was when he walked in. The office manager and I, however, were still in shock over what we had just heard. Mr. CEO got it while the getting was good, and when it was over, he left with no regrets. Another one bites the dust, or did the dust bite the firm?

Typically, I don't pull the race card unless I'm sure race is a factor. However, on many occasions during Mr. CEO's tenure, I could not help thinking, *this would never have happened to a black man*. A black man with the lack of experience that Mr. CEO came to us with would never have even gotten past, if to, the interview stage, let alone, the job offer.

AND THE BEAT GOES ON

Shortly after Mr. CEO's departure, the managing partner came into one of our staff meetings and informed us that Whitt was the new CEO of the firm. He also informed us that the board of directors had every confidence in Whitt and that he had already proven himself at many levels. In addition, he stated that over a three-year period, the firm had employed four CEOs that did not work out. He went on to explain that the board was of the belief that Whitt could not do any worse than his four predecessors. He asked that each of us give Whitt the same level of support we would give him. Some of the administrators and staff were pleased with this decision, some were very leery about it, and others were downright unhappy about it. Whitt's reputation of being a tyrant had long been a concern for many people in the firm. Even though I was very disappointed at how Deja was treated, I was of the belief that it was for the best. Deja would have had a really hard time working with Whitt. I will always believe Whitt encouraged the hire of Mr. CEO so it would open the door for him to have a shot at the position, and, obviously, if this is true, it worked.

Whitt was very skillful with the operations of the firm, but he was weak with finances. He made some very questionable financial decisions in his personal life—all driven by his anger. One example is that he sold a prime piece of real estate in DC, at the beginning of a very high upswing in the housing market, and rented an expensive house in DC, all because he was angry at his old supervisor. His reason, he said, for doing this was because if he wanted to quit his job, he did not need a house holding him back.

One morning while sitting in Whitt's office, he and I were having one of our many fun and relaxing conversations. I always believed that I was comic relief for Whitt. I seemed to be able to make him laugh like no one else. That morning, I was having a heart-to-heart talk with him. I told him his anger was going to cause him a lot of grief if he didn't get control of it. I proceeded to give him my advice on how I would have handled his decision to go from a homeowner to a renter. He sat listening very intently to everything I was saying. After a few minutes of listening, he shook his head repeatedly and said, "I can't believe I am actually listening to financial advice from you." I smiled and replied, "You obviously need it." He then said, in a very sad and embarrassed tone, that he was not very good with his money and that he and his partner blew a lot of money on material things.

Whitt was obviously embarrassed, so to lighten the conversation, I said something like, "Well, don't worry; you're going to be blowing a whole lot more money on that used boat you just bought." We both laughed, and I asked him if he knew the definition of a boat. He said no, with a big smile on his face. He knew the answer was going to be amusing. I told him that one of my old supervisors told me, when I purchased my first boat, that "the definition of a boat is a big hole in the ocean that you pour money into." We both laughed, and he waved me away.

At the beginning of Whitt's tenure as the new CEO, he was confident but very cautious. The ball was now in his court to prove he could not only handle the CEO's position, but that he was worthy of it. He moved very swiftly to get to know each of the administrators intimately. He planned monthly administrator lunches and dinners outside the firm at very expensive restaurants in town. In many cases, our checks (for seven to nine people) would be well over $1,000. We had lots of fun and laughs.

Whitt had a great sense of humor and would joke around with each of us. Initially, many of the administrators were very pleased with Whitt as their supervisor. He and I established a personal relationship outside the office. I was always completely honest with Whitt and willing to tell him the truth about himself every time. He often used me as a gauge. In the early days of his reign over the firm, he needed a crutch, and I was the one to fill that spot. However, when he reached the point where he was totally confident in his position, he did not put up with my painful truths. Whitt was like a brother to me, and, to this day, I still love him dearly.

Cash Cow

ONE OF THE most conniving employees I ever encountered was Varona Bullis. Varona was a real queen butt kisser (QBK), a major manipulator, and a baroness of disingenuousness. She played games with people hard and masterfully. Like Grandpa Harmon, she could fool many people, and she almost fooled me. Varona's family was close friends with the president of our company, and she had previously worked for the company as an intern when she was in college. Before returning to the company, there had been rumors that Varona had been seen having lunch with the president on several occasions. And before anyone knew anything, the guy who was the company's government contracts officer was being asked to leave, and Varona was moving in.

Varona came to our organization after working many years in the federal government. She was hired as the company's government contracts officer. She was about forty-five years old, tall with dark brown hair, and admittedly was a shopaholic. She wore extremely expensive clothes—suits that easily cost $500 to $1,500 each. She was a real looker. And although she was attractive, appeared very confident, and had a lot going for her, she was still very insecure. Employees were buzzing about Varona's return. Those who knew her when she was in college shared stories about how she was always trying to be accepted.

Apparently, Varona was the black sheep of her family and was always on the defensive while at work. Many of the staff expressed their discontent with her returning. However, when she returned, she seemed to be a totally different person. She was far more outgoing and confident than she had been described. She was engaged to be married and in the process of purchasing her first home—a huge house in a posh, swanky area of DC. The handsome salary she received from our company facilitated this purchase greatly. The company, although a nonprofit, was making money hand over fist and had a reputation in town of being a "cash cow," and a cash cow was what Varona needed.

The company paid Varona $250,000 per year with bonuses that ranged from $100,000 to $150,000. Even with that income, she was constantly trying to get more, and expected the company to pay all sorts of ridiculous expenses. She once worked a lot of hours trying to get year-end tasks completed. Thus, she claimed that she could not do her Christmas shopping until very late and felt that because she spent so many hours in the office, the company should pay close to $800 to ship Christmas gifts to her out-of-state relatives. In addition, she charged a $650 personal dinner on the company credit card and wanted to repay it in five payments. Varona had a reputation of doing everything with her personal agenda in mind, and her personal agenda could be summed up in three words: money, money, money.

Not only was Varona hungry for money, she was also hungry for attention and company information, and she went to great lengths to get both—even if it meant stooping low or stepping on others to get it. She was known to hang around the office very late when there was a board meeting. She knew certain board members would spill the beans about everything discussed in those meetings. There were times when she was spotted lurking outside the conference room where the board was meeting. On several occasions, she was also spotted lurking outside the president's office. She would eavesdrop on conversations he was having on the telephone, or behind closed doors. A few employees witnessed this and often talked about it. I always believed Varona needed information to help her maneuver through her mazes of deception and to stay on top of her personal agenda. It was clear that she had an insatiable taste for information, and she did whatever she had to do to get it.

Varona was always in the faces of certain powerful individuals and did not want anyone else competing with her for their attention. A good example of this was shared by one of her peers who, along with Varona, attended a company out-of-state conference. Varona's peer reported that on one night, Varona convinced her to retire early. She said they both should go to bed and leave the board members to bond with each other. At around 9:00 p.m., they returned to their respective rooms for the night. However, the next morning, Varona was bragging about how much fun she had the night before with the board members. When her colleague reminded her that it was her idea to leave the board members alone to bond, Varona told her she could not sleep, so she got up and went back down to the hotel lounge. She bragged about how she partied, gambled, and drank with the board members until the wee hours of the morning. Her colleague was of the belief that Varona wanted all the attention from the board members and used the "let's retire early, so the board members can bond" trick to get her out of the way. Varona was full of manipulative ways.

CARIBBEAN RIVERBOAT GAMBLER

Varona manipulated one of the most masterful plans I have ever seen in the workplace. About two years into her tenure, the company began experiencing a reduction in business. At one point, it got so bad that we started having trouble recruiting strong talent to work for us because people felt the company was too unstable. However, there did come a bright light when we entered discussions about a potentially huge government contract, which, if successful, would have brought in something like $10 million per year over several years. This was a great project for us because we could complete the project without additional overhead. Just the potential of this deal lifted everyone's spirits, and people were suddenly more motivated than ever. Successfully sealing this deal would also have brought in millions of dollars of business from other sources. Sealing this deal would have turned the organization around for the good.

Several months into negotiations, Varona announced that her husband was being transferred to New Orleans to work on a construction project. Yes, New Orleans, Louisiana. People in the office were shocked. Many of them could not see Varona living farther south. However, when people mentioned her moving south, she would say, "Well, New Orleans is really the northern capital of the Caribbean." She and her husband had purchased a new home in New Orleans, and she was going to be leaving the company in ninety days. Varona also announced that she was planning to start a family and that she would not be working when they moved.

B. PHOENIX

People in the office thought this was odd also, because with all the debt Varona claimed to have, she and her husband would be going from a two-income family to a one low-income family. It was common knowledge in the office that Varona lived way above her means and that her husband did not make much money as a construction worker. In addition, she always spoke against having children and seemed way too selfish to properly raise a child. Although Varona's plans seemed odd, quite a few of the other senior staff were very happy to hear the news of her departure because she wreaked havoc on many of them and was always kissing up to the president and the board, and speaking ill of others.

Well, Varona's resignation sent the president into a tailspin. She was the key player in negotiations for the potentially new contract, which would not be finalized for many months. A week later, the news of Varona's departure was spreading quickly throughout the company. None of this was making sense to me. However, the president authorized the events team to start making celebratory plans for Varona. He even authorized staff flying in from other states. And even though Varona stated she did not want a party, plans for a party and gifts were under way. One of her closest friends picked out a piece of artwork for her entitled *Casino New Orleans*. This seemed quite fitting for her new home. The image was two men and a woman sitting at a blackjack table. The work was just what Varona liked—huge in size with a glitzy frame. I saw a subliminal message in the work. Varona was a major gambler. She also gambled in the workplace as well—a real gamester, and, unlike most people, she took unbelievable chances at work.

Albeit Varona was a real gamester and not at all a person of my taste, I began feeling sentimental about her departure and thought that perhaps I had been too hard on her. I was never rude or inappropriate with her but kept my distance and never trusted the QBK. As Cicely used to say, "You must use a long-handled spoon when dealing with some folks," and "fool me once, shame on you; fool me twice, shame on me." These teachings stayed fresh in my mind whenever I was around Varona. The weeks were rolling by fast, and the president, who simply adored Varona, had been walking around for days with a sad face.

Varona, however, was walking around with a look of fear. I saw it for the first time the day the president announced plans for her going-away party. Varona looked as if she had seen a ghost. I began wondering what could be making her afraid. Perhaps it was the fear of no longer having a high-paying job, or the fear of those $1,500 St. John suits and $500 Saint Laurent shoes fading away. Maybe she was afraid she would have to eat flank steak instead of tenderloin fillet. Perhaps the guilt of her scheming was causing the fear. And in the words of William Shakespeare, guilt will spill itself in fear of being spilt.

Before too long, the president accepted the fact that Varona was leaving and began moving on. Varona, however, was walking around sometimes like the cat that ate the canary and other times with a look of fear on her face. She seemed unusually worried and had become more and more adamant about not wanting the company to give her a going-away party. The first time she mentioned not wanting a party, I thought it was strange, but after repeatedly stating she did not want a party, I knew she was up to something. I know it was wrong, but I would bring up her planned departure every time I saw her. This made her visibly uncomfortable. I didn't know what she was up to, but I knew it had something to do with her personal agenda—everything about Varona had something to do with her personal agenda, and you know her personal agenda was money, money, money.

One week before the big party, the president announced to the senior staff that Varona had been admitted into the hospital. She was experiencing chest pains. I cannot tell you how horrible I felt. Here this woman was sick, and I was suspecting her of planning a scheme. I felt bad. And then, the day after learning about Varona's illness, I suddenly started thinking about Grandpa Harmon, who used the old "chest pains" trick whenever he was running from something. This worked perfectly if you wanted to be admitted into the hospital. You could easily get a doctor to support a chest pain admission. Now I'm not saying Varona wasn't experiencing chest pains; I just know she always seemed very healthy. At this point, I, as well as others started to believe that Varona had no intention of leaving. Some of us thought she was just trying to get more money, while others believed her relocation story.

Well, chest pains, or not, it was enough to cause the big party to be canceled. Two days after her hospital admission, Varona returned to work with relief written all over her face. She was acting as if nothing had happened and seemed happier than a pig in poop! And although she seemed relieved that the party was canceled, time was running out, and she was scheduled

B. PHOENIX

to leave very soon. With the new account negotiations, Varona's departure was placing the company in a very awkward position. We were having a difficult time replacing her because most people in town knew the firm was in trouble. Also, it would take a new person far too long to get up to speed, and with a new person, winning the contract would be extremely difficult. Varona knew the company was in a vulnerable position, and she also knew securing this deal would require all the original players.

One afternoon, just days before her scheduled resignation date, Varona came into my office. She seemed very excited and could not wait to break the "good" news to me. She told me the president had asked her to continue working for the company at a reduced schedule from her home in New Orleans. New Orleans was the place Varona spoke of frequently. She and her husband traveled to New Orleans multiple times in one year. She was extremely impressed with the lifestyle in New Orleans. I remember her speaking of a group of people she met there with "phenomenal wealth." The sound in her voice when she said the words *phenomenal wealth* is unforgettable. She sounded and looked as if she could taste the wealth. Well, it looked like Varona was not trying to get more money after all. She just wanted the same money in a new location.

Mind you, Varona, as the government contract officer of our company, was always at various government office buildings in DC meeting with government employees. Now she was going to be living and working in New Orleans. The plan was that her workweek would be reduced to twenty-five hours per week with no benefits. She would work in her home office in New Orleans for three weeks and work in the DC office for one week. This was all at the company's expense. After all, the company needed her. One month later, Varona moved to New Orleans. Two weeks after she moved, she convinced the president that she was working as many, if not more, hours than she was in DC, and thus neither her pay nor benefits were reduced. This was a joke to those who worked closely with her. In addition to full salary and benefits, she could attend to personal matters on the East Coast on the company's dime, be reimbursed for her home office expenses, and earn a salary based on one geographic location while living in another, less expensive location. Along with all the fringe benefits, Varona had access to as much, if not more, company information than ever. It was not enough for her to be in the know; she wanted you to know she was in the know—a real one-upmanship queen.

THE SPONSOR

So, what do you think was going on in New Orleans? One speculation was that Varona was living two separate lives. One as an employee of a DC nonprofit organization telecommuting from New Orleans and the other a woman of wealth whose husband was in the construction business. There were stories Varona supposedly told people about how she wore long blonde wigs, wide brim hats, and very fancy dresses when she was in New Orleans. One person stated that she made it her business to hang around places where the rich and famous frequented. Several people in the office thought Varona was extremely pretentious, a real fake, and a passer, if you will. If she was in fact passing as a rich person, she was doing it with the company as her sponsor. The additional information to which she was given access was just what she needed to help her determine how and when she would roll the dice. She had already told a couple of the employees that she needed a big bonus to help clear up her shopping debt, and she seemed willing to do almost anything to get what she wanted. Her "MO" was sucking up to all of the board members, and she was very good at it! Whatever she did, it worked well for her because that year, she got a *huge* bonus. This was a dream situation for her.

After working from New Orleans for several months, many of Varona's tasks were being left undone, or were being pushed off onto other employees. This made the staff in her department furious. She was constantly making requests for things she could easily access if she was physically in the DC office. Thus a few of the administrative employees complained about how their lives were made miserable because Varona was working from New Orleans. Those complaints, however, fell on deaf ears and nothing was ever done about them. Several of the employees in her department started looking for other employment, and a couple of them left the company very quickly and without giving much notice, but this didn't seem to faze Varona at all. In the words of one of my sisters, "She was the worst!"

Although Varona started this new arrangement on cloud nine, the longer she was in it, the more stressed out she seemed. She knew, just like

B. PHOENIX

many other folks, that her telecommuting from New Orleans was a very poor business decision and that the plug would have to be pulled. She also knew her long-distance contributions were not proving beneficial once the new contract was done. Even though the president's feeling was that she could continue her arrangement forever, I felt sure someone with enough good sense had to pull the plug. Well, one year later, the deal was done, the president was leaving the company, and a new president stepped in and immediately put an end to Varona's sweet deal. For Varona, this was like the stock market crash of 1929, but for many of us, it was poetic justice!

I don't mean to sound too hard on Varona, because she only did what she was allowed to do. I believe she was tired of competing in the workplace (because she competed at a level that was more akin to a very physical athletic sport, which we all know wears the body down fast), but she wanted to continue living a high life with little to no work and more fun. Varona just needed a sponsor to support her shopping and gambling, and this company was the perfect cash cow.

CHAPTER 17

The Controller

WEST POWERS HAD been with the firm for over ten years as the director of quality assurance. He could be such a charming and sweet person. However, he could also torment you like no other. He was very handsome, short, and his hair was prematurely gray. West was promoted to the position of chief operations officer (COO). He was king of the hill. The firm was also in need of a director of operations. After being promoted, West requested that the board of directors allow him to promote one of the young engineers to the director of operations position. This was a major request because the engineer would jump two levels in a very short amount of time and ahead of others who had more tenure. Well, some of the members of the board could not fathom this and flat out rejected the idea. Shortly after, the board decided West was to immediately begin recruiting for a new director. But as Cicely used to say, "There is more than one way to skin a cat." With pressure mounting from the board to hire a director, West decided he would promote Susie Whyten, the young engineer, to the position of operations manager. He was sure this would give him a reprieve from the pressures of the board.

Susie came to the firm as a summer intern in the Quality Assurance Department. She and her brother were interns under West's supervision when he was the director of quality assurance. Susie was offered a regular position, and her brother, who was returning to college that fall, left the firm at the end of the summer. Susie was average height with light brown skin and dark brown shoulder-length hair, and she was extremely competitive. She graduated from one of the top universities in England. She was very smart, but West thought she was a genius. Many of the administrative staff believed Susie was hopelessly in love with West. She was confident in him and everything he did, or said. After many tests of loyalty, Susie proved repeatedly that her loyalty was to West only. He was completely mesmerized by her and could see no wrong in her.

One of Susie's biggest problems was her mouth. She talked way too much. She was compelled to share any information she knew with most people to whom she spoke. At a firm outing, several employees overheard Susie discussing a highly confidential matter about one of the senior engineers that had left the firm. It was reported that Susie was talking in her normal loud voice, and everyone around could hear her. About one week later, the senior engineer contacted the chairman of the board to inform him of what he heard Susie had said. Susie supposedly revealed the exact dollar amount of a settlement the firm offered this engineer. The chairman was livid. He immediately contacted West and blasted him for this. However, West convinced the chairman that Susie was extremely valuable to the firm and that she was critical to quality management in the firm.

Although this was a terminable offense, West convinced the chairman that he would take disciplinary action, document the incident in Susie's file, and ensure that it never happened again. Well, the discipline was a slap on the wrist. It was more like a tap on the wrist, and they went back to work. Insofar as documenting the incident, maybe he did, but I never saw anything in writing about it. However, this disciplinary action worked well because a few months after Susie's major breach of confidentiality, West gave her a pretty substantial salary increase, which I was against. I love Susie as a person, and her technical skills were very sharp, but I felt she had, on too many occasions, behaved inappropriately. And as it turned out, even after her promotion and salary increases, rumors pervaded the office on a regular basis that led back to her. West handled every issue with Susie the same way—basically he did little about it.

Several months after he promoted Susie, the board again began putting pressure on West to fill the director of operations position. Thus, he started the recruiting process. However, he again said he wanted to give the position to Susie, but he knew the board would not go for it. When he told me this, I could not believe it. At that point, I was convinced he was either totally insane, having an affair with Susie (which had been rumored in the office for a while), or he believed promoting her to director of operations would give him even more control. My response to this was, "Have you lost your mind?" He had just promoted Susie from a junior engineer to the manager of operations, and he knew she had issues that would make her a horrible director. And besides, she had already made it very difficult for two of her previous supervisors to manage her. These individuals found it impossible to manage her with West, at every moment, inappropriately defending her. After the board's insistence on hiring a director, finally, there was no more talk about promoting Susie, and West continued the job search.

Several weeks into the recruiting process, West came into my office to discuss a person he wanted to consider for the director position. Her name was Jenny Vogue. West had worked with Jenny at a Chicago firm and, just a few months earlier, had recommended her to a colleague of his. He said she was extremely bright and had graduated top of her class from one of the best universities in the nation, and he thought she would be good for our director of operations position. A few days later, West contacted Jenny and asked her to meet him for dinner to discuss the position. She agreed. They met and, per West, talked for more than three hours. Afterward, he scheduled a meeting for the chairman and me to meet her.

The day I met Jenny, she walked into my office with a very positive attitude. She was extremely polished, well dressed, and conducted herself with the utmost professionalism. She seemed to be a happy person and was very pleasant. Since West did the screening for technical skills, my meeting with Jenny was simply a gauge to see if I thought she would be a fit for our team. She was a classy woman, and I was sure she would fit in with our group very nicely. Each time I tested her human relations skills, she passed with flying colors. She had also been in supervisory roles for many years. By the end of our discussion, I was confident Jenny understood the operations and was up for the task. Our conversation lasted a little over an hour. The chairman also met Jenny and gave West the green light to hire her. West made her the offer, and she accepted.

Shortly after Jenny began working with us, she came to me with complaints about Susie. She thought Susie had a "personality defect." Several months later, Jenny began telling me stories about how Susie totally disregarded her as her supervisor. Susie, in an indirect manner, made it very clear she had no intention of reporting to Jenny. If Susie was planning a vacation, she would coordinate her absence with West. If she needed to be off work unexpectedly, she would call West, not Jenny. She never recognized Jenny as her supervisor, and West allowed her to get away with this behavior. If Jenny was not bucking Susie's system, Susie got along fine with her. Jenny, however, was becoming more and more frustrated. She would bring her concerns to me for advice. I counseled her and suggested that she first speak to Susie about these problems. I told her if they continued, she would have to speak to West.

Finally, Jenny spoke to Susie, to no avail. When she confronted Susie about her problems, Susie would agree to do whatever Jenny asked of her, but as soon as she walked out of Jenny's office, it would be business as usual. Susie continued ignoring Jenny as her supervisor, and her behavior became worse. With Jenny, she was constantly rude and quite honestly downright insubordinate. Jenny was not comfortable speaking to West about it because she felt he would side with Susie. So, she decided to continue speaking to Susie, and if she did not improve her behavior, Jenny would document it in her performance evaluation. Although Jenny struggled with Susie's behavior, she kept moving forward and tried to stay focused on her work.

By the year's end, Susie's behavior was no better, and Jenny began preparing her evaluation. Prior to completing the evaluation, West told her he wanted to review it before she met with Susie. In a nutshell, the evaluation stated that Susie had good technical skills, but she had horrible people skills. When Jenny took Susie's evaluation to West, he told her he would review it and give her his feedback. Near the end of the evaluation process, Jenny sent West a reminder that she had not heard back from him. Meanwhile, Susie continued to be as rude and insubordinate as ever. West told Jenny he wanted to add his comments to the evaluation and wanted the two of them to meet with Susie to discuss it. Jenny found this to be very odd, especially since West had not made this request for any of her other direct reports. Nonetheless, no matter how odd she thought it to be, she did not question him.

Jenny believed Susie and West were involved intimately, and she became afraid to go against West on anything involving Susie. After reminding him for the third time they needed to do Susie's evaluation, Jenny decided she was going to leave it alone. The evaluation process came and went, and Jenny never heard any more from West about Susie's evaluation. And, yes, Susie continued the inappropriate behavior. Later, Jenny learned that West had spoken to Susie about some, if not all, of her comments on the evaluation. Susie, in a very passive aggressive manner, made sure Jenny knew West had shared this information with her. She also became more impossible to deal with, and West began to treat Jenny differently—just a little cool at first and then very cold. At this point, things were getting out of control.

West and Susie attended a weeklong out-of-state conference that Jenny and Susie should have attended. The conference was designed for high-level operations folks, but Jenny, although she was the director of the Operations Department, was not allowed to go. Most of the senior staff, among themselves, questioned why West was doing this. I knew he was angry with Jenny because of her comments about Susie, but I was in disbelief that he would make his feelings so obvious. When he and Susie returned from the conference, Susie made it a point to tell Jenny all about the partying and drinking that she and West did while they were at the conference. She also began snooping around Jenny's office, eavesdropping on her conversations, and, per certain staff, plotting to turn the department employees against her. Things the employees should have gone to Jenny with, Susie would tell them to bring to her. It was all very petty and was spiraling downward fast.

Finally, Jenny came to me totally frustrated and ready to go off on West. I encouraged her to sit down and calmly list her concerns on paper. I then set up a meeting with her, West, and me. The meeting was wilder than I could have imagined. Jenny did not hold back on anything. She told West that she believed he and Susie were having an affair, that he allowed Susie to disrespect her and her position, and that he had condoned Susie's inappropriate behavior since she began working there. She brought up the out-of-town conference that he did not allow her to attend and reminded him that he recruited her to come to the firm, and she was, at that point, of the mind that he was using her as a figurehead because he rarely involved her in any of the high-level operations issues.

Well, West went crazy! He began yelling and screaming at Jenny, telling her that he needed Susie and how she would be one of the last employees there. He told her that if he had to choose between her and Susie, he would pick Susie repeatedly. West was yelling so loudly, out of control, that I had to break in and ask him to please speak more quietly. He began to calm himself and apologized for raising his voice. Jenny spoke up and said, "West, listen, I am not asking you to fire Susie. I just need you to support me as her supervisor." He said he would speak to Susie, but he needed both her and Susie to help him get through two major projects. He said the firm could not afford to do anything that might cause Susie to quit because they were dealing with a lot of complex issues, and he needed everyone to remain in place. Jenny said she understood and would try again to work with Susie.

After our meeting, Susie seemed to do everything she could possibly do to make Jenny's life more miserable, and West did nothing about it. At one point, things got so bad that I went back to West to complain about Susie's behavior. He told me Susie was very frustrated having Jenny as her supervisor because she was performing at a much higher level than Jenny. He said Susie knew more about operations than Jenny and had proven it to him. He told me Susie had generated a report in which she purposely included errors to see if Jenny would catch them. Supposedly, Jenny did not catch the errors. After telling me this, West looked at me and reminded me that he had told me Jenny was not that bright.

Well, I thought my head was going to spin off my shoulders. I looked at him and said, in a very angry voice, "You have got to be kidding me. You told me this woman had one of the brightest minds in the area. You bragged about her education and her accomplishments before coming to the firm, and now you're telling me she is not that bright. What is wrong with you? You need to be hauling Susie in here and raking her over the coals. She can't set her supervisor up to fail. That's wrong. And you actually condone this behavior?"

Although my comments seemed to make him uncomfortable, West looked me square in the eye and said, "I would have done the same thing." I could not believe what I was hearing. Then I was sure, the stench that was in the air truly was a conspiracy. West and Susie wanted Jenny out, and they seemed to be working hard to get her out.

THE LAST STRAW

That following summer, the company rehired Susie's brother as part of a summer internship program for future engineers. The entire summer was a real challenge for a lot of folks in the office. Many people found themselves having to choose between following the rules and honoring Susie's special requests for her brother. Susie was flying high, and it was very clear that we were in for a bad nepotistic ride. She, with West's support, was requesting special exceptions for her brother at every moment. One of the exceptions was that her brother be given after-hour access to the operations administrative suite. The confidential nature of the information in this suite required that access after regular working hours be limited to only those who worked in that area. Even the other directors were restricted from accessing the suite after hours. Susie wanted her brother to have after-hours access because they carpooled together, and she did not want to walk twenty-five feet each night to open the door for him. Her request was honored because West gave her whatever she wanted whether it was right or wrong. The fact that West favored Susie caused many of the staff members to do whatever Susie told them to do.

By midsummer, Jenny was at the boiling point in frustration with Susie's behavior. She reached out to West several more times looking for guidance on how to deal with Susie, but instead of giving her guidance, he ridiculed her. He continued defending Susie. The clincher for Jenny came during a program that was put together for the summer interns. The interns were divided into small groups. Each group was to create a video about their impression of the company. All the directors and managers were invited to preview these videos, which were ultimately going to be shown to the entire company.

Well, guess who helped plan the video for Susie's brother's group? If you said Susie, you're right. Not only did she assist with the production of this video, it was very clear she wrote much of the script. I can't remember the exact words, but there were lines in the script such as, Susie the operator is in total control of this firm; Susie is the main operator because West Powers gave her the control, and no one can come between Susie and West; and I know everything about the firm because my sister the operator is in control. This video, with Susie's brother as the star, went on and on mostly stating that Susie was calling the shots at the company's operations level. I must tell you, most of the directors and managers sat with their mouths wide open. None of us could believe what we were hearing.

At the end of the video, one of the directors stated that we should destroy it so no one else would ever see it. West was not present for the viewing, but I went to him and told him about it. I also told him he needed to speak to Susie and put her in her place. Most of the directors came to my office afterward.

B. PHOENIX

They all felt the video was nothing but a message for everyone, especially Jenny. I remember looking over at Jenny during the video, and she looked as if all the blood had drained from her face. West had allowed Susie to get away with murder, and whether it was true or not, many of the staff felt sure she was "in control."

About one month later, Jenny left the office on a Friday never to return. The next week, I received a call from her husband. He informed me that Jenny was so upset about what she said had gone on in the firm that she was literally unable to return to work under the conditions in which she had been working. He told me she was extremely upset the entire weekend. He said Jenny had shared with him a one-inch-thick stack of notes she had taken about her and others' experiences with West and Susie. He knew just about everything that had gone on, and much of what he was saying, I knew to be true. Jenny must have taken very copious notes because in speaking to her husband, it was as if he had observed this behavior firsthand himself.

I reported this information to the chairman of the firm. He asked me what I thought about it, and I gave him my true observations. I told him that there had been a lot of inappropriate behavior going on in the Operations Department; I believed Susie was the root of much of it; I had gone to West on several occasions about Susie's behavior to no avail; some of the other staff truly believed Susie had some serious problems; there were rumors of West and Susie having an affair, and that I had asked West about the rumors; I let West know that if he had some type of relations with Susie and was afraid of what she might do or say, I would help him as best as I could; and that West gave me no response and sat looking at me and remained silent. The chairman looked at me with a very puzzling expression on his face. He was lost for words.

The next day, West called me into his office and said, "I just want you to know I have not had an affair with Susie." I thought I was in the twilight zone again. I didn't think West had an affair with Susie, but giving me his answer twenty-four hours later just didn't touch my believable senses. I don't think the chairman's believable senses were touched either. He told me to contact the chairman of the Risk Management Committee, give him the information about Jenny and Susie, and notify West of Jenny's claims. I immediately called the chairman of the Risk Management Committee and told him everything that was going on with Jenny's claims, and he was obviously very concerned. He instructed me to contact the company's outside labor attorney and to meet with West.

I reported the matter to the labor attorney and met with West as instructed. My meeting with West was not easy. I told him everything Jenny's husband told me, everything I told the chairman, and that we had reported this issue to the Risk Management Committee and the outside labor attorneys. West became very agitated and began accusing Jenny of making up a reason to leave because she couldn't handle the job. I told him I believed Jenny had a legitimate complaint. She had been subjected to Susie's insubordination for over a year. I also told him he did not help the situation, because he could have controlled Susie, and he chose not to deal with her appropriately. At the end of our meeting, West was visibly numb.

Days later, Susie and a few of her buddies began gossiping about Jenny and what they thought, or had been told, was going on with her. No one should have known anything about Jenny except West, the firm's chairman, the chairman of the Risk Management Committee, the labor attorney and me. I e-mailed West and told him he needed to get a grip on the folks in the Operations Department. Susie had called his secretary on speaker phone with one of the other operations people, discussing Jenny's absence and attempting to make plans as if Jenny would not be returning. It was obvious Susie knew more than she should have known. West needed to put a stop to all the gossiping. And later that day, he informed me that he told Susie and the other people who were gossiping with her to "sit down and shut up."

The next week, West sent me an e-mail thanking me for being a friend and apologizing for getting agitated. He said, "I feel really badly about what happened to Jenny and my role in it." He also said that it was all he thought about for days and that he was upset and very irritated about everything that happened with Jenny. He knew he had wronged this woman and condoned inappropriate behavior by Susie. In addition, West had been in the same hot seat on a couple of other occasions about his inappropriate behavior, and the firm had to pay. He was worried this may be the end of the road for him. After all, how many claims would the firm receive before they seriously looked at West as the problem? One of the things I used to tell managers I trained was that no matter how good an employee is, if you keep getting the same type of complaints about the employee from different people, you must look at the common denominator.

B. PHOENIX

West and Susie began reassigning responsibilities that were previously Jenny's to others in the department. Up until that point, they had been saying Jenny made no contribution to the firm. However, suddenly, she played such an important role that steps were immediately taken to monitor her voice mail and e-mail for "business purposes." Well, the reassignments and monitoring continued, and Jenny never returned to the firm. She was paid, West was tapped on the wrists and told to get back to work, and nothing happened to Susie. Along with time, we all moved on. Jenny and her husband opened a very upscale furniture store in one of the beach resort areas in Florida and were very happy.

WHAT GOES AROUND COMES AROUND

West, in one of his staff meetings and in an extremely nasty tone, told each of his direct reports that he could care less if they left the firm. Coincidentally, the plant director received an offer and resigned days after West's rage. He gave the firm two weeks' notice and moved on. To my knowledge, none of the board members questioned why this high-level executive was leaving and why he was not giving the company more notice. Most of us knew the plant director was leaving because of West. West was a problem with which the firm refused to deal. Now, in addition to the plant director's position being vacant, no efforts were being made to fill the director of operations position (Jenny's old position). At this point, and for all intents and purposes, West was running everything—just what he wanted but what everyone knew was the wrong thing for the firm.

About six months later, West informed me he was considering giving Susie the director of operations position. He asked me if I had noticed a change in her behavior. I told him that although I had seen a small amount of improvement in her behavior, it was not nearly enough to justify promoting her to the director position. Susie had continued to leak confidential information, and West continued defending her. One of the other directors also supported promoting Susie, suggesting that with some professional coaching (which cost the firm a cool $10,000), Susie would be ready for the promotion. I did not agree with West's decision, but, at this point, I disagreed with a lot he was doing. Some of the other directors felt the same as me but never expressed their true opinion to West about Susie.

Earlier that year, after trying unsuccessfully for a couple years, Susie became pregnant. Many people in our office wondered if she was pregnant with West's baby. She was due in the fall of that year. However, by the end of summer, the baby was born. Everyone wondered why the baby came so early. One of the rumors in the office was that West was the father of Susie's baby, and she lied about the due date to confuse her husband. Wow! I was there, and I am still finding this stuff hard to believe. Another rumor in our office was that Susie convinced her doctor to induce labor early, so she would be able to return to work before the Operations Department got busy with new projects. During this time, many celebrity wives were inducing labor early to fit their personal and professional schedules. It was speculated that West participated in this decision.

Susie delivered twins, two beautiful baby girls, without incident. She and her daughters left the hospital with a clean bill of health. Several weeks later, Susie attempted suicide. She took an overdose of pills and was admitted into a psychiatric hospital. She was in bad shape for several months. Her husband reported that she was incapable of caring for herself or their newborn daughters. West tried to keep the suicide attempt quiet, but several people from the office called Susie's home, and her mother told them Susie had attempted suicide.

At the office Christmas party that year, one of the directors who was always in support of West's decision to promote Susie came up to me and talked about how she was not at all surprised at the suicide attempt. At one point in the conversation, she said, "We called that one; didn't we? We knew she was unstable." I could not believe what I was hearing. This woman was always in support of each of Susie's promotions, and although others in the office often said Susie was unstable, I never once heard this director mention that she thought Susie was unstable. Per West, this director felt Susie was young but very capable and just needed someone to give her a chance.

It is ironic that Susie would attempt suicide almost one year to the day that Jenny left the firm. One could say Susie tried to drive Jenny crazy but was unsuccessful. One could also say, "What goes around comes around." I'm not saying that Susie's attempted suicide was her payback for the way she treated Jenny, but it is possible. Grandpa Harmon used to always say, "Every dog has its day." And you know Grandpa Harmon's payback, for coning so many people, was brutal.

B. PHOENIX

CHAPTER 18

Blackballed

ONE OF MY supervisors, Simon Ballton, was so cocky that he tried to control everything. One summer, his cockiness reached an unprecedented high. His behavior became so inappropriate that most of his direct reports began seeking other employment. I signed up with an executive search firm in DC and met with one of its agents about my job search. After an initial screening interview, the agent scheduled a meeting for me with an international law firm that was looking for a director of HR. The agent told me they had worked with this firm for over fifteen years, and they knew exactly what the firm liked and needed. They told me I would be a perfect match for the firm. After the interview, the agent informed me that everything went extremely well. They said the people with whom I met gave me rave reviews, and the firm was going to be making me an offer that week.

A couple days later, I was at a meeting with a group of administrators from other DC law firms. A very close friend of Simon's attended this meeting also. Throughout the entire meeting, I found this person's eyes on me. We were not sitting close to each other, but I could tell he had something to say to me. After the meeting ended, he quickly made his way through the crowd to speak to me. He prefaced what he said with, "I want you to know I have not told Simon about this and will not mention it to him, but do you know Gerald Lookings?"

I said, "I don't know a Gerald Lookings."

He then asked, in a tone of total disbelief, "You don't know Gerald Lookings?"

B. PHOENIX

I said, "No." At that point, my tone quickly changed from being calm to being irritated. Then I asked, "Is this someone I should know?" I was totally confused and had no idea about what this man was talking.

He proceeded to belt out profanities, saying he knew the guy was lying. Again, I asked, in total puzzlement, "What are you talking about?" He explained that Gerald Lookings was a headhunter who placed him at his firm, and he also placed Simon at his old firm. He said the guy called him the day before and told him he was very close to placing me at another law firm. Simon's friend said he told the agent there was no way he could recruit me from my firm. He said he knew that Simon could not live without me and that if he knew this guy was trying to recruit me, he would never use their agency again. At that point, I told him I did not know what he was talking about. Again, he said, "I knew he was a lying SOB. He is a real bastard." He shook his head in total disgust, and we both left.

In the taxicab ride back to my office, I continued wondering about what this friend of Simon's could have been talking. Suddenly, exhaustion took over my body. This conversation, in addition to the heat of a DC summer in a taxicab with no AC, was wiping me out. I was drained. Then it hit me, and I thought, *"Oh my God. I'll bet Gerald Lookings is somehow affiliated with the agency I'm using."* When I reached my office, I dropped my bag and rushed over to the kitchen to get a cold glass of water, quickly returning to call my agent. I asked if the agency was affiliated with someone named Gerald Lookings. The person I was speaking to hesitated before answering my question and then said no. However, she never asked any other questions about Gerald Lookings. I told her about my earlier conversation with Simon's friend, and she again denied having any affiliation with Gerald Lookings. So, I dropped it and assumed, for as crazy as it seemed, that maybe it was all a fluke.

One week after, I had not heard anything from my agent or the law firm that was to be making me an offer. When I called my agent, I was unable to reach her, so I left a message. Two days later, I still had not heard from her, but I received a letter from the law firm basically saying thanks but no thanks. I knew right then that someone had blocked the job offer. I had been blackballed. I could not believe it. As I later learned, the agency I was using was, in fact, affiliated with Gerald Lookings's company, and although I can never prove it, I will always believe Gerald Lookings canceled me as a candidate for fear of losing two big accounts.

THE OVERSIGHT

During one of the coldest winters on record, all hell was breaking loose in the DC office. Till Foxx, the COO, missed a major deadline in the firm's lease, which was going to result in a $1.2 million loss for the firm. The managing partner was livid. He raked Till over the coals, but Till blamed the oversight on the facilities manager. Fortunately for him, the landlord took pity on the firm and compromised on the loss. After it was all said and done, Till convinced the managing partner that the facilities manager was at fault, and he needed to hire someone to supervise her more directly. Even though Till was the one who worked on the lease with certain members of the board of directors, he was the one the board assigned as the keeper of the lease, and he was the one who housed the lease in his files; he refused to take the blame for this oversight. Till was so outside of his mind, he seemed to be convinced that he was not at fault. When he told me his side of the story, it made no sense to me. So, I went to the facilities manager and asked her what happened. She told me she had no idea she was responsible for the firm's office space leases. As she and I discussed the matter, it became clear to me what happened.

At one point, Till moved to a new office. Due to the lack of file space in his new office, he asked the facilities manager to keep the lease files in her space. Well, that proves it. Till was right. How dare the facilities manager overlook a huge clause in a six-year-old lease in one of many files which she was asked to keep a few months earlier due to a space issue. This was so ridiculous. As you can imagine, the facilities manager lost all respect for Till. As time moved on, they became like oil and water. Till started accusing her of being lazy and incapable of handling the tasks for which he wanted her to become responsible. He made her life pure hell. He pulled problems out of the air. Minor infractions such as a few small marks on one of the conference room walls, coffee cups he felt were too small, and a telephone that was not connected properly in one of the conference rooms all became major problems. Now mind you, the telephone that was improperly installed was not even the responsibility of the Facilities Department.

After all that had gone on, the facilities manager decided she had to get out as soon as possible. She began interviewing and received a job offer quickly. After submitting her resignation, she had a very candid conversation with a member of the board about Till's inappropriate behavior but nothing really changed. A couple of weeks later, the facilities manager was gone, and Till was happy about her resignation. This was his opportunity to hire someone he felt could handle more of the operations tasks for which he was responsible. Meanwhile, after the facilities manager left, it became more difficult for Till to run all of the general operations of the firm. Although very busy, he immediately began interviewing candidates for the facilities position.

CANDIDATE OF FAVOR

During the interview process, Till brought in a couple of candidates for the position. The first candidate was someone he said would be perfect for our team. He asked several senior staff people, including me, to meet the candidate. Well, let me tell you. When I walked into the conference room, I could not believe my eyes. There sat a young white male approximately thirty years old. He had a completely bald head, with a gold hoop earring in his left ear about the size of a quarter. He was wearing a very shiny, silky, button-down shirt, of which he left the top three buttons open. Of course, you could see his chest, and it was hairier than many people's heads. I could barely focus on the interview because this guy's chest hairs were popping out of his shirt looking like taco meat. He also wore other gaudy jewelry, which was shining like new money.

In addition to his inappropriate attire, he admitted (and his resume verified) that he knew nothing about most of what the position required. When asked about his lack of experience in several specific areas, his response, very confidently stated, was, "I'm sure I can learn." I was in total shock and could not believe what I was seeing or hearing. This guy made numerous bad statements, and even his posture was not what you'd expect from someone interviewing for a job. At one point, he began slouching down in his chair with one arm over the back. I don't think he wanted a job. He behaved like a spoiled little rich kid who turned into an adult and became a spoiled adult whose daddy is rich. It baffled me how anyone could present this person as a serious candidate.

After the interview, I told Till I did not see this guy fitting in with us, but I was not as candid as I normally would have been. The way he treated the facilities manager and the fact that he could get away with it, and everything else he could get away with, was starting to take something out of me. That same day, Till e-mailed the other administrator and the member of the board that interviewed this guy, asking them to let him know how they felt about the candidate. For some reason, Till wanted to move very quickly on this hire. Well, the other administrator gave him a written response (copying the board member) for which he was unprepared. The response was painfully honest and extremely candid.

Basically, the facts as the administrator stated were: (1) the candidate was not polished at all, (2) he started his interview by stating he had spent forty days prior to the interview drunk at his father's beach house, (3) he swore repeatedly during the interview, (4) he admitted he was virtually computer illiterate, (5) he had very limited senior-level facilities experience, and (6) he was no match for our firm. Till was beyond livid. He cursed the administrator for days over this. However, it was the right thing and a good thing the other administrator did. Thank God, we didn't let that horse out of the barn! I later learned that the candidate was the son of an executive director of another law firm.

The second candidate was a woman who responded to our ad in a national legal association's job bank. As it turned out, the candidate was a woman with whom I worked at another law firm. Diora Day was the perfect candidate for the position. She had worked with a couple of major DC law firms and was an excellent facilities manager. Diora was well versed and full of experience in all aspects of facilities management, leasing, budgeting, and major office moves. Her experience as well as her personality, I thought, would have fit in with us very nicely. Diora came in and met with Till and several other senior staff people.

After the interview, I saw Till and asked him what he thought of Diora. He looked at me with this crazy grin on his face and said nothing. I asked again, and he said, "You are kidding me, right?"

I replied, "No. Did you like her or not?" At that point, he looked me square in the eye and said, "She reminded me of my mother, and I don't mean age."

I then said in a very disgusted voice, "What are you talking about?"

Till said, "If I wanted someone to bake cookies, then I would hire her." With that said, I just walked away. He claimed he didn't mean age, so what was the problem? One of the other administrators told me Till thought Diora was "poor white trash." All I could do was shake my head and walk away.

After Diora met with Till, she left the firm and called me immediately upon reaching her destination. I asked her how the interview went, and she began to pour out one of the most unbelievable stories I had ever heard about an interview. She said, "Till never sat down during the entire interview." Then she corrected herself and said, "It actually was not an interview at all." She said he continuously looked out the window, he never asked her one question, and he did most of the talking. Supposedly, he told her that all the partners had full trust in him, that he and the managing partner were like brothers, that the board had given him carte blanche to run the firm as he saw fit, and that the other partners did whatever he told them to do. She said he told her the firm paid its employees extremely well, and he used himself as an example. And what a good example.

At the time, Till was earning more money than some of the partners in the firm. Considering how he got his salary, what he was doing to keep it, his severely weak people skills, the fact that he constantly placed the firm at risk of a lawsuit, and his lack of prior experience in this type of position, his salary would have been considered obscene by most standards. I'm sure if certain partners had known Till's salary, all hell would have broken loose. It was all about Till's skill of disingenuousness. He really would have continued working in that position for a lot less money, but the chairman was able to get the board to buy in on taking Till's salary from the high $200,000s to more than one half million dollars in one jump. They must have thought he was Superman. This was a perfect example of my theory that not only does he who has the gold rule, but he who is close to the one who has the gold rules also.

The way in which Till described to the applicant how well the firm paid its employees is unbelievable. Had I not known the information to be correct, I would have thought Diora Day made up the entire story. Till did not directly divulge his salary, but Diora's account of his example went something like this: "I earn so much money that my wife, who had worked in a Fortune 500 company, earning a very large salary herself, could quit her job and become a stay-at-home mom for our five children. I could purchase my wife's dream house (a very large house in Annapolis, Maryland), and a boat. I am leasing an apartment here in DC, so that I don't have to make the commute to Annapolis on nights when I work late. I'm also able to work from home on Fridays. As I told you, the firm takes care of its employees. Well, thank you for coming in." Diora could not believe her ears. She was in shock. She told me she had never been on a more bizarre interview in her entire life. Even though she walked away knowing she was not going to get the job, she was very interested in learning more about Till and why he treated her so unprofessionally.

After the interview was over, Diora shared her experience with a friend who happened to know someone who had worked with Till in the past. Her friend arranged a phone call with her and this person. Diora got an earful. She said the guy told her that he was not at all surprised Till behaved the way he did. She told me he said that Till would never hire her for that position because he would consider her too old and not attractive enough. He also told her Till has issues with women—particularly women who are older and who he feels are unattractive. Well, Diora knew Till had some issues, but she didn't know the seriousness of them. She had her suspicions, but hearing it from another source made it all clear. She knew she would never hear from our firm again. And even though she was highly qualified, and I know she would have made a real contribution to the firm, Diora did not get the job, and like she said, she never heard from our firm again.

Several months later, Till decided he was going to promote the person who had been the facilities assistant to the facilities manager. This was a very strange move because he had always said he did not like the facilities assistant. In the past, he would never approve promoting her even though she was an effective, hard worker. Well, as we later learned, the firm was hot and heavy into discussions with another law firm about a possible merger, and Till did not want to spend any more money than necessary. He also knew it would be very difficult and impractical to hire a senior-level person when the firm was so deep in merger discussions.

So, promoting the facilities assistant made sense, and he could give her a pacifier. He could not afford to have her leave also. He gave her the manager title and a small salary increase (relatively speaking), with which she was pleased. She also thought this would put her in line to be promoted to the senior-level position if she did a good job. Till worked this individual like a slave until after the merger. He only needed her to hang around for another six months. She stayed with the firm and did a great job with minimal

B. PHOENIX

support. At the end of the six-month period, Till hired another person for the top facilities position. The facilities manager was very hurt, but she, as always, continued to provide a high level of support to the firm until she eventually left.

CHAPTER 19

The Midyear Checkup

MY SUPERVISOR, SAL Midwin, requested to take me to lunch for a "midyear checkup." I had never heard him speak of a "midyear checkup" before, and to my knowledge he had never done one in our office. I knew this midyear checkup was a crock, but I played along, much like the crock I participated in that Harmon was feeding the guy having a fake photo taken. Sal and I went to one of the most popular restaurants in DC. There was a spectacular view through thirty-to-forty-foot-tall windows that enclosed one side of the restaurant. It was a relaxing yet elegant atmosphere. As we sat talking about nothing, I noticed he suddenly had this crazy look on his face. I had seen this look before, and it normally meant Sal was about to say something that was total nonsense, but he needed to work himself up to it. So, I broke the ice for him and asked, "What is this palaver all about?"

He laughed. Then he said, "I called one of the other managers about his midyear checkup, and he asked me if he was in trouble."

Sal never answered my question because he knew this "midyear checkup" was nothing but a farce. I let it ride because I knew he was trying to build himself up to be able to say what he wanted to say to me. I also felt very strongly that none of the other administrators were going to have a "midyear checkup." I was right. Later, when asked, three of the other administrators said nothing was ever mentioned to them. We ordered lunch and finished the meal before Sal could bring himself to say anything to me about this "checkup." I guess he wanted to spring the news on me after I had a full stomach. Finally, he proceeded to tell me that a few of my peers had complained to him about my "attitude." He said these individuals asked him, "What is her problem?" These complaints could only have come from a couple of places. If anyone complained, it had to have been Liz or Carlayin.

Liz oversaw client services and was one of Sal's favorite employees. She was smart, attractive, and willing to do anything for Sal. Carlayin was a real bully to some and a suck-up to others. Her role was assisting certain high-level partners with administrative practice group matters. Liz and Carlayin had become very close and were Sal's closest allies. Carlayin got very close to Liz because she was Sal's baby and could be very useful to her. Also, anything that belonged to Sal automatically received a butt kissing from Carlayin. Sal was kissing Carlayin's butt because he felt she was extremely close to the powers that be, and Liz was kissing Sal's butt on GP. Also, Liz was a messenger. Anything Carlayin wanted Sal to know but did not want to tell him herself, she would tell Liz. Liz told Sal everything, and most people knew it. There was a lot of nonsense going on in the office at this point. So, the way I figured, the so-called complaints had to come from either of these two people, or no one.

Sal never made a move without first running it by a few folks. I believe he discussed my midyear checkup with someone and probably rehearsed what he would say several times. It would not surprise me at all if he ran it by Carlayin and Liz. Finally, he began telling me about his concerns. He said: (1) I was very defensive and seemed "disengaged" from the group; (2) there was a lot of tension in our administrators' meetings because of me; (3) whenever it was my turn to give a report, everyone in the room became very tense; and (4) because the firm was looking at hiring real powerhouses, he needed our group to be brought closer together. He said he felt I was the only one in the group who could bring everyone together, and he wanted me to lead this effort by being the positive force.

I believe Sal's biggest concern was that he needed to look good for the new powerhouses. At this point, I had no more patience for him, and there was nothing I was willing to do to help him with his personal agenda. Near the end of our lunch, Sal began giving me a rundown on each of his direct reports—who he knew to be looking for a new job, who was happy and unhappy, who he felt might leave the company and the fact that he could care less if they did, and one of the folks he felt would continue a relationship with the firm. I knew this was all nervous talk, and I had no response to any of it.

However, Sal's request of me was answered when we returned to the office, and I never spoke a word or moved a muscle to pull his staff together. I told you there was a lot of nonsense going on. Sal picked the one person who was "disengaged" and had a bad "attitude" to rally everyone together. I couldn't believe what I had heard.

The entire "midyear checkup" was utterly ridiculous. My performance reviews from Sal had always been stellar, even the one I received just several months before the "midyear checkup." There was only one concern mentioned during my performance review prior to the "midyear checkup." Although not in writing, Sal said he wanted me to "try to get along with Carlayin." I was confused about his request because I had always been extremely professional in my dealings with Carlayin. I told Sal I didn't understand to what he was referring and he just looked at me with this poop-eating grin on his face. At that point, I realized Sal did not mean I needed to get along with Carlayin; what he meant was that he wanted me to kiss her butt—*I would not ever!*

THE ELEPHANT IN THE ROOM

For many months, in our senior staff meetings, there was a huge amount of tension in the room; you know, the elephant in the room that nobody talks about. Everyone sees it, but no one says a word about it. In all honesty, it was the elephant in the room that was causing a lot of tension among my peers. Most of them would discuss the elephant with me but would not say anything publicly about this huge animal. Thus, our meetings continued twice a week as if nothing was wrong. Discussions were being held about issues that would never come to fruition, but everyone played the game anyway. I mean most of my peers jumped right into discussions with Redlet Stone, the president, as if business was as usual. Business was nothing close to "usual." As I began feeling as if I could not take another day of this farce, I had an epiphany at five thirty one Monday morning in November. I was in my workout room on the treadmill sweating like a pig. Suddenly, it was as if someone walked into the room and began speaking to me. I felt as if I could hear a voice saying, "Today is the day you put all the cards on the table. You are to reveal everything you know. Do not allow another meeting to go by without bringing the tension to a head." This was stirring so deeply in me that I knew I had to say something. And as one of my colleagues stated, "This was going to be a red-letter day"—a day we all would remember forever!

The company, as we knew it, was in financial trouble, and it was obvious to most of the senior staff. I can remember sitting in a conference room eating breakfast looking around at all the beautiful furnishings. As my eyes passed each senior staff member, I remember thinking, "There are some real kook-a-loos in this room." The way they played along with Redlet as if everything was good and dandy was *A-mazing* to me. I just shut down. There was no way I could play that game. In my world, it is crazy to carry on a conversation pretending that something is what it is not. I know the other senior staff members knew better, but for some reason they felt compelled to play along. After every meeting, at least two or three of my peers would come to my office and vent their frustrations with Redlet's decision not to include all of us in on the true state of the company. I became more and more frustrated with the way things were being handled. Redlet was extremely deceptive in the way he dealt with most of the senior staff.

VPs were leaving the company in record numbers. Although some were being asked to leave, many of them were leaving on their own. For those who left on their own, Rosemary, the SVP of operations, would report to the group that the departures were "positive moves for the company." She did not realize that we all thought she was losing her mind. Her justification of some of the VP departures was like trying to justify someone driving down a smooth road leading to a pot of gold that you could see and for no good reason turning off that road onto a rocky, winding road with no gold in sight. The VPs were all speculating about what was going on in the company, but again, no one would ask Redlet about it, or bring it up in our senior staff meetings. It was obvious that Redlet had included Charlotte, the senior VP of finance, and Rosemary on everything that was happening. At almost every meeting during that summer, Redlet, Charlotte, and Rosemary would openly discuss issues the rest of us knew nothing about. It wasn't bad enough that they did this; they did it in code.

Charlotte and Rosemary would say things such as, "If we are still around," suggesting a downfall of the company. Or when someone mentioned having to make a completely customary purchase of some sort, Rosemary would say, "We might not need it. Redlet, do you want me to call Mike and ask if they already have one." At this point, the other SVPs and I are sitting at the table wondering "who the hell is Mike" and "who are *they*?" Then, Charlotte would chime in with information she knew. Charlotte and Rosemary would volley statements back and forth, sometimes for five or more minutes, which officially meant nothing to anyone in the room other than them and Redlet. It was beyond crazy. When this behavior became ridiculously out of control, I would give Redlet a look and, without opening my mouth, say, "You have got to be kidding me. You cannot possibly allow this to continue." At that point, Redlet would say something to Rosemary and Charlotte such as, "All right, all right." The sad part about all of this is that most of the SVPs knew there was trouble in paradise, but we had not received any official notification or information as to the depth of trouble.

The other SVPs were very offended by this behavior. I, however, could care less about the way they behaved. And as Cicely taught me "every dog has its day" and that "what goes around comes around." And the beauty of these lessons is that you don't have to do a thing. Sometimes you witness the day and/or the come-around, and sometimes you don't, but rest assured, it will happen! Redlet, Charlotte, and Rosemary's behavior in these meetings became so bad that some of the other directors would look at me with pleading expressions on their faces. They wanted me to say something that might end these code discussions. You know, let the air out, release the pressure, and let the river flow. Although it was obvious the SVPs wanted someone to end these horrible code discussions, most of them continued to play this ridiculous game. And thus, Redlet thought he, Charlotte, and Rosemary were the only administrative staff that knew anything about the state of the company. It was unbelievable!

As normally scheduled, the senior staff meeting began at 8:00 a.m. And on this Monday morning, the decision had been made for me. This was the day the charade, which had been going on far too long, would have to stop, and I was used to do it. It was also just a couple days before the company's annual board retreat, and rumors were flying like crazy about what the board would be discussing. The telephone rang, and it was Rosemary. She was unexpectedly off that day. I wasn't sure whether she would be calling in to the meeting, or not, but I was glad she did. I wanted everyone to hear firsthand what I had to say. Redlet began the meeting as usual. Normally, he went around the table and gave each person an opportunity to report on what was going on in his or her department. I was never called on first, but on this morning, Redlet called me first.

B. PHOENIX

I was happy to start the meeting because I knew that after my comments, there would be no time to discuss anything else. I went on to explain that I did not have a report, but I had some things I wanted to bring out in the open. My peers perked up. A few of them looked as if they were thinking, *Oh God, please let this be it.* Several of them had already told me I was their only hope for breaking the ice. I continued, saying, "For months, we all have been showing up for these meetings pretending everything is normal. Redlet, we all know something is going on, but no one wanted to ask." Redlet, looking confused, asked me to clarify my statement. I said, "There are lots of rumors floating around the company, some of which I believe have merit, but no one is saying anything to the senior staff. It is obvious that Charlotte and Rosemary are privy to what is going on, but the rest of us are being left in the dark to speculate."

Redlet spoke up in a very irritated, angry voice, yelling, "There is nothing to tell! There is nothing to tell!"

Then, very calmly, I said, "Well, if there is nothing to tell, I would like to share some of the rumors that most of us have been hearing."

Redlet said, "Go ahead. I want to know everything you have heard." I proceeded to share the following rumors, some of which most of us had been hearing:

1. One of the officers on the board resigned from the committee responsible for hiring because he could not bear to look applicants in the face and try to convince them to come to work for us given the horrible state of the company.
2. The chairman of that committee had resigned for the same reason, but Rosemary and another board member begged him to change his mind. This individual supposedly agreed to remain the chairman with the stipulation that he would not have to meet any of the applicants.
3. The company was in merger discussions again.
4. The company was considering going out of business.
5. A letter had been sent to the interns that were scheduled to return the following year, explaining that the company may not be the same when and if they returned.

Redlet's initial reaction to my comments, again, was anger. In a very loud and hysterical voice, he repeated several times, "There is nothing to tell! There is nothing to tell! There is nothing to tell!"

I said, "I know for a fact a letter was sent to the interns, and I don't understand why they, who are not even employees, have been given information about the state of the company when our own senior staff have not been told anything." Redlet, ignoring my comments about the interns, denied the rumors about the hiring committee and repeated that there was nothing to tell. I said "Okay," and sat quietly. Redlet then asked if anyone had heard anything else. I did not respond. He repeated himself again, but this time he said, in a very nasty, angry tone, "If there is anything else, I want to hear it right now!" No one said a word.

Finally, I said, "There is one more thing, but I should discuss this with you in private." Redlet lost it.

Again, he began yelling and screaming, saying, "If we are putting all the cards on the table, I want everything out right now." Everyone knew all the yelling and screaming was because Redlet was embarrassed. He had not handled the situation properly, and it was coming back to bite him. Well, I knew the last thing I had to say was going to put him over the top. However, Redlet was so adamant about hearing everything right then and there that I decided to give him what he wanted, and since "Mr. Nasty" insisted on having all the cards put on the table, I gladly obliged him.

In a very calm voice, I said, "I saw the agenda for the board's retreat, which verifies some of the rumors that you have denied."

And as I expected, Redlet lost it this time. He went completely out of his mind. He was enraged. He began yelling and screaming again, banging his fist on the conference room table and saying, "That is impossible! There is no way you saw that agenda! There are only two people who have copies of that agenda, the chairman and me!"

I responded, still in a very calm manner, saying, "Well, then one of you must have mishandled the agenda."

This made Redlet's head explode. In a very angry voice, he said, "If you saw the agenda, what was on it?"

I knew Redlet was 100 percent sure I was bluffing. Again, I said, "Redlet, perhaps you and I should discuss this in private."

B. PHOENIX

And again, he started banging his fist on the table and yelled out at me, "I want to know what you saw right now, because I know you did not see the agenda for the board retreat!" All the other SVPs were looking very confused but intrigued by the whole exchange. They seemed convinced that I must have seen something other than the agenda. They were still falling for the nonsense. I repeated almost verbatim what was on the agenda, including the fact that the board was going to be discussing possibilities of a merger with another company as well as full dissolution of our company. This discussion had become so action-packed that the other SVPs' heads were moving back and forth looking at Redlet and then me and then Redlet and then me again. It was as if they were watching a very intense tennis match. Redlet began to hyperventilate. Finally, he took several deep breaths and began to simmer down. After about five minutes of him composing himself, he began to speak very calmly. It was like a Dr. Jekyll and Mr. Hyde type transformation.

Although Redlet repeatedly denied there was anything to tell, he was now exposed. Not having much choice, and everyone in the room knew it, he broke down and told us everything. He confirmed the merger discussions as well as the discussions about dissolution. A couple of the SVPs looked shocked. Redlet, in no more than fifteen minutes, had taken them on the worst roller coaster ride of their lives. I spoke up and said, "I would have appreciated hearing officially from the company, rather than from rumors and outside sources."

Redlet's response was, "I probably need to take the blame for not informing you guys." I thought, *You think?* Although he sort of took the blame, most of us knew he had received bad counsel on how to deal with the SVPs. I'm sure you know who was probably counseling him. It was very odd that he did not include all of us on these merger discussions because he had included all of us on information about other merger discussions without any problems.

After Redlet accepted the blame for not including us, he said, "I guess I didn't say anything to you guys because I did not want to have to apologize to Robert." Robert was the new CIO. He had only been with us about six months and was already depressed about the state of the company. After Redlet's comments, Robert looked as if he needed to shake the fuzzy out of his head, and he appeared to be sinking deep into depression right before our eyes. He had been suffering for months, worrying about whether he was going to have a job or not. Looking at Robert's face was so sad to me. He sat in a complete daze. I imagined he was hearing Redlet's voice repeating over and over, "I did not want to have to apologize to Robert." The other SVPs were now looking like they needed to shake the fuzzy out of their heads as well. It was obvious they had no understanding of why Redlet needed to apologize to Robert.

Robert, on numerous occasions, told me he believed Redlet had flat out lied to him during his interview. Redlet hired him under false pretenses. Robert told me he asked Redlet very specific questions about the state of the company during his interview and was told the company was stable and a very secure place to work. This was all unfortunate because Robert was very happy at his old job, but through a cold call from an employment agency, he pursued the position at our company. It was a promotion for him with a substantial salary increase. He was married with three lovely daughters, all under the age of ten, and he was the sole breadwinner for his family. Thus, he said he was very careful about asking the right questions during his interview.

Robert told me he asked Redlet about rumors of merger talks, and he was told the company had decided against a merger. In addition to promising Robert stability in the company, Redlet told him all the principals had committed to stay and make the company work. Redlet convinced Robert to accept the offer. Shortly after starting, he was detecting signs of trouble, but he convinced himself that Redlet could not have blatantly lied to him. Obviously, he did. Redlet's only concern was getting someone in to do the job. He needed someone in that position, and he knew making a hire at that level would send signals that the state of the company was good. Although the CIO's position was a critical function for the company, it was not critical enough to rock someone's world. There were other options.

At the end of our staff meeting, Redlet asked us to keep the information confidential. About forty-five minutes later, he came to my office asking me to tell him how I came to see the agenda for the board retreat. He was drilling me hard for the information. It was like a police interrogation. I told him I would not reveal my source. He then began drilling me on who had shared the information with me about the letters to the interns. He asked if it was a board member's secretary. He asked if it was an administrative person. The only thing I shared with him was that the information about the letter

B. PHOENIX

sent to the interns came from an outside source. He looked as if he did not believe me and again began asking about the agenda for the board retreat. He reiterated that the only people who had the agenda were the chairman of the board and him. Again, I told him, if that were true, one of them had to have mishandled the agenda. When he realized I was not going to reveal my source, he left my office. Well, the truth of the matter is, he lied again. Rosemary also had the agenda, and she was the one who left it in a copy room. The person who found it said Rosemary left it in the copy machine, but they could not find her, so they brought it to me. The next year, the company closed, and we all moved on in separate directions.

CHAPTER 20

Changing Tides

BY FALL OF the year, the law firm was very close to a final merger deal. It was not a merger, but an acquisition. We were being swallowed by a big fish. Price & Little (P&L), a very large New York-based international firm, was taking over my firm. In late October, West met with all the administrators and informed us that P&L was going to keep everyone except one administrator. Insofar as my group was concerned, he informed me that everyone in the HR Department would move on to the new firm. This seemed odd to me because I had six employees in my department, and P&L had four in its DC HR Department. In my mind, there was no need to have eleven HR employees in the combined firm's DC office. Nonetheless, we all moved into gear, working like crazy to make the transition happen smoothly. By the end of November, West announced that Leroy, the manager of legal support, was not going to be kept. P&L offered Leroy a position to manage the legal support teams in DC and New York, which would require him to travel to New York for one week each month. He respectfully declined the offer, which seemed to please West very much. I immediately knew this was a setup and felt other tricks were coming down the pike. West was good for offering people things he knew they would not want, all the while making them think he was looking out for them. I saw that skill all the time in Harmon. West did not want Leroy to stay with the new firm, and I'm sure the terms of the position were designed so that Leroy would not want the job. He had several children, and everyone knew he did not travel because of his children. I believe West was banking on those children to help him.

At one point, Leroy was kissing West's butt at every moment, and West loved it. It was absolutely sickening to see. I remember going to West's office one day, and Leroy was there sucking up to him so hard that I just walked away in disgust. Later that day, West commented that he had not seen me all day. I told him I stopped by his office earlier that day, but Leroy was in there sucking up so hard that I walked away. West laughed and said, "Oh yeah, he was doing a really good job, wasn't he?" He had always supported Leroy in the past, but, suddenly, they were like oil and water. West started treating Leroy as if he was a third-class citizen. He found something wrong with everything he did. Leroy, after having kissed West's butt for years, was now threatening to sue the firm because of how West was treating him. It is amazing how quickly the tide changes. Just as West was pleased that Leroy declined the firm's offer, Leroy seemed equally as pleased to leave, especially with a nice severance package.

West and I began working very closely with P&L trying to resolve all the HR and benefits issues for both firms. At times, it was difficult to work with him and the staff from P&L because he was bitter about the changes that were taking place. He was losing power to folks that were nowhere near as sharp as he was, and he hated it. One morning, West called me into his office for a conference call with some of the staff from P&L. We were hashing out issues regarding the benefits. It was an exhausting conversation that lasted two long hours. After we ended the call, I told West I was surprised that P&L's senior HR person did not seem as experienced as I expected. I also told him that because P&L had made several acquisitions in the past, I expected them to have the process down to a science, but they did not. West agreed.

Then, without skipping a beat, he said, "Well, I guess if that is how you feel about them, you wouldn't be upset if you didn't go?"

I responded, "What do you mean?"

He said, "You wouldn't be upset if you didn't go with them."

Now realizing West was referring to me going to P&L, I said, "I guess it would depend on where I was going."

He said, "Well, what if you could go home for a few months?"

I then asked, "What are you trying to tell me?"

He said, "P&L does not want you to join their firm, and February 28 will be your last day." He was telling me this at the end of January.

Although, I was not surprised, I could not believe the firm allowed West to give me this notice so late in the game. I wonder if he thought I would quit, or not be productive if I knew sooner. Either one of these possibilities is not me. He should have known I am not dumb enough to quit if the firm offered me a severance package, and he should have also known I am not the type to renege on my obligations. I was being given a thirty-day notice when I believe West knew well before that they were not going to keep me. For some reason, he chose to give me less notice than everyone else. Nonetheless, I was ahead of that curve. For as convincing as West tried to be, I didn't fall for the "okeydoke." From the beginning, it was clear to me that P&L would not keep all the HR staff. I also knew that they would not keep two high-level HR professionals. It just wasn't smart business.

So, early on, I started making plans to leave. And what a good decision this turned out to be. I witnessed so many folks being mistreated during the planning phases of this acquisition, so I knew it was time for me to get out. West had no idea I was planning to leave. What he also did not know was that before he broke this news to me, one of the secretaries who worked for a member of the board of directors had already told me she read a document that clearly stated that the firm could not justify having two highly compensated HR professionals and that I would not be kept. She also stated that others who were not aware would not be kept either.

While still in West's office, he proceeded to tell me about the severance package the firm was proposing to give me. It was six months' pay. I felt this was not enough. Under normal circumstances, I would have considered it fair. However, I felt I had been used. West and the P&L staff repeatedly told me I would have a job. Even though I was planning to leave, I felt I deserved more than six months' pay. I wanted them to know they were wrong to repeatedly tell folks their livelihood was secure, even if there was a slight bit of uncertainty. Also, I felt that, at my level and with more than fifteen years' tenure, I should have been compensated more for being given such short notice.

All the other administrators were given three- to six-months' notice with a six-month severance package. I was being given one month notice, and it was less than one month. There were even staff members who were given six months' notice. What was more unfair was the fact that the firm was willing to give a secretary, who was being fired for cause, a much larger period of severance than me. Believe it or not, this secretary was someone who should have been fired years before. She worked for one of the partners and was found to have divulged, on more than one occasion, highly confidential information. During the merger discussions, she informed several people of sensitive details regarding attorneys that were being terminated.

When West and I reported the secretary to the chairman, he would not allow us to fire her. He said he could not let anything get in the way of the pending merger. Although the secretary was not a good employee, the firm gave her ten months' salary in exchange for her quiet resignation. Both firms wanted to "keep her quiet." About what, I don't know. When I told West how outrageously unfair I felt the firms were, he gave me two "good reasons" why the secretary was being given a larger severance package than me. The first reason he gave was, "She is crazy, and the firm is afraid she might go running to the press with who knows what." The second reason was that the new firm's directive was to "do whatever needed to be done to make her go away quietly forever."

West thought this would make me feel better. It didn't. I couldn't resist asking, "If I promise to act crazy and threaten to run to the press, will I get a larger severance package?"

He said, "No. You are not like that." I told him I was extremely insulted. Basically, both firms were giving no regard to the positions the secretary and I held, nor our value to the firms. This clearly made no difference. It was the firms' fear of the secretary and their lack of fear of me that made the difference. However, in the end, West agreed to go back to the chairman with my concerns, relay my displeasure with the severance offer, and get back to me.

Several days later, West reported back to me. He said the chairman was very sorry, but the firm could not give me more severance. He said the merger documents had already been finalized, and all the documents would have to be redone if they changed my severance amount. This was very interesting to me because they didn't seem to have this problem when unexpectedly they decided to give the secretary a special hush package. This is what I call "royal" nonsense. They were willing to give someone who had for many years been a horrible employee far more than they were willing to give me, who had been loyal when many people would have been disloyal.

I had always performed at the highest level and was loyal to West and the firm. In a sick effort to console me, West told me he felt the six months was fair. He said that most people didn't know, but he was not going to be staying with the new firm either. He said he agreed to work with P&L for the rest of the year (which was ten more months) and that, at the beginning of the next year, he would receive six months' severance and move on. Again, West reiterated that he felt six months' pay was more than fair. He said, "I will be happy to get it." Well, I looked at him like he was crazy. Right before my eyes, he had turned into Sam Sausagehead. How dare he compare his deal to mine?

Then I said, "You have got to be kidding me. If I made more than a half million dollars a year and was given almost one year's notice, I would be happy with six months' severance also." West had ample time to plan a new life for him and his family while earning an extremely high salary.

West knew this was crazy! In a nutshell, the abject way my layoff was handled is inexcusable. This entire process was handled very poorly. The five remaining members of my staff were so discontented that they all left the new firm shortly after me. In the end, all the staff, who were told repeatedly that the firm would look out for them, and they would be kept by the new firm, were either booted out openly, booted out through some type of nonsense, or kept on and demoted and eventually moved on, but there was one exception.

A NEW START

As originally promised, the director of finance was laid off with a six-month notice, and six months' severance pay. Her severance pay was huge due to the unbelievable salary increase she received from West right before information was passed on to P&L for the merger. I told you, "There is more than one way to skin a cat."

As you know, the legal support manager was booted out through a nonsense offer that worked out in his favor because he was planning to leave anyway. When he declined the offer, he was given a three-month notice and six months' severance.

The marketing administrator was given the position of DC marketing manager for a small practice group. However, when she was told about the position, she was also told that the head of the group stated that his group was far too busy to deal with marketing issues. So, basically, she was given a position to work with a group that did not want her services. Shortly after the merger, she resigned and moved on to a great position.

The new chief information officer was demoted to the DC director of information technology. He decided that because he had recently changed positions, because he was the sole breadwinner for his family, and because of the fact that he did not lose income, he would stay with the new firm for some period, which turned out not to be that long.

The library services administrator was demoted to a library manager, but was allowed to keep her "administrator" title for the remainder of the year. However, she was not eligible for any of the "administrator" benefits. This arrangement lasted only a few months. I was told by a P&L employee that the firm eventually offered her a severance package and asked her to move on.

The office administrator was the one exception. She was the only administrator to be "promoted." She was made a "regional administrator." Her region was DC; yes, just DC. They didn't want to keep her, but West fought to get her a "promotion." The tide was going out fast. However, this administrator decided she wanted out, so she agreed to accept a bonus and leave. Last I heard, she had convinced her old firm to hire her back, and she was working in its DC office.

West was demoted to the DC administrator of operations. He was given two options for employment with the new firm: (1) he could keep his same salary for the remainder of the year, and at the end of the year, he would leave the firm with a huge bonus and six months' severance pay, or (2) he could keep his same salary for the rest of the year and at the beginning of the new year, continue working indefinitely at a much lower salary. Per West, he wanted to move on and was taking the first option. Before I left the firm, he had already found major fault in his new supervisor and was calling this guy a whole rack of bad names. I believe West went on to work for a small law firm in Philadelphia.

MY NEW START

I gladly left the firm and began my new journey. I knew I did not want to return to a regular nine to five, and was looking forward to helping people who needed me. When West thought he was creating a shock factor for me, what he didn't know was that I was literally days away from resigning. I had not told most of my peers, but my family, those in whom I confided, and a few close friends knew about my plans. As it turned out, the firm paid me the equivalent of one year's salary to do what I was going to do for free. My plans were to do HR consulting from my home office. When West informed me that I would not be kept on, it was only days before I was going to turn in my resignation. I was starting a new journey on my own.

With all the drama surrounding the relationship between the new firm and mine, I was happy to move on. The businesses I planned to target for HR consulting were those with less than 100 employees. The firm was not going to be able to take one of its wholly owned subsidiaries and thus would leave it without any administrative support. This seemed to be a perfect group to approach about my new business. They were extremely profitable, and everyone expected them to do very well on their own. The subsidiary specialized in public relations, and many of their clients were very well-known politicians. Because the company was a subsidiary of the firm, my department had been providing HR support to them as well. Continuing to provide them with HR support would be a natural transition.

I spoke to the CEO of the company about my new business. He thanked me and agreed that it was a perfect solution to both our needs. We entered a verbal agreement and decided we would meet later to discuss the details. This guy was very excited that I would be continuing to assist him with his HR needs. I was excited as well because not only did I have my first client lined up, I was looking forward to the continuity of working for someone with whom I had worked for five years. After confirming with the CEO of the company that I would be counting on them as my first and only client, I began taking steps for a smooth transition.

A couple weeks before I was scheduled to leave the firm, I called the CEO on several occasions. He never returned my calls. Finally, I left him a message saying he needed to call me immediately. After that message, he came to my office one Monday afternoon. He apologized for not returning my calls. He said he was not sure if his business was going to last more than one year, and he was becoming very concerned about it. There was no need for concern in my mind because his company was making a lot of money. Also, I would be assisting him with HR issues, and West had been working to employ a company to assist him with financial matters. With this type of support, he would be able to focus more on the business.

About the transition, I told him we needed to make some final plans. He thought I was referring to our business agreement, and he said, "I know, you want something in writing."

At that point, I said, "Yes; that would be nice." He told me he would give me a call no later than that Friday. Well, Friday came and went, and I did not hear from him. I left one message after that and still never heard from him. Assuming he was so overwhelmed by the new changes, I thought he did not have an opportunity to get back to me. To date, it has been well over fifteen years, and I still have not heard from him. Do you think he will ever return my call? Great public relations, huh?

About two weeks after I left the firm, I was told that the CEO, "my first real client," had hired another HR consultant. This guy entered a verbal agreement with me. We even shook hands on it. You know, the old-fashioned way of doing business. I had no reason to be concerned that he would not keep his word. After all, he told me he would be writing me a check. As a matter of fact, his exact words were, "You just let me know when you are ready, and I'll write the check." After all that said, he had the audacity to go out and hire someone else. Even worse, he never said a word to me. Well, if you think that is despicable, you totally won't believe this. The HR consultant he hired was West's best friend. This makes me think of a story told by the elders in my family about Grandpa Harmon.

Grandpa Harmon was famous for entering deals with people and not keeping his end of the deal. Supposedly, he once sold a home to a couple and took $2,000 in cash from them as a deposit. Well, a week or so later, the couple showed up at the house, a prime piece of real estate on Capitol Hill in DC. They were so excited; they wanted to show some friends their new home. However, when they arrived at the house and knocked on the door, they got a bomb dropped on them. They were not allowed to enter the house. As they quickly learned, the house did not belong to their seller. The owner told them that she had owned the house for over twenty years and was not in the market to sell.

The couple told the owner their side of the story. They described the person who took their money, as well as the inside of the house. It was obvious they had been in the house, but the owner did not recognize the description of the person who took their money and had no idea about any of it. The couple left the house in obvious despair. Well, guess what? The owner was Cicely. Members of my family, although it was never proven, were convinced that the salesman was someone in cahoots with Grandpa Harmon! Harmon had pulled this horrible scheme and left these poor people out of the money that probably took years to save. So needless to say, you should be very careful when entering deals with people, even when you think you know them. Also, like the biblical story of Joseph, you must be careful to whom you tell things. If Joseph's brothers sold him out, then you know outsiders will sell you out.

After I learned what the subsidiary CEO had done to me, I too was in despair and initially could not believe it. Then, after a short while, I thought about something Cicely used to say about brides that were "left at the altar." Her belief was that the woman should be thankful to God, and the man, if this happened to her. She felt the man was doing the woman a favor, because if he did not want her and married her anyway, the marriage would be bad and/or would never last. With that in mind, I said, "Thank you, God." Some lessons are hard to accept, but we have to accept them and learn from them all. Hopefully, the couple Harmon scammed learned a lesson also.

Insofar as West's best friend getting the gig, I'm not saying West had anything to do with it, but you know it is possible. Nonetheless, all things happen for a reason. After all that drama, I decided to focus on the completion of this, my first book. I realized that the text had been handed to me on a silver platter, and all I needed to do was show up, and God would do the rest. Therefore, I started getting ready. I packed my bags and headed down the path that was laid out for me. If history is indicative of what God will do for me, I have nothing to worry about.

"When you learn teach, and when you get give."
—Maya Angelou

Bloopers: Go Ahead and Check

MYSTERY VOICE. One morning at a directors' meeting, the new COO told us about a strange voice mail message he received. He had no idea the identity of the caller, and was so baffled about the message; he repeatedly mentioned it during the meeting. Finally, one of the directors asked, "Can we hear the message?" Well, I knew this was a bad idea. I could feel it in my bones, but I kept my mouth shut.

The COO replied, "Sure." He dialed into his voicemail box and played the message on speakerphone. It was not clear to any of us who the caller was, but we knew by what the person was saying that it was one of the owners of the firm. It was also clear that this owner thought he was talking to someone who was a nonowner and was reporting what happened at an owners' meeting the night before. The caller was not happy with the outcome of the meeting. He was trashing one of the founders of the firm. Yes, one of the guys whose name was on all the paychecks. The voice on the message was referring to the named partner as multiple really bad names, and then some more.

We were all horrified listening to this message. Finally, one of the directors, for as mortified as he was, spoke up and said, "The message was left for me." We were all shocked. Then someone asked, "Who is the person leaving the message?" I was hoping the director would not reveal the caller's name, but he did. I couldn't believe he did this. Even worse, as we later learned, not only did the COO receive the voice message, someone had forwarded the message to the entire board of directors. What a way to find out how your partner feels about you. We believed, even though it couldn't be proven, that the director's secretary (who was known as the Wicked Witch of the West) had forwarded the voice mail message. For those of you who give others access to your voice mail box, remember this—it can help you, but it can also bite you in the butt. There was hell to pay that day.

A JOB FOR A CLERK. Early one spring morning, I walked out of my office heading down the hall to speak to one of the other directors. When I arrived at the director's office, her door was shut. As usual, I lightly tapped on the door a couple of times and walk in. You know, I'm HR. There is nothing I can't see. This morning, I received more than an eyeful. There the director was sitting at her desk with one of the clerks. Well, the director was sitting in her desk chair, and the clerk was sitting on her desk facing her with his legs spread wide open. The type of job she was giving him was very daring or very something!

PRESTIGIOUS TERMINATION. One of the firm's legal secretaries had been creating problems for months. She was constantly pushing the rules to the limit. Finally, she pushed one time too many. She requested assistance from one of the backup secretaries because she had too much work to do. As it turned out, she gave the backup secretary her work while she spent the day working on preparations for her wedding. Once we verified the information, I called the secretary and her supervisor to one of the conference rooms and told the secretary that we were terminating her employment immediately. She did not make a fuss, and the meeting was very brief. Her supervisor was going to escort her back to her desk to get her personal belongings, so she could leave the office. As she and her supervisor got up to leave the conference room, she looked back at me, and her final words to me were, "I've been escorted out of more prestigious firms than this one."

I couldn't help saying, "Good, now you can add this one to your list."

FREE BACKGROUND CHECKS. One firm ran full background checks on all new employees. A senior manager, who was authorized to request background check information, decided to offer this service to her friends. So, she ran credit and criminal background checks for her friends at the firm's expense. You know, just helping her friends.

FILE CABINET INSPECTION. After one of the office "thank God it's Friday" parties, there were a couple of managers who had to stay a little longer to test the file cabinets. These individuals were checking to be sure the hall file cabinets were strong and safe. So, they decided to stand up against them and have sex—forceful sex. That's right. They were standing right in the middle of the hallway as I walked by. I stopped and asked in a very strong voice, "What are you doing?" One of them spoke up and said, "We were just checking the file cabinets." Both inspectors fled the area in different directions.

GIRLFRIENDS. Early one morning, I heard a very loud voice in the courtyard below my office. I looked out the window, but I didn't see anything. Moments later, one of the employees came rushing into my office saying, "You have to go down to the courtyard. Ms. Smith is lying on the ground screaming and crying. I think she's having a nervous breakdown." Well, I'm thinking, *God what have I done to deserve this?* I know, you're probably thinking I'm cold and inconsiderate. What you need to know is that I spent the week prior to this incident in meeting after meeting with Ms. Smith. She had just ended a long-term, on again, off again relationship with a former employee at the firm. Now she was in a relationship with one of the clerks, and there was trouble in paradise. Several of the employees had complained about the clerk spending too much time chitchatting with Ms. Smith whenever she had to conduct business with her. Well, in the end, I learned that the clerk was breaking up with Ms. Smith because she was starting a relationship with, no other than, Ms. Smith's Ex. It was far too much drama for me. I had heard enough about the voice mail messages, love letters, dear Jane letters, and wet T-shirts hung on Ms. Smith's home front doorknob. It was all too much for me. When I reached the courtyard, Ms. Smith was lying on the ground screaming, "I can't live without you; I can't live without you!"

This was the kind of stuff I had no patience for, so I said, in an extremely firm voice, "Ms. Smith, get up off the ground. You are making a spectacle of yourself. Get it together and either go home or go back to work." I tried to deal with this patiently for an entire week. Now, I was unable to take another minute of the drama. No more drama!

COKE BREAKS. There was an entire practice group of attorneys, legal secretaries, and paralegals that frequently traveled out of state to do client work. In some cases, these folks would be away from home for weeks at a time. They often worked eighteen to twenty hours straight. Their meals were always brought in, and the only time they would stop working would be for coke breaks—I'm sorry, I mean cocaine breaks. This group sniffed so much cocaine that their collective bill was reported to be well over $100,000 in one year.

PRIZE APPLICANT. As you can imagine, I have conducted thousands of interviews over my career. One of my all-time favorites, for its unbelievable nature, happened one spring afternoon. After receiving an exhausting number of resumes, we narrowed the applicants down to about six or seven strong candidates. The HR manager conducted the initial interviews and recommended the final three candidates to me. The first two candidates came in without incident. The third candidate reported right on time. The HR manager could not be available for the third candidate, so she had the receptionist call me when the applicant arrived. I went out to the reception area to greet the candidate. She was a very tall, attractive woman with model-like qualities. I welcomed her and proceeded to escort her to the testing room. On the way, I realized something about this woman seemed familiar to me. I thought perhaps she had interviewed with us before.

So, I asked, "have you been to our firm before?"

She responded, "No, I don't think so." At that moment, the feeling of having seen this person before grew stronger.

I asked again, "Are you sure you've not been here before?"

Again, she said, "I don't think so. Perhaps it was my sister. She is a legal secretary as well." Although I have an unusual ability to remember faces, I let it go.

While the candidate was in the testing room completing her paperwork, I began to review her resume and application. It was at this point that I was sure I had seen this person before. I couldn't remember specifics, but there was even something familiar about her resume. Also, I was very suspicious when I asked her if she had been at our firm before, and her answer was, "I don't think so." Wrong answer. People never visited our office and not remember it.

The location and our office space were unique for the DC area. And besides, we were one of only two law firms with office space at that location. I couldn't take it anymore. I went to the file where we kept all former applicants' paperwork, and sure enough there was a packet in there that was much like the one I had on my desk. After carefully reviewing both packets, I learned it was in fact the same person. She had written her name differently. The old packet had first name, middle initial and last name (Jane B. Doe). The new packet had first name initial, middle name and last name (J. Betty Doe). She had moved some of the previous employers around and basically tried to disguise who she was. She even had a hairstyle that was drastically different from the year before when I interviewed her. The clincher for me was that she had listed the exact same three personal references (with the same addresses and telephone numbers) on both applications in the exact same order.

I went back to the testing room, walked in, and said, "I'm sorry, but you have to leave." She looked up at me in total shock and I repeated, "I'm sorry, but you have to leave, now." I told her that she lied to me and that because she lied, she could not continue with the interview. She began to boo-hoo crying and asked if I could give her a moment to get herself together. I told her she could have one minute, and I stood there waiting for her to leave. I have no patience for folks who purposely try to trick me. This premeditated scheme may have worked in some places, but not in mine.

A CLIP AND A NAP. A very high-level executive in my office was known for clipping his fingernails during meetings in his office. Some of my colleagues and I always feared being popped in the eye with one of these fingernails. One of my colleagues and I were in this person's office discussing firm business. The executive, after clipping each one of his fingernails, neatly placed the nail clipper in his desk drawer, leaned back in his chair, and proceeded to take a nap. I mean this guy literally went to sleep. We could not believe it. We started doing things like clearing our throats, but that did not wake him; dropping a pen on his desk did not wake him; and my colleague's attempt to hit the desk without shocking the guy into a heart attack did not wake him either. We were both uncertain as to what else we could do. My colleague wanted to shake the guy, but I told him he could not do that. Then, he and I began having a whisper fight, which I lost. My colleague gets up from his chair, walks over to the guy, and begins to shake him.

He said, "Hey, man, wake up. Do you need a cup of coffee, or something? Maybe you should take a walk around the block, man. I'm just saying ..." This was one of the funniest things that ever happened to me in the workplace. My colleague and I laughed about this for years.

UNDESIRABLE BLACKS. A black secretary came to my office very upset about a comment that had been made to her by one of the white paralegals in our office. The secretary said the paralegal walked up to her and asked if she could have some of the jelly beans that were in a jar on the secretary's desk. The secretary replied, "Sure, just don't take the black ones; they are my favorites."

The paralegal then asked, "Who likes the black ones, aren't they inferior?" When I spoke to the paralegal to explain to her how she should be more sensitive to such comments, she said she thought the comment was perfectly okay because she was "just kidding." She's lucky she didn't get punched in her face. *Just kidding* just doesn't get it with some people.

BAKE ME A CAKE. Two of our senior managers needed a new secretary, and they learned that one of our secretaries was available. They approached me about the possibility of the secretary being assigned to them. I told them the secretary was earning $65K per year, and the COO would have to approve the assignment. When requested, the COO approved the assignment with the stipulation that we did not add another secretary to the general pool. We made the assignment change without having to hire a new person. Many months later, the COO came to me complaining that she had to reduce the administrative staff budget. She was very concerned that the board would be upset with her about the excessive administrative overhead, which was due to overstaffing in two other departments that the COO allowed to get out of control. Although the secretary did not work with the COO, suddenly, she began complaining about the secretary. At first, I wasn't sure why the COO was complaining. I had not heard of any problems the supervisors were having with the secretary. Then, suddenly, I realized it wasn't the secretary at all. The COO had just found an easy way to save $65K. She told me the secretary was doing a terrible job. When I asked her how she knew that, she told me to speak to the secretary's supervisors.

After speaking to the supervisors, I went back to the COO and told her that they did not have any real problems with the secretary. About two weeks later, the COO came back to me again voicing complaints about the secretary and telling me she wanted her fired. We had no grounds to fire this person, but again she told me to speak to the supervisors. I knew this was a game, so I began to communicate in writing only. I e-mailed both supervisors asking them to let me know about any problems they were having with the secretary. They both stated, in writing, that they had no problems with her, or her performance. When I told the COO what the supervisors said, she went crazy. About a half hour later, I received an e-mail from one of the supervisors stating that he had not understood my question earlier. He said the COO explained it to him, and he would provide me with a list of problems he was having with the secretary. The following is verbatim what I wrote in my e-mail message:

> "I am checking with the two of you to see how things are working out with you and your secretary. If you are having any problems, or performance-related issues with your secretary, please let me know."

The COO came to me the next day and told me she wanted the secretary fired by the end of that week. This cake was baked and pulled from the oven.

CYBER SEX. One afternoon, I received a telephone call from one of the partners. She was calling to complain about one of the employees she said was behaving very inappropriately with her husband, who was also a partner in the firm. She went on to say that this employee often stands too close to her husband and other men in the office as well. She said the person wears her blouses cut too low, and her breasts were often exposed for everyone to see. She went on to say, "This woman purposely leans over her desk so the men can see her breasts. I am fed up with this woman flirting with my husband, and if she doesn't stop it, I'm going to personally speak to her about it." The partner was very upset and angry. She called the employee very unprofessional and said she always behaved inappropriately with the male clients and employees. Finally, the partner, who had reached the boiling point, said, "She literally has sex with Jonathan Parker over the PA system." If you remember the rendition of "Happy Birthday" Marilyn Monroe sang for President John F. Kennedy, then you have an idea of how this person sounded when she paged Jonathan Parker—"Jonathan Parker, please call the operator; Jonathan Parker, please call the operator." The partner calmed down and apologized for sounding off on me and said she knew it wasn't my fault and that the employee was being protected by several of the "doggish men in the office."

CHRISTMAS CHEER. At one of the office Christmas parties, I just happened to be walking to the back of the restaurant looking for a restaurant manager to find out if we could extend the party hours. As I approached a very narrow hallway, who do I find stretched out on one of the long folding tables, stuck together like two dogs in heat, but one of the partners and one of the young interns. Yes, on a table in a hallway in the restaurant.

At that same Christmas Party, I was wearing a beautiful red suit. It was very conservative in style and not at all revealing. However, one of the partners (a different guy) walked up to me and said, "You look so good in that red suit, I could eat you." I looked at him, rolled my eyes, and walked away. I guess it was just the season. Twas the season to be horny!

HAND WASHABLES. Shortly after I started working at one firm, I began receiving complaints from the staff that one of the hospitality workers had extremely bad body odor. Folks were appalled by this because this person handled food daily. After experiencing the odor myself, I called the employee into my office. This is always a hard conversation to have, and it was my first, but I thought it better to just get it out as opposed to trying to beat around the bush. So, I told the person that several employees had complained about their body odor. The employee was very upset at first and explained that they bathe regularly. I asked about the frequency of doing laundry and discovered the culprit. The employee told me they could not afford to go to a laundry service and therefore was hand washing all their clothes in the bathtub (heavy jeans and all). I suggested that perhaps this method was not getting the heavy items clean enough and that maybe they were holding an odor which people could smell. This was an older person who was mean and crotchety with most people, but was always very nice to me. I said I would check to see if I could get some help for this problem. The employee was very appreciative and left my office. The first thing I did was check compensation history in the personnel file. Well, I can't tell you how shocked I was at what I found. This employee was making less than minimum wage and had not had a raise in four or five years. I immediately went to the managing partner and requested a 50 percent raise for this person. The managing partner thought I had lost my mind until I told him the employee was earning less than $10K a year. This was during a time when the market was paying a minimum of $15,000 per year for this position. In addition, I requested that we provide the hospitality staff with uniforms that the firm would pay to have cleaned on a weekly basis. The managing partner agreed, and all was well. When I informed the staff person of the firm's decision, I got hugged so tight I thought one of my ribs was going to break. It was a very happy day!

FIRST-ROUND KNOCKOUT. I was sitting in my office one afternoon, and I received a frantic call from one of the younger attorneys. He informed me that one of the legal secretaries and one of the file clerks had gotten into a fight. It was not a fight. They apparently were arguing about a Girl Scout cookie issue they both were involved in outside the firm. The male hauled off and slapped the female just as the managing partner was walking down the hallway. The managing partner immediately escorted the male out of the building and notified me that he was never to return. No hitting at work!

DAILY POLITICAL SWEEP. As the HR assistant, I worked with a very young executive aspirant. This young woman was desperate to succeed at a level far beyond her reach. She was desperate for many things. She had a need for attention akin to a diabetic's need for insulin. She was a professional disingenuous artist and would make at least one of what I called a daily political sweep (DPS). This was a walk she made through the firm each day, purposely passing the offices of the top owners and feeding them a bunch of nonsense. At first, I didn't know what she was doing, but after a couple of months, I realized she was basically trying to suck up to the owners. She would pour it on especially thick during evaluation and bonus times. Some days, she would make two DPSs—one in the morning and one in the late afternoon. This was nothing but a psych game. It was her way of ensuring that she would be on the minds of the powerful owners. I'm sure she was taught to do this. I always thought she probably attended one of those career seminars. You know, something like, "How to Get Ahead through Office Politics." For as crazy as this may sound, I have seen it work. The only problem is that it causes the individual engaging in this behavior huge amounts of stress. They are constantly on edge worrying about whether people see through them or not. I have never succumbed to this type of behavior, but I've known plenty of folks who have done so proudly. The sad part about this behavior is that many of the people who are served the nonsense eat it up.

I knew this person, although most people thought differently, had esteem issues. She could never pass a reflection of herself without looking at it. I mean it could be a tiny strip of metal—if she saw her reflection, she could not resist checking it out. She would look at herself, it seemed, at least one hundred times each day. We could be sitting in a restaurant, and she would try to look at her reflection in the silverware. She smoked like a fanatic and was known to tipple into oblivion. She also had her fair share of the young attorneys in the office. Her love affairs often interfered with work progress, but the firm accepted this behavior. She was, for the most part, a very nice person, but one with low self-esteem.

AMACING. Here we go again; another HR nightmare telephone call. This call was from the security guard in the building. He wanted to inform us that an ambulance was on its way to take one of our employees to the hospital. As the story goes, our employee was driving into the office one morning, and there was a slight incident on the road not far from our building where another driver yelled out profanities at our employee. As fate would have it, they both parked in the same building. As our employee stood waiting for the elevator, in comes the other driver. This person was still very upset at our employee. The other driver accused our employee of cutting her off on the road and wanted to talk about it. Our employee, reportedly, told the other driver, "Leave me alone. I don't have time for this. I have to get to my office." They both got on the elevator, and the other driver pressed the button for the first floor, and our employee was going to the twelfth floor. When the elevator reached the first floor, and the doors opened, the other driver reached in her pocket, pulled out a can of pepper spray, sprayed our employee all over her face, and fled.

I'm sure you're thinking how horrible this must have been. Well, truth be told, for as horrible as it was, many people in my office felt our employee deserved what she got. Some people said it was poetic justice. This employee had a reputation of being rude, obnoxious, and looking down on people she felt were beneath her. One isolated population was the people who worked in one department. They were, supposedly, frequently subjected to this employee's rude behavior. Well, on this morning, I was called by a couple of people informing me that there was a lot of disturbance in this department. I rushed over to find several of the employees playing loud music, dancing, and singing. When I asked what was going on, one of the employees shouted, "You didn't hear; Missy got pepper sprayed in her face, and we are celebrating." I made them stop the celebration and get back to work. Although the music was turned down, and the employees went back to work, they were convinced that justice was served and seemed to continue celebrating inwardly.

RACIST MANAGER. When I first started working at one firm, I kept receiving complaints from several black employees about how their white manager spoke to them. The comments the manager was reportedly making were things such as, "you people," "Did you go to school?," and "That is a stupid question," when a legitimate question was being asked. The manager would also yell and speak to the blacks in a very degrading manner. As I began to closely observe this manager, it was clear to me that blacks were being treated differently than their white counterparts. I decided that before I took my concerns any further, I would check a little deeper. I attended one of the managers' staff meetings, and it was even more obvious that the manager had some real issues with black people. In addition, the records clearly showed a pattern of black males being terminated at an unusual rate under this manager's supervision. In a period of about six months, nine black males either resigned or were fired under this manager.

I reported the matter to our labor attorney, informing him that I felt this manager was a racist. I also informed him that the other employees had made the same claim about the manager. Our labor attorney launched a full investigation focusing on the evaluation results of blacks versus whites. At the end of the investigation, he reported back to me that he had, in fact, found some "discrepancies" in the evaluations and that he was going to handle the situation. How, I never knew, but the manager continued working at the firm for many years and in a very inexplicable manner continued his racist behavior. I just figured, hey, they probably sent him to some sensitivity class, and instead of him atoning for his sins, he just changed into an oblique racist.

THE ELEVAPOR. While sitting in my office working on that day's drama, I received a telephone call from the director of facilities. She informed me that there had been an incident in the building that had occurred shortly before she called me. The building manager called her and wanted to meet with her and me immediately. I could not imagine what was going on, but I left my office and went to the location where I was to meet them. It was in the elevator lobby on the seventh floor of our building. The building manager saw me coming and began speaking into a walkie-talkie. He was telling the person on the other end to send the elevator up. "John, send the elevator to the seventh floor now!" This guy was clearly very upset. I still could not imagine what was going on in the elevator. Was there something on the elevator for us to see? Was it a dead body? Had someone dumped a bunch of our office files in the elevator? Was it a bunch of trash on it? I could not imagine what it was, but the facilities manager and I both knew it must have been something bad.

Well bad it wasn't. It was horrible and totally disgusting. Some nutcase had taken a paper plate, which the building traced back to our firm, and pooped on it. Yes, feces—a huge pile of it on a paper plate. Can you imagine having to trace the origin of a paper plate with feces on it? What do you do? Do you take the plate from office to office? No way. Maybe the building "investigators" took a photo of the plate and went from office to office in search of that exact type of plate. Well, this plate was the same type of paper plates we used in all our kitchens. None of the other tenants used the same plates. We were busted—caught red-handed. A sick person was running around the building, and that person worked for our firm. Believe it or not, this happened twice—a huge pile of poop riding up and down the elevator on a paper plate. What message was this person sending?

THE PURSUIT OF A MAN. One direct report of the managing partner was the firm administrator. About five years after working in one firm, the firm administrator was just ending her second serious office relationship. After this break-up, she immediately started dating other guys, beginning her pursuit once more for a husband, but none of them worked out. The administrator then decided, based on an article she read in a magazine, that it was easier to get a husband in the Midwest. So, she began a job search in Phoenix, Arizona. She found a Phoenix law firm that was in search of an administrator. She flew out to their offices, interviewed for the position, and received an offer. She returned to DC, packed her bags and relocated to Phoenix. In addition to starting a new job, she would begin a new pursuit for a husband. After living in Phoenix for one year, she met and married the man of her dreams and was living very happily, last I heard.

HELLO—GOOD-BYE. One of the attorneys contacted me to say he believed his secretary had miscoded some charges that were billed to his client. Because the secretary was on medical leave when I started working at the firm, I had never met her. The attorney asked the accounting department to reconcile the client's account. As it turned out, the secretary had paid her mortgage with firm checks for three consecutive months. She simply submitted a check request to the Accounting Department with her mortgage company as the payee. After paying her mortgage the third time, she went out on medical leave and was out for about two months before the firm knew about these charges. I will never forget the day the secretary returned from medical leave. When confronted with the matter, she sat in my office and explained how the HR person before me had been having an affair with her husband. She told me she had been confiding in this person for months and had no idea she was the one with whom her husband was having an affair. "I poured my heart out to her and when I learned the truth about what was going on, I lost it," she told me. At this point, she began crying hysterically. Once she calmed down, she said, "My husband took all the money we had in the bank, moved out of our house while I was at work and took all of our furniture, including my eight-year-old son's bed, and he ran off with Ms. Steal" (the former HR person). This was a very sad story, but I thought the woman was crazy. She stole money from the firm and expected us to understand. If her story was true, I believe the firm would have tried to assist her if she had not taken it upon herself to freely dip into the firm's bank account. Well, the day she returned to the office from medical leave, I had to fire her. It was the first time I laid eyes on this woman, and I had to say hello and good-bye in the same meeting.

B. PHOENIX

ANTHRAX IN THE OFFICE. One afternoon, I was working quietly in my office. It was a very hot day in DC and about an hour after most people had finished their lunch break. My telephone rang and it was the director of facilities telling me that one of the employees had reported a white powder-like substance on the floor in one of the restrooms. The employee was very upset because she thought it might have been anthrax. This was right in the heat of the anthrax terror, which had practically paralyzed the DC metropolitan area. We immediately called security and roped off the restroom so no one could go in. About one half hour later, the world's slowest security guard showed up on our floor. This guy was about seventy years old with an extremely arrogant attitude. He was very thin and medium height—a real Barney Fife (one of the lead characters in *The Andy Griffith Show*) type law enforcer. When he arrived, we told him what had been reported. We asked if he thought we should call one of the local emergency agencies. He, in a very cavalier tone, said, "No. I'll check it out." Then he saunters into the restroom (gun in holster and all, which appeared to be heavier than he was soaking wet) and was in there a little more than five minutes.

Well, the director of facilities and I were on pins and needles with worry. When the security guard returned, he looked at us in total disgust (as if we had bothered him for some nonsense) and in the same cavalier tone said, "It's nothing more than some of that feminine powder."

We were totally confused about how he knew so quickly what it was. I then asked in total amazement, "How do you know?"

His reply was "Lady, I have many years of experience in dealing with women, and I have smelled enough of that feminine powder to know what it is."

The director of facilities asked, "Did you actually smell it?"

Again, in the same tone, Barney Fife said with pride, "Yes, I did."

At that point the facilities director said, "Okay, great; mystery solved," and we went back to our offices and continued working as if nothing ever happened. Some detective work, huh? This could have been a deadly substance. However, due to the security guard's "expertise" in white powdery substances, he was confident enough to do a sniff test just to solve the mystery.

HOLY PATRIMONY. I worked with one individual who married a guy that worked in our office as well. The office gossip was that the gentleman's parents paid this female $25K in cash and gave her an all-expense-paid trip to Europe for two weeks to marry their son, so he could become a United States citizen. Did she agree to a phony marriage for $25K and a trip to Europe? It seemed crazy to me, but there were several women in the office who said they would have done the same thing. Some said they would have done it for $10K.

STAPLER TOSS. One of the legal secretaries called my office one afternoon very upset that one of the attorneys was in his office screaming and having a very bad temper tantrum as he often did. This day he went too far. He threw a stapler out of his office into the hallway and just barely missed the secretary's face. The impact was so great that it left a big hole in the wall. He got a little slap on the wrist, was made to apologize to the secretary, and life went on. Tempers can be dangerous.

THE QUESTION OF THE HOUR. At the end of an executive staff meeting, everyone was beginning to leave the conference room, when, suddenly, my supervisor said, "Oh I'm sorry, but would all men please stay after the meeting. I have a question to ask you." Well, not only did the women think it was strange, the men thought it was strange as well. However, all the women left, and all the men stayed. Later that day, one of my male colleagues came into my office to show me a gift he had purchased for our supervisor. He had gone out, purchased a watch, and had it gift wrapped. When I asked why on earth he would do that, he reminded me of the earlier meeting where our supervisor asked all the men to stay behind. Well, the question he asked them was, "Do any of you have a spare watch I can borrow?" My colleague found this so pathetic that he went out and purchased a watch for him.

SECRETARY OR BANKING CLERK? One of my many investigations involved a secretary that was stealing money from her attorney's bank account. This attorney used her to do his personal banking. This went on for years. The attorney's biweekly paycheck was larger than the secretary's annual salary. One month, the bank contacted the attorney because a lot of cash withdrawals were being made, which was unusual. As it turned out, the secretary had stolen money from the attorney to the tune of $50K.

ALL OR NONE. Over a very hot, steamy summer, one of the young male professionals was assigned to oversee the summer intern program. This man turned out to be an old-fashioned overseer. Twelve students were in the program that year. Of the twelve, nine were females and three were males. The program ran for three months, from June through August. It wasn't enough that the young overseer had sex with one or two of the female interns; he had sex with all nine of them. Wow! What a busy summer for this guy—having to do so many contracts, and interns as well, must have been hard work.

TAKE YOUR CHILD TO WORK DAY. We were very lenient about children visiting the office. The employees enjoyed bringing their children in for visits, and the children enjoyed coming. It was very nice to see the little ones from time-to-time. And all was well until the little rascal children showed up. These children seemed possessed. They would chase each other through the office as if they were running an Olympic marathon. One of these little darlings took colored markers, went into an attorney's office and proceeded to mark on everything on his desk, and not just the items on the desk. These children marked all over the beautiful hardwood desk as well. That still wasn't enough. They went into one of our most popular conference rooms—beautiful and exquisitely decorated—took soda cans, shook them up, and sprayed dark-colored soda all over the conference room walls, furniture, and carpet.

The furniture and carpeting required special cleaning, and the very expensive wall covering had to be removed and replaced. The grand finale was that these little rascals spread feces all over the walls in one of the men's restrooms. That's right—human feces. We knew it had to be them because they made handprints on the walls. Now in my world those little darlings would have gotten a good butt whuppin'! From that day forward, I decided that bringing children into the office was not a good idea unless there was some control, and guess who was designated to be the one in charge of children in the office. *Me!*

DUMPSTER DIVING. One of the partners and his secretary filled two standard-size record boxes with client files, which they were going to send to the client the next day. These boxes were stacked beside the secretary's desk when they left for the night. The next morning when they arrived, the boxes were gone. The secretary asked the partner if he knew the whereabouts of the boxes. The partner jumped up in a panic and began looking for them. He called me, but I had not seen them, nor did I know anything about them. I told him I would call the office manager to see if she knew anything about the boxes. When I called the office manager and explained what happened, she was sure the cleaning people had probably trashed them. After checking with the cleaning crew, we learned they did, in fact, trash the contents of the boxes. When I reported this to the partner, he went ballistic. The office manager rushed over to his office to apologize and assured him that the cleaning people were going to go down to the garbage bins and find the papers. After meeting with the partner, the office manager came to my office looking as if she had seen a ghost. I asked her what had happened. She was clearly very upset and nervous. She informed me that the partner insisted that she personally dive in the garbage bin for the papers. And off she went diving in the garbage bin; digging through tons of all kinds of trash, for hours, until she found every document.

NO DRINKING AND DRIVING. One morning while sitting in my office, I received a telephone call from the office manager. She said the owner of the taxicab service used by my firm called her about an issue they were having with one of our employees. He told her they were receiving daily calls from an employee for taxi pickup service from our office to her home. On many occasions, however, he reported that they were also making pit stops before taking the employee home. She was having the drivers make one or two stops along the way. I asked the office manager to call the taxicab company and request copies of all the signed taxi vouchers she used. Well, there were at least fifty of them over a 2½-month period. After considering why the employee was using so many taxi vouchers, we discovered she was also reporting overtime on those nights. The staff could have a free taxi ride home if they worked overtime past 7:00 p.m. during the week. This person was reporting overtime almost every night. After checking with her supervisor, we learned that she was not working overtime as often as she reported.

As it turned out, the employee was a regular at one of the bars in downtown DC. She would go down to the bar, drink herself into oblivion, and have the firm's taxi service drive her home. Her pit stops were mostly to pick up her fourteen-month-old child from the day-care center. Worse yet, she would sometimes stop at her local liquor store before getting her child. And just think, all of this while she was as drunk as Coota Brown. To show how drunk she was, many of the taxi vouchers we received barely had her full signature—some would have her first name and the first letter of her last name, some would have the first letter of her first name and the first letter of her last name and everything in between would be missing. We later learned that this woman, in addition to being an abuser of alcohol, was a habitual abuser of the Virginia taxi system and that the State of Virginia had a warrant out for her arrest for taxi fraud. Interestingly, she did own a vehicle, but no drinking and driving for her!

THE JAILBIRD. One of our employees went to her supervisor to report a conversation she overheard between two new employees in the employee lounge. This employee was very nervous and upset. She told her supervisor she had overheard one of the new employees say he had murdered someone and escaped from prison. She also reported that the new employee was not using his true name. She was so nervous and upset she wanted to leave the office for the rest of the day. Before leaving, the supervisor brought her to my office and asked her to tell me exactly what she heard. She repeated the same story to me, and because she was so upset, we decided it would be better to allow her to leave the office until we could get to the bottom of the story. Moments after the employee left, we began receiving calls from other employees who were concerned about "the escaped convict" working in our office. The woman had told this story to several employees before going to her supervisor. Well, the new employee had, in fact, been to prison. He had been a counselor in the prison system and left (escaped) because the job became too stressful. What this guy said was that he had worked at a prison in Virginia for five years, but he was afraid he would have to "kill" someone, so when the opportunity presented itself, he "escaped." The only thing the woman heard was prison for five years, kill someone and escaped, and she started a wildfire.

A LEGAL BEAT DOWN. I received a telephone call from a HR director at another DC law firm. This person informed me that inappropriate e-mails from someone in my office were being sent to someone in her office, and her firm was particularly concerned about the messages. Apparently, one of the young male attorneys in my office was dating a young female attorney in her office. The e-mails confirmed that several weeks before, the attorney from my office had, in one of the popular bars in Georgetown, beaten the female attorney to the point she had to be taken to the hospital and was hospitalized for several days. The other law firm requested we notify our attorney that if he continued sending e-mails to this woman at their firm, they were going to notify the authorities. The attorney was sending pleas for forgiveness to this woman. Her refusal to accept his apology and her request that he not e-mail her again, clearly, from his e-mail messages, made him very angry. We told the attorney to stop the nonsense immediately, or he would be terminated. I'm glad we could intervene on this!

EMPLOYEE ASSISTANCE ON PORN. The company that administered our employee assistance program (EAP) called to inform me that we needed to send out a communication to all employees regarding the inappropriateness of accessing pornography in the workplace. Apparently, the government discovered that this issue had become so prevalent in the workplace that they needed to conduct a study. The results of this study were staggering. It showed a huge percentage of the workforce was accessing the Internet for personal use in the workplace. The study also showed that many employees were accessing pornography from the workplace. Our EAP representative contacted me immediately after the results of this study were published. The EAP representative knew employees in my office were accessing pornography, but due to the confidential nature of the relationship, they could not give us the names of the employees. Thus, we immediately issued a notice to all employees stating that they would be subject to disciplinary action, up to and including termination, for accessing pornography in our office. This communication also stated that accessing child pornography would be grounds for immediate termination. Apparently, many of our employees, attorneys, and staff were accessing pornography from the office. This was confirmed by our IT Department. They were often required to assist employees who found themselves in a situation where their computers would lock up, and they needed the IT staff to unlock their computers. No reboot here!

BONNIE AND CLYDE. One morning, I received a telephone call from a nearby federal penitentiary. The prison official was trying to track down the sender of a package they received for one of their prisoners. The package was sent in an envelope with my firm's name on it. I didn't think too much about it at the time because employees, although they were not supposed to, had been known to use the firm's envelopes. The caller began to explain the contents of the envelope. There were five one-hundred-dollar bills in the envelope. Again, I thought it was strange, but so what, someone sent their loved one money in prison. I was so dumb; it didn't hit me right away why someone would need cash, especially $500 cash, in prison. As the caller continued telling me about this package, I realized that this was serious business. The sender had placed a fifty-page book of sheet music in the envelope. The one-hundred-dollar bills were taped individually to the back of certain sheets of music. Using an envelope from a law firm was very calculating because, per the prison official, they don't normally open mail from a prisoner's attorney. This package, however, looked very suspicious to them. It was covered in postage stamps and this was a huge red flag because normally law firm mailings have meter postage. Also, the package had been mailed from a different city than the law firm address. Thus, the prison official opened the package.

As it turned out, the prisoner had been charged with armed robbery and attempted murder. He was being held in a federal prison awaiting his sentencing. The prison official gave me the name of the prisoner to whom the package had been sent and asked me if the name meant anything to me. Initially it did not, but I agreed to check our employee roster and call them back. Immediately after I got off the line, it occurred to me that it might be someone in our office. This one employee had used a couple different names during her employment, one of which was the same as the prisoner's last name. I felt very befuddled about all of this because the person was one of the firm's most respected employees. She was extremely dependable and was always a very hard worker. She was very well put together, extremely articulate, and came across as a model citizen. She was a mother and a wife.

It was very hard for me to believe this woman was at all connected to this situation. I initially thought that perhaps this was some relative of hers (a cousin, uncle, or brother) to whom the package was sent. I pulled her personnel file and checked the emergency contact information. The name she listed as her first emergency contact was the same name as the prisoner. Not only was he listed; he was listed as her husband.

Suddenly, I felt my heart racing, and my stomach sank. I could not believe what I was seeing. I looked at the emergency contact form off and on for about ten minutes before I was convinced that my eyes were not playing tricks on me. I could not imagine what had gone on. I reported this to our risk management attorneys. At their direction, I called the prison official and notified them that we had an employee with the same last name as their prisoner. They informed me that because the package had no name of sender, they were going to keep the money. I tried to convince them that since the firm name was on the envelope as the sender, they should send the money to the firm. This was such a horrible situation that I was hoping to get the money back to this poor woman, but the prison flat out refused. Perhaps I should not have tried to get the money back for her, but I could not help it.

We notified the employee's supervisor of the situation and the supervisor, also, could not believe it. He told me he had just inquired about the employee's husband and was told he had gone out of town for a car race. The supervisor had no idea anything was going on with his employee's family. The employee had worked for him over twenty years and was always a loyal, hardworking person. He was shocked. After speaking to the supervisor, the COO and I spoke to the employee, who initially denied everything. Then she changed her story and claimed the prisoner was her cousin. I told her I had confirmed that it was her husband. I also told her the firm's only issue with her, in that matter, was that she inappropriately used firm stationery, which was a violation of firm policy. I told her that because she had always been a model employee, we would excuse the offense that time only. She was extremely humiliated and assured us this would never happen again. The supervisor and I were feeling very bad for her and believed it was unfortunate this wonderful person had been forced into single parenthood with several children. Per the prison officials, her husband was going to be in prison for a very, very long time.

After I returned to my office, I could barely get any work done. My thoughts were consumed with this woman's horrible situation. She was such a nice person and a very hard worker that I could not help feeling sorry for her and her children. Then, suddenly, my grandfather Harmon popped into my head, and I started remembering how many people thought he was something that he was not. Then a very different picture began to form in my mind. Past conversations and certain facts about this employee began to replay in my head. I started to recall things about this woman that made my imagination go wild.

The employee worked many hours of overtime on a consistent basis. No matter how busy, no matter how slow, her overtime remained consistent. At one point, the firm decided that the amount of overtime employees could work had to be drastically reduced. This caused several employees to realize a pretty substantial reduction in compensation. In this employee's case, the reduction was about $30,000 per year. She was extremely upset about the cutback in overtime and the new overtime policy, which eliminated 99 percent of all firm chargeable overtime. Most of the overtime this individual worked was firm chargeable.

Many months after the firm's cutback in overtime, there were a string of bank robberies in a nearby community, and the persons had recently been caught. I never heard the details of the apprehensions, but it was all feeling like it could be related to this employee. Several months later, and out of nowhere, the secretary began to show signs of degradation in her personal appearance. Her hair was no longer as well groomed. Her clothes were no longer as well cared for as before. She was no longer parking in the parking garage, which was very expensive. She parked on the streets of downtown DC, which required her to run outside every two hours to feed the parking meter or move her vehicle. Suddenly, the very expensive car she had been driving was gone, and you could often hear her complaints about things being so expensive. People in the office started making comments about the difference in her appearance. Most people thought it was stress from losing the overtime that was dragging her down. Perhaps it was the stress of this dark secret and the loss of her husband that was dragging her down. The whole situation was so very sad.

One morning, I saw the secretary driving to the office in, what appeared to be an extremely racy Camaro from the 1960s. This car looked like it should have been on a professional racetrack. It was souped up and very loud. She was driving like a bat out of hell—dodging in and out of lanes, maneuvering that car like a true professional race car driver. As I was remembering this, suddenly, the voice of her supervisor entered my head. It was as if he was sitting beside me saying, "She told me her husband had been training to become a race car driver." It was at that moment my imagination went completely wild. When I arrived at work that morning, I sat in my office staring out the window in a daze. I imagined the loss of overtime caused the secretary and her husband to cut back on more than they wanted. So, did someone decide they could rob a bank and get away with it? If you are going to rob a bank, you must have a getaway car and a person to drive it—Bonnie and Clyde taught us that. Her husband took race car driving lessons. Did she take lessons also? Did he teach her everything he learned about race car driving? This is the story my imagination told me:

After many months of race car driving practice, they decided it was time to put it to the test. So, they planned their first big heist. A friend of her husband decided to go along with this grand plan as well. Since one of the local banks had been robbed successfully on several occasions in the past, they decided that bank would be a perfect trial run. The trial run was very successful, and they felt prepared to go for the real deal. When they arrived at the bank, her husband and his friend went inside and left her in the running car. When they came out and jumped into the car, she sped off, and they were safe. When they reached their home, their adrenaline was so high it took them all night to calm down. They had gotten away with lots of cash and could hardly believe it. After the first robbery was so successful, they were convinced this money was far too easy to get. The second time out, it was Christmas in April. The third time out, something went very wrong, and Clyde was faced with getting caught red-handed or shooting someone. He chose the latter. Bonnie escaped with not even a trace of evidence that she was ever involved.

When I snapped out of my daydream, I thought I had just come out of a nightmare. However, Bonnie remained at the firm for many years afterward without incident.

OFFICE ENTREPRENEUR. One of our employees had been with the firm a very short amount of time, I believe no more than a year. She was a very impressive worker, and her supervisors had nothing but good things to say about her and her work product. This woman showed up to work every day, was always early, and would often stay late. One afternoon the receptionist called me to say that an unusual number of visitors were coming to the office for this employee, and she thought I should know. In addition, the facilities staff began reporting that this same person was often seen taking outsiders into empty attorney offices. As it turned out, the employee was running a catering business and was using our office to meet with her clients and to host taste tests. She would go into an empty office, spread a tablecloth over the desk and set up china, silverware, wine glasses and the works, and have people come in and taste samples of her food. That entrepreneur had to move herself and her business elsewhere!

ANOTHER ONE BITES THE DUST. One of my responsibilities was to recruit secretaries for several attorneys that just could not keep a secretary. One attorney had eight different secretaries in six months; another changed secretaries every other month for almost one year; and the grand prize winner is the person who, in one year, had twenty different secretaries. Collectively, some of the reasons for so many changes were: accusations by secretaries that the attorneys were "crazy"; the attorneys claimed the secretaries were crazy and incompetent—incompetence was one of the main reasons given for needing a change; some of the attorneys were yellers and screamers, and in some cases yelling and screaming profanities; some were downright abusive—mentally and emotionally; and some were accused of being "pure buttholes." One of my colleagues from another law firm convinced her managing partner to implement a policy that required the attorneys to pay all the recruiting expenses for hiring new secretaries after the third request for a change. These expenses would run thousands of dollars. My office adopted that policy, and it reduced the number of unnecessary requests for secretarial changes.

LOVE OR LUST? The first issue I had to deal with at one of the firms was an owner that had been sleeping with one of the employees. The employee claimed to be in love with the owner. Well, I didn't think it was love. I was of the belief that the employee was fascinated by the owner's power and money. Prior to me starting at the firm, they apparently had a steamy relationship and were a hot item in private. They were never in public together, but he frequented her very expensive townhouse near the office. In fact, one morning another owner was walking into the office and spotted this owner and the employee passionately kissing on the employee's front porch. This relationship became so intense that more and more people were beginning to talk about it, so I had to bring the managing partner in to control the owner. A fine job he did—a week after speaking to the owner, someone found a note on the employee's desk from the owner with a wax candle on top of the note. Don't ask!

SCOPE OR LISTERINE? Several employees came to me to report a bad odor they smelled on one of the employees. They felt the employee had a drinking problem. I called the employee's supervisors to find out if they noticed any unusual odors, but they had not. I found this to be strange because the supervisors worked very closely with the employee. However, because of the number of complaints and the fact that the secretary had begun to miss work quite frequently on Mondays and Fridays, I spoke to her about the complaints. She denied drinking on the job and stated she was merely a social drinker and nothing more. She told me she was having some dental work done, and people must have smelled the medication she was taking, which had the scent of alcohol. I told her if she could get a note from her dentist verifying this information, I would put it in her personnel file, and this issue would end there. She said, "Sure, no problem."

Several weeks and excuses later, I decided to unofficially check with someone in the dental profession. The father of a good friend of mine had been in the dental profession for over forty years. So I called him. Without telling him what the issue was, I asked if he knew of any type of medication prescribed for dental work that would have the scent of liquor. He said in a very serious and professional manner, "In the dental profession, we call that Scotch." Well, a couple of weeks later, the secretary did in fact bring in a note from her dentist stating that she was being treated by their office, but nothing about medication that smells like liquor. I put the note in her file and decided if I did not receive any more complaints about this, I would drop it, but if I did, I would have to take further action.

A few weeks later, the estranged boyfriend of the employee called me. He knew all about our request for a doctor's note and wanted me to know that the employee had given us a bogus doctor's note. He said that she had a drinking problem and that she was worried she would be fired, so she paid a dentist $500 for the note. Don't know how true this is, but I found it odd that he would call at the time he called and give me the information he gave me. We received no more complaints about smelling liquor on the employee, and eventually she left the firm.

FINDING NEMO. One of the employees in the office was very "crafty." She was a craft queen. She made everything—holiday wreaths, miniature Christmas trees, jewelry, pillows—you name it, she made it. She came into the office one Monday with a gorgeous tall glass bowl with very rich-colored stones in the bottom and a beautiful live green plant bursting out of the top. There was water in the bowl with a spectacular-looking Japanese fighting fish gracefully swimming around and around the bottom. She put the bowl in a prominent place on her desk. This was her advertisement, and it worked. Many of the employees wanted one of these bowls for their desk. I had no idea this was the hot new item in the office until all hell broke loose.

Within a couple of weeks, there were several major disasters. One of the attorneys called me, and he was enraged because his secretary had knocked her fishbowl over on her desk and ruined some client documents; a supervisor in one of the administrative departments called me extremely upset because he was trying to get work done, and an employee in his department was in the ladies' room for a half hour cleaning her fishbowl; and the grand finale happened when the cleaning lady's glasses were broken and one of her teeth was chipped. Someone had cleaned a fishbowl in one of the kitchen sinks, and a couple of the stones had fallen down the drain. When the cleaning lady hit the garbage disposal switch, out flew the stones, one cracking her glasses and the other hitting her in the mouth, cracking one of her false teeth. That did it for the fishbowls. The firm paid to have the cleaning lady's glasses and tooth repaired, and I sent out a notice that all fishbowls had to be removed from the office by close of business that day.

YOU HAUL, PLEASE. One afternoon an e-mail flashed across my screen from one of the owners. This person was having an addition put onto his home and was giving away several items on a "first-come, first-serve" basis. The items were mostly kitchen appliances. Well, at the time, I was having my basement finished and was just at the point where I was ready to purchase appliances. The list of items being given away included an overhead oven, a cooktop stove, a marble tile wall cabinet, and a few other pieces. The item that sparked my interest was the cooktop stove. I immediately called the owner and arranged to look at the stove. When I told my husband about it, he was initially hesitant. However, I convinced him the items would be fine because one of the firm's owners was giving them away. I told him I could not believe he would offer anything that was no good. So we trucked over to his house on that Saturday and found the cooktop, which was with all the other items in his backyard, uncovered and in such horrible condition that I could not imagine anyone wanting any of these things. They were dirty and rickety. My husband was so angry he told the owner, "We can't do anything with this stuff. It's no good."

I could tell the owner was embarrassed, but I also knew he was embarrassed only because my husband told him the items were no good. I guess he expected us to like them and be happy to have them even though he knew they were only good for the trash. When my husband and I returned to the car, he said, "Don't ever tell me about anything those owners at your firm are giving away." My husband believed the owner was too cheap to pay someone to haul it away and decided to offer the items for free to the staff. It seemed as if he was banking on firm employees hauling his trash.

MIRACULOUS RECOVERY. One of the secretaries in my office had been out on medical leave for about eighteen weeks. I contacted this individual to let her know she had exceeded the time her position had to be held. At the onset of the conversation, the employee immediately began telling me how sick she still was and that she did not know when she would be able to return to work. I told her the attorneys she worked for were growing concerned because they needed to have a regularly assigned person. I offered her an additional two weeks of personal leave and informed her that if she was unable to return to work after the two-week period, we would have to terminate her employment. Miraculously, the employee could return to work that next Monday with a doctor's note stating there were no restrictions.

PUT YOUR CLOTHES ON. The director of our Computer Department came to my office to show me a large stack of papers that had been printed from one of our employee's e-mail boxes. In one communication, the employee was engaged in a discussion with her boyfriend about why she had not removed her nude photographs from the Internet. There were also communications between this employee and others where the employee was clearly speaking in code. However, there was nothing we felt we should be alarmed about. Then one afternoon I received a telephone call from a gentleman who would only identify himself as the live-in boyfriend of "Scope or Listerine?" Remember her, the secretary who claimed to be on medication that caused her to smell like liquor? Well, this was her boyfriend (once again providing me with information) telling me that "Put Your Clothes On" was dealing drugs in our office. He said he knew this because "Scope or Listerine" used to purchase drugs from "Put Your Clothes On" for him. So, this person was definitely a nudie online, but was she a drug dealer also? Well, drug dealer, or not, "Put Your Clothes On" got herself fired for inappropriate use of firm technology.

BEAUTY IS ONLY SKIN DEEP. One of the young women in the office had a bad reputation for wearing inappropriate clothes to work. Her reputation preceded her. When I finally met her for the first time, she was wearing a long (right above the ankle) black skirt that was made from yarn and in a window pane pattern—an open window pane pattern. Under this garment was a very, very short black satin lining that perhaps came to the middle of her thigh. I could not believe my eyes, but I let it slide because it was my first day on the job. As I later learned, this woman was very skilled at going right up to the line and in some cases crossing over the line of the office attire policy. Finally, the day came when I was done with her inappropriate attire.

I was walking past her desk one morning, and she was sitting with what appeared to be an extremely short skirt. The way she was sitting, I could see her panties. When I kindly and quietly told her that her skirt was too short, she stood to show me that, in her opinion, it was not. I told her that although it did not appear too short when she was standing, it was far too short when she sat down. She was adamant that I was wrong, and finally I asked her to come to my office. I needed to read her the riot act in private. I told her she pushed the limits on more than one occasion and that I could no longer tolerate her inappropriate attire. I also told her she could not wear that skirt in the office anymore, and she would be sent home if there were any more violations of the firm's office attire policy. This woman, with a very serious look on her face, said, "I can't help it if I am beautiful." So does that mean beauty trumps inappropriate attire? From that day forward, although she got close to the line, I did not have to speak to her about appropriate office attire.

POSTMASTER GENERAL. Our facilities manager received a telephone call from the postmaster general's office. They informed her that they pulled five very large boxes from the tarmac at a national airport in the area being shipped to Africa from our office. These boxes had stale postage on them from our postage meter. Stale postage is when the date on the postmark is far earlier than the date the package goes out. The Facilities Department did some research and found that one of the employees had been taking postage from the firm's postage meter. The total was something like $780. The executive director, facilities manager, and I met with this young man and told him what had been reported by the postmaster's office. Initially, he denied everything. We told him that the return address on the packages was his home address. The executive director pleaded with him to tell the truth, and he confessed. We immediately terminated his employment. About six months after he was terminated, he filed a claim with the EEOC Office charging me, the one who had the least to do with it, with terminating him because he rejected my sexual advances. The EEOC ruled the claim unfounded. It was all a big lie, and he knew it. For some reason, he took this whole thing out on me. Why me?

A BURNING JOB SEARCH. One Saturday afternoon, I walked out to my mailbox to check that day's mail. When I opened the mailbox, I found a folded newspaper. Why would a newspaper be in my mailbox? It appeared to be the classified section. As it turned out, someone had put the employment section of a local newspaper in my mailbox. What was unbelievable about this situation was that a hole had been burned right through the middle of the paper. I took it as a message for me. Several weeks before this incident, I fired an employee who forged my signature on a letter to an insurance company. The letter was verifying lost wages that were being claimed—lots of lost wages of which were not her correct salary. I'm not saying that the terminated employee burned the employment section of the local newspaper and put it in my mailbox, but it is possible. I reported the incident to my office, and the police and kept it moving.

B. PHOENIX

THE SUPREME SUPREMES. A white employee who worked in one of the administrative departments came to me very upset and turned in her resignation. When speaking to her about why she was resigning, she said she felt discriminated against. She told me on many occasions the black manager over her department would take the two black employees to lunch and leave her behind. She also claimed that the black manager was always treating her like she was a low-class citizen. The straw that broke the camel's back for her was when the manager and the other two employees were preparing to portray Diana Ross and the Supremes in an office talent show. The white employee wanted so badly to participate but was told by the black manager she could not. When she asked why, the manager stated, "We are portraying the Supremes, and you could not portray either of the Supremes." That being the final straw, the white employee quit.

WHO'S WHO. A highly educated senior partner of the firm came into my office one afternoon to meet with me about an employee-related issue. He walked in and looked over at a photograph I kept on my bookcase. He, in a very pleasant voice, asked, "Who is that distinguished-looking gentlemen? Is that your grandfather?"

At first I thought he was kidding, so I said, "Yes, it is."

Then he replied, "Very nice photo." I thanked him, and we went on with our business, and he left my office. At that point, I realized he was not kidding. The "distinguished-looking gentlemen" in the photograph was Frederick Douglass. And mind you, this was a very common image of Frederick Douglass. Go figure.

HOT POLKA DOTS. The facilities manager had been in the office of one of the partners many times and was always curious about these white polka dots that were on his beautiful black leather chair. This had been bugging the facilities manager for months, but she never said anything about it. Finally, she was in his office one day and could not take it any longer. She asked him why the polka dots were on this beautiful chair. He explained that he was meeting with a female client in his office one day and she apparently became so hot that the polka dots literally came off her dress and stuck to his chair. She thought he was kidding, but he was not. Can you imagine? Her butt must have been oven hot. I mean those things baked into the leather. The facilities manager asked the partner how long ago this had happened. Believe it or not, those polka dots had been infused in that chair for about seven years. Finally, the facilities manager brought in a company that specialized in upholstery cleaning, and they removed all the polka dots.

SECRETARIES—WHO NEEDS THEM? One of my former supervisors was so outside of his mind that when discussing the secretaries in our office being displeased about a merger possibility, he began screaming at the top of his voice, saying, in profane words, that he did not care about the secretaries. "If they want to leave, they can go. I will have all of them replaced in one hour after they are gone." This was said in a meeting with all my peers, most of whom were horrified at these statements. One of my peers, however, agreed with my supervisor. She said the only group the firm could not afford to lose was the associate attorney group because they billed their time. Can you believe these people? The firm employed at least seventy to eighty secretaries. We may not have needed all of them, but I assure you, the firm would have collapsed if all or even most of them walked out.

RAT RACE. One year, my office suffered several floods. There was water and mud everywhere. After all the water and mud had been cleared from the building, we had to wage a war on the rats. Rats and mice were running all over the building. You could be in your office quietly working, and suddenly, you would hear a scream—a rat would have entered someone's office and frightened them. We had to deal with this problem for weeks, and those people who stockpiled unwrapped food in their desks and offices suffered the worst.

SAVE OUR CHILDREN. As you have read, I've heard all kinds of stories over the years in my career, but this was one of the saddest. One of our employees did not report to work one Monday, and we were all very concerned. On Tuesday when he did not show up, I checked with one of his work buddies, who agreed to try to track him down. When the missing employee called me, he said his twelve-year-old son had been shot in the head over the weekend and was in critical condition. He gave me a telephone number to reach him if necessary. Well, I could not get this child out of my mind, so the next morning, I called to check on him and reached the child's mother. I poured out all my sorrow and offered aid from the firm, but the mother, in a very irritated tone of voice said, "Miss, what are you talking about?" I told her we knew that her son had been shot, and we were all so very sorry and prayed that he would pull through this tragedy. In the same tone as she used before, the mother said, "Lady, listen, I am in a rush to get to work. My son is perfectly fine. He is at school as we speak. He and some other boys were playing with an old broken BB gun, and my son hurt his finger trying to fix it. He was never in the hospital, and he is perfectly okay. I don't know where you got your information, but I have to go to work." She hung up the phone, and I sat in my office in total shock.

SCORNED WOMAN. One morning a beautiful, very well-dressed, sexy, hot momma came into our office. She identified herself as a client of one of our partners. When the receptionist called the partner to let him know his client was there, the partner told her to tell the woman he was busy with another client. The next day, the woman came back to the office looking for the partner. Again, he refused to see her. This beauty tried a third time, later that same day, to no avail. On the fourth visit, the woman was very irritated and began making a scene in the main reception area. The receptionist called me to come out and speak to this woman. When I approached her, it was obvious to me she was more than a client. This woman acted as if she had been loved and left, and she wanted her man back. All I could think was that the partner must have laid it on her. She was desperate for him. I convinced her to leave by promising I would track the partner down and ask him to call her if she promised not to return to our office. I kept my promise, and she kept hers. She did not return to our office, but she made it her full-time job to hang around the courtyard of the main building looking for her man.

The partner did not want anything done to this woman, but the COO was so freaked out about it that he decided the "smart" thing to do was to move the partner to a "safe office location." So, he moved him to our other building directly across the street. A real safe place, huh? The partner still ended up being in the main building just as much as he was in the "safe location" without incident.

GO AHEAD AND CHECK. One of the supervisors came to me because an employee had been charging overtime each night. Someone in payroll, however, had been seeing this person on the bus leaving the office an hour before he reported leaving. The supervisor and I called the employee into a meeting to discuss the matter. He emphatically denied leaving before his overtime ended. He stated very firmly and specifically, "I work every night until eight o'clock." There was nothing about this person that would make you think he was lying. We told him someone reported seeing him on the bus each night at seven o'clock. He said, "There has been a big mistake, because I never leave at seven. The other people who work with me know that I am here every night until eight o'clock." At this point, I knew there must have been some mistake. The employee was too sincere. So I asked him if he would mind me checking with the other employees to see if they would verify the time he normally leaves. He said, "Sure, go ask them. They'll tell you." So, I did.

I left the employee in the office with his supervisor, and I went to his department to find the other two employees. They both were there and when asked, they both said, "He normally leaves at around five minutes to seven, because he takes the seven o'clock bus each night." I asked them both if they were sure, and they both said yes. I could not believe what I was hearing. This guy either thought these people did not know the time he left or thought they would lie for him. They both acted as if this guy's departure time was common knowledge. When I went back into the supervisor's office, I said, "I'm sorry, but the other two employees said you leave every night at around five minutes to seven, because you take the seven o'clock bus."

He looked me square in the eyes and said, "Okay, so am I fired?"

The supervisor and I said simultaneously "Yes." I told him I would get his final paycheck, and his supervisor would escort him to his desk to get his personal belongings and see him out. I guess sometimes you can roll the dice, and it works, and sometimes it doesn't.

PETTY CASH. It was about 9:00 a.m. one Friday when one of the accounting clerks came into my office with a very frightened look on her face. She said someone had broken into the petty cash office and stolen the money from the petty cash box. The safe had been tampered with, and the office had been trashed. There was about $5K in the petty cash box, but it was now gone. After the word about the petty cash theft started spreading throughout the office, we received a telephone call from one of the partners who had heard through the grapevine that one of our employees had been terminated the day before. The partner called to inform us that the terminated employee had entered the office with him the night before. I'm not saying the terminated employee came back to the firm at nine o'clock the night he was terminated to steal the petty cash money, I'm just saying …

YOU'RE UNDER ARREST. One of our attorneys was married to a Maryland state trooper. This man was the perfect stature of a stereotypical state trooper. His presence commanded respect. He was tall and extremely well built, almost a giant of a man. Several of us had previously met him outside the office. One afternoon, one of the guys from the mailroom came up to the reception area and said that a state trooper (a friend of someone in the office) was on his way up and that they were going to play a joke on one of the guys in the office.

When the state trooper arrived, just as planned, he walked up to the receptionist and stated that he was there to see John Doe. The receptionist called John Doe and told him someone was there to see him. John told her he would be right up. He came whistling and singing down the hall, as he often did (not sure who he was expecting to see), and when he spotted the state trooper, without a word spoken by anyone, he turned and made a beeline and began running down the hall away from us. The person who pranked him went running after, trying to convince him that it was a prank, but it took a lot of coaching to bring John down off his fear high.

YOU WANNA GET AWAY? One morning I showed up at a law firm in town where I was teaching a supervisory class. When I walked into the room, I noticed a woman that had not been there before. She looked very familiar to me, but I couldn't figure out why. This was a six-week class, and we were already halfway through it. Therefore, it was strange that a new person would be signed up right in the middle, but I carried on. Before the class got started, I asked the new person to give her name and to tell one thing about herself that she thought the group might find interesting. She introduced herself and said that she had just returned from vacationing in Europe. She had a very odd name, and I recognized it, but I didn't say anything to her at the time. I decided to wait until our first break. When we took our first break, she disappeared so quickly from the class I was unable to say anything to her. During the lunch break, she and I and a few other folks were leaving out at the same time. She looked at me and smiled. It was obvious she did not remember me, but I remembered her very well. It had probably been about fifteen to twenty years since we saw each other, but we had spoken on the telephone several times over the years. She was in the HR profession as well and had just been hired by a very large law firm that sent all its new managers to my class.

As we walked out of the class, I said, "Pat, you don't remember me, do you?"

She looked at me and smiled, saying, "No, I'm sorry, I don't."

I said, "I'm B. Phoenix," thinking this would trigger something, but it did not. Again, I said, "B. Phoenix."

Again, she looked at me, but this time she had a semifrown on her face. She said, "I know a B. Phoenix, but it is a different person."

"Are you sure?" I asked.

She looked at me with wrinkles in her forehead and said, "The B. Phoenix I know, she and I are very close. I speak to her on a regular basis, and I see her quite frequently."

So I, still totally confused, said, "Well, it must be someone else because I have not seen you in at least fifteen years." Then she said with a little indignity, "Oh, no, I only know one B. Phoenix, and I talk to her all the time."

Well, at this point, I'm thinking in the words of my baby sister, "What-the-what"? So I said, "Okay. It must be someone else." She smiled and started to walk away, when I said, "Pat, from where do you know your B. Phoenix?"

She looked at me as if she was referring to the president of the United States, and said, "The B. Phoenix I know is the director of HR for Wilcox & Andrews."

What was this woman doing? Was she name-dropping? I could not believe my ears. I looked her square in the eyes and said, "Pat, I am B. Phoenix, the former director of HR for Wilcox & Andrews."

The expression on her face only reminded me of the airline commercial, "Wanna get away?" She could not say a word and after about thirty seconds, she just walked away. Wrongly dropping my name on me! Who does that!

GOOD COP, BAD COP. I promoted one of the legal secretaries to my department as the new HR manager. This woman was extremely intelligent and had been a valued employee for years. She attended law school and did very well, but for personal reasons did not continue her pursuit in practicing law. We had known each other for many years when I promoted her. During her first week in the new HR manager position, we had to terminate one of the employees for insubordination. This guy was an excellent worker and very smart but had only been with the firm for a little over a year. His supervisor, however, was just pure dumb—I mean dumber than a box of rocks. This supervisor was constantly complaining about anything and everything the guy did. Well, the day came when the employee could not take it anymore. The supervisor showed up to work one morning in a foul mood and called the employee into his office with some real nonsense. The employee, who was at his wit's end, told the supervisor he was the dumbest jackass he had ever met. He threw a folder on his desk and walked out. The supervisor reported it to me and wanted the guy terminated immediately.

I gave the new HR manager the details of the termination and told her that I wanted her to sit in on the discussion, but that she was not to say anything—just listen and observe. The guy came in to the HR conference room, and we all sat down. I explained that, although he had been a good worker, we had to terminate his employment for flagrant insubordination. He totally understood and knew he would be terminated, but, understandably, he was still hurt. I explained that we were giving him a generous severance package, that our employee relations person would have his personal effects delivered to his home, and that he needed to leave the office then. The new HR manager was very sad about having to let this guy go, and as we got up to see him out, she stretched out her arms and said, "Awwww, let me give you a hug." I could not believe my ears. I told her not to say a word! When the guy left, I looked at her and in a very stern voice said, "I told you not to say a word! I should punch you in your face!" The HR manager was sad for this guy, and in a sad voice, she said, "I'm sorry. I felt so bad for him, and besides I thought we should be good cop, bad cop." At that point, we both laughed and continued with our day.

EXCUSED TARDINESS. One employee was working for me as my administrative assistant. This individual had a very odd personality, but it did not stop me from giving her a fair chance. She was about five feet tall and wore a very bad-looking long black wig. Her upper body was very small and narrow in structure, but her lower body was huge. She had a butt so big you could use it as a tray. She was in her midtwenties, but she spoke with a very childlike voice—extremely high-pitched and very squeaky. She was no dummy by any standard. Odd, yes; dumb, no. She had not done a great job for me, and there were a couple of incidents that would have caused most people to throw in the towel, but I felt strongly that I wanted to work with her and teach her. At the end of her first six weeks, I could tell she was getting very nervous about whether I was planning to keep her or not. She suddenly was overly apologetic whenever she made even the slightest mistake. I tried to calm her by telling her when things were not a big deal.

One morning, this young woman came to my office door. She had this look on her face like she was coming to tell me something that would not make me happy. She stood at the threshold of my door and in that baby-like tone of voice said, "Can I come in and talk to you?" I said yes. She then asked if she could close the door. I said yes again. Her body language was telling me this was going to be something wild. She began repeating over and over, "This is so embarrassing." After she repeated "this is so embarrassing" about five more times, I said, "Just spit it out." My tone was harsh because I was sick of her performance. I knew this was a big act. I always believed she thought her baby-like voice would get her more attention. So, I never fed into it. I never showed any emotion. I always looked at her with a very straight face and dealt with her in a firm manner. As she began to tell her story, she moved to the very edge of her seat and grasped both hands and began rubbing them together. I pretended I didn't see any of this.

Finally, she was telling her story. She said, "Um, um, last night, my boyfriend and I, we, we were, we were; this is so embarrassing; okay, okay, we were, this is so hard for me, but I need to tell you; we were, oh God, we were ..." (By now, I am contemplating either throwing my stapler at her or stabbing her with my letter opener). Her voice was getting squeakier and squeakier, and it was getting on my last nerve; however, I refused to let her know this was bothering me in any way. So, I remained calm with a blank face and said, "Just spit it out. I have to get back to work." She started all over again. "Um, um, last night, my boyfriend, my boyfriend and I, we, we were, we were having sex" (she took a very deep breath and paused for, I know, twenty seconds) "and, and, and his condom got stuck in me."

I thought I was going to vomit all over myself. The thought of this was making me sick to my stomach. After another very long pause, she said, "I was so embarrassed that I did not want to go to the hospital, so I just waited until this morning and called my doctor, and he told me I should drink lots of water today, and the condom would come out of me on its own." I thought about the psycho technology person and suddenly could relate to her feelings of violence. I found myself thinking, *Should I choke you now? Should I choke you now?* But I kept my poker face on and said nothing. I just looked blankly at her. Then she said, "But I was standing at the bus stop this morning, and I suddenly had to go to the bathroom, so I rushed to the burger shop. You know, the one downtown near the metro station. I went in there to use the bathroom, and guess what?" (She was looking at me as if she expected me to guess.) I just stared at her. Then she said, "The condom came out of me in the toilet, so I rushed back out, but I had missed my bus. I'm so sorry, but that's why I was seven minutes late this morning."

IT WAS A BIG MISTAKE. On a cold day in December, I was called by one of the employees at the firm. The person told me that Liza was caught on camera stealing a five-carat diamond ring from her supervisor. She was fired. This left her supervisor crushed and in disbelief for a long time afterward. Many of Liza's colleagues were in shock too—some believed it, and some didn't.

Shortly after the fallout, I ran into one of her close friends at another law firm, and she informed me of the situation and explained that "it was all a big mistake." She said Liza took the diamond ring mistakenly. She explained that the ring had been delivered to Liza's supervisor, but Liza thought it was something she had ordered. People reportedly saw Liza wearing a very expensive-looking diamond ring. She was fired and made to return the ring; however, her friend explained that the reason Liza was fired was because she refused her supervisor's sexual advances, and he used the "mistakenly stolen ring" as an excuse to fire her.

THANK GOD I'M FIRED. I fired a lot of people over my career, but I only got a few different reactions—one reaction, I only got once. One of my assistants was a very good person, but she was totally distracted with her personal and outside interests. I warned her on at least five or six different occasions that she needed to improve, or I would have to fire her. Well, the day came, and I had to fire her. After she left my office, I could hear someone yelling and screaming outside my window. I looked out, and it was the woman I had just fired. She was yelling, screaming, and dancing through the courtyard, saying, "Yippeee, woo hoooo!" Her hands were raised in the air waving like she just didn't care. At first, I was feeling very sad that I had to fire her, but when I saw her out my window, I thought to myself if I had known it was going to be that good to her, I would have fired the little hussy weeks ago.

Epilogue

IN THE BEGINNING, God gave me unbelievable strength. For nine months, I survived being in a womb that was totally constricted. Miraculously, I was born a healthy, beautiful baby weighing close to ten pounds out of a pregnancy that should not have gone full term. In addition, I enjoyed all the pleasures of a happy young girl. It is ironic that I, as a fetus, had nothing; as a child and adolescent had everything; had to start my adult life with nothing, but reached a point where I was one of the highest-paid individuals in my profession, and got there without education beyond high school; and have people in my life who love me unconditionally. I know I have always had the favor of God on my life, and I am eternally grateful to Him!

Thus far, my personal adult life has been very interesting. The loss of Cicely was extremely deep and everlasting. I married at an early age and suffered the death of my firstborn child when she was just one year old. Years later, I gave birth to two other children, both beautiful and healthy. I survived divorce after thirty-five years of marriage (thirty of which were very happy and good years). I have always held positions in my career for which, under normal circumstances, one would not have qualified. And although I grew up in the church, it wasn't until 1999 that I gave my life to Christ and began a new journey.

In late 2000, the one-plus packs of cigarettes I was smoking each day went away, the ten to fifteen cups of coffee I was drinking each day went away, the foul language I was using on a regular basis went away, and the neglect I bestowed upon my body for many years ceased. I decided I had to take further action to get to where God would have me. So, for the next three years, I began studying the Bible, fasting, praying, and taking better care of my body. In the summer of 2004, I registered for college. By 2013, I was in divorce court, and in 2014, I completed a master's in business administration. During the first five years after I gave my life to Christ, God began revealing to me what was already there—that all things truly are possible with Him. This journey began with the restoration of my mind, body and soul, and it is a great pleasure to still be a work in progress. Another great pleasure I have is restoring old furniture and relishing in the results. I can't wait to see what the results are when God completes His restoration of me!

LETTER TO CEOS

Dear CEOs:

I encourage you to pay very close attention to everyone who has any control over your business. Having said that, although you must give people the autonomy to manage when they can do so, you still need to hold them accountable. And remember, everybody, including you, needs to be held accountable to somebody, and some folks need to be held accountable to somebodies. Additionally, you must be sure these individuals do not allow their personal agendas to negatively affect your business and ultimately your bottom line. When this happens, I call it a personal agenda disorder (PAD). This is a situation whereby managers and/or those who have the power to make decisions allow their personal agendas to negatively affect their decision-making process. Please note: employees at all levels of an organization may suffer from a PAD.

It is my experience that far too many decisions in the workplace are clouded by personal agendas, especially when the full prosperity of the organization is flaunted in the faces of those who have no "need to know." This problem, in my opinion, is multiplied when those individuals (who have no need to know but know) believe they are unfairly compensated. I caution you to take very seriously this "need to know" statement. Some folks are tricky enough to make you think they "need to know" certain information, but examine very closely who and what you put in a "need to know" category. This will help you avoid individuals with a PAD.

Anyone who demonstrates that his or her personal agenda comes before the best interest of the business and/or its employees needs to be released from your employ **immediately**. If you have employees in your company who are managers (of a function or people) with any of the following characteristics:

Vindictive, Acquisitive, Envious,

you may need to make some changes, or keep a very close eye on these individuals. If you find that any of your managers, particularly those in high-powered positions, have two or more of these characteristics, you are dealing with a lethal combination and immediate action should be taken to remove them from your employ. Keep in mind, however, that these characteristics may never clearly reveal themselves to you as the CEO. However, for the overall good of the business, I believe it is your responsibility to smoke them out.

Unfortunately, you may find individuals with PAD characteristics at every level of your organization (i.e., owners, presidents, vice presidents, chiefs, directors, managers, supervisors, and employees). These individuals will cause you more grief than you need, and you may find that many of your employees are treated unfairly because of this inappropriate behavior. Ultimately, everyone in the organization relies on you to ensure that all are treated fairly. Therefore, if you identify someone with a PAD (putting his or her personal agenda before your business goals and objectives), and you are the least bit hesitant about letting them go, please remember the old true saying, "One monkey don't stop no show," because that monkey is never guaranteed to be there anyway.

Sincerely,
B. Phoenix

LETTER TO MANAGERS AND SUPERVISORS

Dear Managers and Supervisors:

I am of the belief that when you hire individuals, it is your responsibility to do everything in your power to keep them. Many of you have fallen far too short on nurturing and training your employees. As part of your responsibility, you must ensure that your employees have the proper tools and training needed to be effective workers. More importantly, please be sure to make your expectations clear. This will not only be good for the employee, but for the overall business as well.

The following are a few important points to remember:

1. treat all your employees fairly and equitably;
2. don't ever show favoritism and hold everyone to the same standard;
3. don't give, or allow any employee to be given, preferential treatment for no good reason (you may believe an individual employee can do more than a full team; however, unless you are staffed incorrectly, this will never happen); and
4. figure out a way, in your absence, to learn about the behavior of your "favorite employee"—your "Wonderboy," your "Girl Friday" (you may be very surprised to learn that some of these individuals are not the person you think they are; some of them put on a facade just for you; and remember, in many cases, the phonies are being controlled by their personal agendas.

In addition, don't ever allow an employee to hold you hostage. If an individual should be terminated, don't hesitate to let him or her go, especially if that person has a problem controlling their personal agenda. This is what I call a personal agenda disorder (PAD). A PAD is behavior where the employee puts his or her personal agenda before the business goals and objectives.

The power of someone's personal agenda can be great. It will make an employee do all sorts of crazy things, such as charge the company for time he or she didn't work, or submit expense reimbursements for things he or she never purchased for the business. And some of these individuals will flat out lie to you. In my experience, this does not apply to most employees, but it does apply to enough of them that you should pay close attention to PADs. And please keep your own personal agenda in check by not allowing it to affect your decisions regarding the business and/or your employees. I suggest you use a theory I have used for many years—the JB squared theory (JB squared).

JB squared is a practice used by very experienced law firm administrators that I love and have always admired and respected. JB squared offers ten concepts for managers and supervisors to follow. Basically, it:

1. calls a spade a spade,
2. accepts that things are what they are—it is what it is,
3. has no time for foolishness,
4. stops you dead in your tracks,
5. does not sugar coat an issue,
6. is painfully honest,
7. holds all employees to a high standard,
8. does not give *special* kudos to anyone for doing what he or she is paid to do,
9. does not play political games of any kind, and
10. treats all employees fairly and equitably.

JB squared says that most employees are like children—you must keep expectations high; you sometimes must swallow a bitter pill; you must remember the importance of communication; and you sometimes might just have to step on their necks (not literally, of course).

For the most part, properly managing people puts you in a very difficult world, and I totally understand that, for sure. However, you must be strong, able to fight tough fights (many times alone), recognize when an employee's personal agenda negatively affects business operations, keep your personal agenda in check, and stomach the fact that the world of management can sometimes be a very cold and dark place. It can be a lonely place. Also, remember that being part of management very rarely allows you to be friends with those whom you supervise. However, keep in mind that if one of your employees is a true friend, you can treat him or her like everyone else in your employ, and he or she gives you full respect as the supervisor, you have found, in the words of one of my mentors, "a diamond in the rough."

Sincerely,
B. Phoenix

LETTER TO EMPLOYEES

Dear Employees:

I strongly encourage you to remember what you agree to when you accept a position with a company. Also, you should remember that unless you and the company agree to changes in the original terms of your employment, you must continue upholding your end of the bargain. Too many times in the workplace, I found a scenario such as the following:

An employee is hired to work nine to five and is paid X dollars. Shortly after being hired, the employee reveals a personal need to leave work fifteen minutes early each day, freely does so, but expects no adjustment to his or her leave or pay. This is what I call a personal agenda disorder (PAD). This is a situation whereby you allow your personal agenda to violate company policy or alter your original employment agreement. If this is you, *stop it!*

It is very important that you keep your personal agenda in check so as not to put you in a place of dishonesty that ultimately will negatively affect you, your company, and all other employees. Just as your employer should pay you for the time you work, you should not charge your employer for time you did not work. You may be easily tempted to stretch your time, but don't do it. If you are not earning enough money to support your lifestyle, consider additional employment, a new career, or a new lifestyle. Also, please remember that you are providing your employer a service. Stay fresh on your skill level and don't find yourself on a job for ten years with two years of experience.

To the contrary, your employer should also uphold the agreed-upon terms of your employment. They should respect you as a human being and take care that you are treated fairly and judged based on the merits of your performance and the content of your character only. And finally, never let an employer abuse you or hold you hostage. You should be at peace in your workplace. And in the words of my great-grandmother, "peace of mind is worth a million dollars."

Sincerely,
B. Phoenix

LESSON FOR HR PROFESSIONALS

Dear HR Professionals:

There are many things I could share with you from the HR arena, and perhaps later, I will, but for now, I offer you this: You *must* be able to recognize signs of danger. When those employees who attacked the HR professional referenced in this book began missing work, that was a sign of a problem. When their personal appearance began to change, that was an even bigger sign. When other employees began complaining that these individuals were acting "strangely," that was yet another sign. You must sit up, pay close attention to signs, and act in a timely and appropriate fashion. These employees clearly had problems much greater than the normal day-to-day employee relations issues. Please don't allow signs to go on for too long before taking action.

Additionally, when you terminate an employee, you *must* immediately deactivate his or her access to your premises. You must notify your building's security office and all your employees when individuals are no longer employed by your company. Also, you should let active employees know when individuals should not be allowed on the premises. I recommend this in all cases of terminations. However, I strongly make the recommendation if there is the slightest reason to believe that harm could be caused to anyone.

And last, but certainly not least, please do not give a terminated employee a legitimate reason to return to your place of business. I always recommend giving an employee his or her final paycheck immediately upon termination. It was always my practice that the notice of termination and the final paycheck go together. I understand that you may not be required to give final paychecks on the day of termination; however, in my many years of experience, I can tell you it is much better to do this.

I know the story of the attack on the HR professional shared in this book was horrible; however, it should give you some food for thought. And although I hope this is something you never encounter, if you do, I pray you are ready!

Sincerely,
B. Phoenix

B. PHOENIX has over thirty years of experience in business and law firm administration, most of which has been in human resources. She was born, raised, and educated in Washington, DC, receiving a certificate in professional human resource management, a BS in management, and an MBA. She has held such positions as legal secretary, retirement specialist, vice president of human resources, executive director, administrator, and professional trainer. B. Phoenix is available for speaking engagements on topics such as leadership, HR management, employee training, performance management, and business administration. In addition, she has devoted a substantial amount of her time to volunteer work in her church and community. B. Phoenix has three children and a grandson and enjoys spending time with them, reading, shopping, and dining out. She is a third-generation Washingtonian currently residing in Prince George's County, Maryland.

Printed in the United States
By Bookmasters